Advance Praise for DAUGHTERS *of the* BUDDHA

"*Daughters of the Buddha* is a much-awaited pioneer work on the early Buddhist women of ancient India who strove for their own emancipation guided by the Buddha, contributed to the historical and philosophical aspects of Buddhism, and became the source of inspiration for hundreds and thousands of women to save themselves from the drudgery of worldly life as 'a woman.' We have many works on the early Buddhist nuns of the *Therīgāthā*, but Bhikkhu Anālayo's perspective is quite different from the existing ones. It is the first ever to have all the teachings given by early Buddhist women collected together, providing us with access to all the important information from the major primary sources. This was possible for Bhikkhu Anālayo because with his scholarship he had comfortable access to all these sources in the original languages. His presentation is simple and lucid, and the content is comprehensively supported by an analytical study. This book is a successful addition to the list of works on women and Buddhism by Bhikkhu Anālayo. Needless to say, it will be enlightening research material for other scholars and will give moral support to the daughters of the Buddha of the present day."

—Professor Shobha Rani Dash, author of *Mahāpajāpatī: The First Bhikkhunī*

"On behalf of all daughters of the Buddha (if I may), I wish to express my deepest gratitude toward our brother (again, if I may) Venerable Bhikkhu Anālayo for his everlasting support through his solid academic studies to present these precious and inspiring teachings by our venerable ancient Indian sisters. It's been both an enjoyable and enriching read—I'd like to encourage all my sisters to get a copy of it! With these great woman role models, both lay and monastic, we daughters of the Buddha in our time should never feel alone nor unconfident in any way. Thank you, Venerable Anālayo!"

—Dr. Christie Chang, joint president, International Buddhist Confederation; former president of Sakyadhita International

"Bhikkhu Anālayo brings his deep knowledge and reading of the Buddhist texts in the (now) relatively familiar languages of Pali and Sanskrit and casts a new, shimmering comparative light from the translations of Chinese and Tibetan Buddhist texts that he has accessed through his skill with languages. In *Daughters of the Buddha*, he brings perspectives from these texts on stories about, and statements of, the earliest Buddhist nuns and laywomen. The comparative data sometimes helps confirm the meaning or reference of a term or phrase, as in the issue of Mahāpajāpatī Gotamī's seniority among the early nuns, or it casts light on a new understanding of the Buddha's first refusal of her request to establish an order for nuns, while he accepted that women have the ability to reach the highest stage of the Path. The book is thus a rich tapestry of comparative data from the ancient Buddhist discourses on issues faced by Buddhist women then and especially Buddhist nuns in different parts of the modern world today."

—Ranjini Obeyesekere, PhD, author of *Portraits of Buddhist Women*

"In the early Buddhist community, the ability to teach well was of paramount importance. We are fortunate, therefore, to have this new book by Bhikkhu Anālayo, the monk-scholar and prodigious translator of early Buddhist texts, which highlights the 'teachings given by women who were the direct disciples of the Buddha.' The twenty-one women featured here (seventeen nuns and four laywomen) were well-known practitioners who were singled out during their lifetime for being foremost in possessing specific qualities, skills, and talents. Most noteworthy, they were all considered to be extraordinarily gifted teachers. Beyond merely recounting their life stories here, this group of translations gives testimony to these early women's abilities, agency, and important—and even singular—contributions to what we know of today as Buddhist Dharma."

—Jan Willis, PhD, author of *Dreaming Me: Black, Baptist, and Buddhist* and *Dharma Matters: Women, Race, and Tantra*

DAUGHTERS of the BUDDHA

TEACHINGS BY ANCIENT INDIAN WOMEN

Bhikkhu Anālayo

Foreword by Bhikkhunī Dhammanandā

Wisdom

Wisdom Publications
199 Elm Street
Somerville, MA 02144 USA
wisdomexperience.org

Library of Congress Cataloging-in-Publication Data
Names: Anālayo, 1962– author. | Thammananthā, Phiksunī, 1944– writer of foreword.
Title: Daughters of the Buddha: teachings by ancient Indian women /
Bhikkhu Anālayo; foreword by Bhikkhunī Dhammanandā.
Description: First edition. | Somerville: Wisdom Publications, 2022. |
Includes bibliographical references and index.
Identifiers: LCCN 2022013447 (print) | LCCN 2022013448 (ebook) |
ISBN 9781614298410 (hardcover) | ISBN 9781614298625 (ebook)
Subjects: LCSH: Women in Buddhism. | Women—Religious aspects—Buddhism. |
Buddhism—Doctrines.
Classification: LCC BQ4570.W6 A63 2022 (print) | LCC BQ4570.W6 (ebook) |
DDC 294.3082/0934—dc23/eng/20220607
LC record available at https://lccn.loc.gov/2022013447
LC ebook record available at https://lccn.loc.gov/2022013448

ISBN 978-1-61429-841-0 ebook ISBN 978-1-61429-862-5

26 25 24 23 22
5 4 3 2 1

Cover design by Gopa & Ted 2. Interior design by James Skatges. Set in DGP 11.25/14.9. The index was not compiled by the author.

As an act of Dhammadāna, Bhikkhu Anālayo has waived royalty payments for this book.

Wisdom Publications' books are printed on acid-free paper and meet the guidelines for permanence and durability of the Production Guidelines for Book Longevity of the Council on Library Resources.

Printed in the United States of America.

To Myozen and Uppalā

The teaching I call the charioteer
With right view forging ahead.
Whoever has such a vehicle,
Whether being female or male,
By means of that vehicle
Is close to Nirvana indeed. (SN 1.46)

Contents

Foreword

Bhikkhu Anālayo has long been an advocate for women in Buddhism. For instance, his thorough research on the legality of bhikkhunī ordination has been an obstacle for critics of the efforts to ordain nuns and his work on this topic has been translated into several languages. The bhikkhunīs in the Theravāda tradition are grateful for his academic work to support the ground upon which they stand.

For this present work, a very beautiful book, he studied leading bhikkhunīs and lay Buddhist women who were disciples of the Buddha. In the Theravāda tradition, to which I belong, discussion is usually limited to the thirteen bhikkhunīs who were praised by the Buddha for being foremost practitioners. In *Daughters of the Buddha*, we are given access to information regarding far more women than those thirteen foremost bhikkhunīs.

Additionally, and very importantly, Ven. Anālayo allows us to have a glimpse of material from the *Ekottarikāgama*, which is extant in Chinese and thus something many of us would not have access to. This is very important; it allows the readers to have a more complete understanding of the role and important contributions by women recorded in early Buddhist texts.

For instance, Bhikkhunī Soṇā is usually known only as someone who entered the monastic life late; she was disappointed with her children and awakened with a special blessing from the Buddha when he appeared to guide her toward her awakening. But the information we can find in this book gives us much more than that. Here, Bhikkhunī Soṇā is the only one who is able to face and challenge the six teachers—contemporaries of the Buddha who held various mistaken beliefs—and she does so in such a spectacular manner that none of them dares to respond to her challenge. This puts her in a most outstanding status, much more than the material provided in Pāli sources.

Daughters of the Buddha is yet another important scholarly contribution from Bhikkhu Anālayo that gives direct support to the emerging bhikkhunīs in Theravāda Buddhism. This new sapling of the Theravāda bhikkhunī sangha would be weakened without support from authentic scholars in Buddhist studies.

Bhikkhu Anālayo's monumental book not only provides new material for the tiny pockets of Theravāda bhikkhunīs that are spreading in various countries but also further emphasizes the necessity to explore other traditions and not limit ourselves to the Pāli tradition. This work also connects and strengthens the Theravāda bhikkhunīs and the Mahāyāna bhikṣuṇīs to support each other.

As a Buddhist academic who became a bhikkhunī, I know that the support of our brother bhikkhus is essential. Bhikkhu Anālayo has done his responsibility as a bhikkhu, as intended by the Buddha, well. My great appreciation is not just that he is supporting the bhikkhunī cause but that he has taken the duty given to him by the Buddha seriously to study the teaching and to put it into practice. After the Buddha, it is the bhikkhus who have the duty to take care of the bhikkhunīs. Authority to give ordination to bhikkhunīs depends on the bhikkhu sangha. The rise and fall of Buddhism also depends on the harmonious work of the fourfold Buddhist communities. This book stands as a symbol of this true spirit of a bhikkhu.

As an academic, Bhikkhu Anālayo is very particular in searching and examining objectively. His access to Chinese is very important for the study of the issue at hand; the references used by traditional academia have not covered this area. Thus, his book has broadened the academic horizon in a way for which I am most appreciative.

I personally bow to him with deep gratitude.

Bhikkhunī Dhammanandā
(Dr. Chatsumarn Kabilsingh)

Acknowledgments

I AM INDEBTED to Laura Cunningham, Bhikkhunī Dhammadinnā, Linda Grace, Sarah Kirchberger, Yuka Nakamura, and Vimala for commenting on a draft version of this book, and to the staff, board members, and supporters of the Barre Center for Buddhist Studies for providing me with the facilities needed to do my practice and writing.

Introduction

This book brings together textual reports of teachings given by women who were direct disciples of the Buddha. It is meant to be a testimony to their important contributions and thereby provide a source of inspiration to Buddhist women in today's world.

The main source materials used in the ensuing pages are the early discourses extant in Pāli and their parallels in Chinese, Tibetan, and at times Gāndhārī or Sanskrit fragments. The comparative study of these texts takes us back to the earliest period in the history of Buddhism that can still be accessed today.[1] My survey in the following pages, which combines new translations with texts already translated in some of my other publications, also includes material from discourses that either do not have a parallel or else have counterparts in later texts. For ease of presentation, even though I mostly translate texts from the Chinese in order to make these more widely accessible, I nevertheless give proper names in Pāli. This is merely a matter of convenience and does not intend to convey the impression that the originals I translate were based on a version in that language.

Whenever possible, I begin a chapter on a particular woman with a quote from a listing of eminent female disciples found in a numerical collection of discourses extant in Chinese translation, the *Ekottarikāgama*, as a way of putting a spotlight on what tradition considered to be particularly remarkable in the case of the nun or female lay disciple in question. In line with this pattern, the book cover features a mural from Pagan depicting several of the eminent nuns listed in the corresponding Pāli version.

My translations of the texts taken up in the ensuing chapters are supplemented by discussions and explanations in an attempt to draw out the doctrinal implications of the teachings in question. As a result, the present book becomes something of a tour through early Buddhist thought and practice from the viewpoint of ancient Indian women.

The resultant survey covers a range of different perspectives, due to which not every single instance will be equally inspiring to all readers. Some may not be taken by episodes highlighting supernormal feats; others may have less interest in some doctrinal points. In such cases, my suggestion would be to stay simply with the overall picture of the broad variety of achievements in which, according to these texts, ancient Indian women excelled, and based on that, then give special attention to those episodes that speak most directly to one's personal interests.

The early discourses in general evince little interest in the personal and subjective, even lacking a complete biography of the Buddha himself. Whatever can be gleaned about his life stems from bits and pieces that have been employed to convey a doctrinal point. Even proper names are treated with relatively little interest, and it is not at all unusual to find parallel discourses disagreeing about the names of their main protagonists, even though they are in concord on the actual teachings given. In the same vein, the voices of the daughters of the Buddha collected here are less concerned with sharing their subjective experiences; instead, their overarching interest is the path to liberation from craving and ignorance. As a result, the present book can serve as a complement to publications focused more on the individual stories and experiences of Buddhist women, mainly based on the information found in later texts and hagiographies.

It is a sad truth that even today Buddhist women are still regularly confronted by androcentrism and even at times misogyny, a heartbreaking heritage unfortunately shared by the different Buddhist traditions.[2] In a range of other publications, I have studied examples of such androcentric and misogynist tendencies, examining them from a historical-critical perspective. In the present book, my main concern is simply to bring together passages that can serve as a source of encouragement and support for Buddhist women to face the challenges of having their voices heard and their practice respected in a setting that continues its longstanding and depressing failure to provide equal opportunities to women.

Gotamī

> The foremost of those nuns who have gone forth to train for a long time and are thus respected by the king of the country is the nun called Mahāpajāpatī Gotamī.[3]

THE ABOVE QUOTE stems from the already-mentioned listing of eminent female monastics in the *Ekottarikāgama*. The text eulogizes fifty-one nuns and thirty-one lay women for an array of impressive qualities. This listing has a counterpart in Pāli that is shorter in the case of both female and male disciples.

Mahāpajāpatī Gotamī was the Buddha's maternal aunt who nursed him after the death of his mother and took a central role in the events leading to the founding of the order of nuns. She is mentioned in both listings of eminent female monastics; according to the Pāli account she was foremost in seniority.[4] The Pāli listing of outstanding monks employs the same qualification for the monk Koṇḍañña, who reportedly attained stream-entry at the time of the delivery of what according to tradition was the Buddha's first sermon, the Discourse on Setting in Motion the Wheel of Dharma.[5] Elsewhere the Pāli discourses use the same expression to designate the seniority of six well-known non-Buddhist teachers who were contemporaries of the Buddha.[6] In addition to being regularly used for monastic seniority, the same term can also be applied to Buddhist lay disciples.[7] Given this broad range of usage, the reference to Mahāpajāpatī Gotamī's foremost quality in the Pāli version need not intend to convey that she was the most senior nun. Nevertheless, this would be the most natural interpretation, as monastic seniority is the most common occurrence of the term in question.

In the parallel passage from the *Ekottarikāgama*, translated above, monastic seniority is beyond doubt the intended sense. This is evident in the reference to her having "gone forth" for a long time, terminology that reflects monastic ordination. In addition to her seniority, the *Ekottarikāgama* version also highlights the king's respect for her. In the ancient Indian setting, receiving such respect was an important asset for members of a mendicant community whose lifestyle depended on having harmonious relationships with the political authorities.

The First Nun

According to the traditional account, Mahāpajāpatī Gotamī was indeed the most senior of all Buddhist nuns, as she played a crucial role in the developments that led to the founding of an order of nuns.[8] The story of this important event is rather complex. In another book publication I have tried to unravel some of the strands of this narrative, based on a comparative study of the various extant sources, most of which are texts on monastic discipline (*Vinaya*).[9] In the context of the present exploration, my focus is on Mahāpajāpatī Gotamī's request for the Buddha to start an order of nuns, as reported in the relevant discourse versions. The exchange between her and the Buddha takes the following form in two discourses extant in Chinese translation, presented below one after the other:[10]

> (*First Chinese version*:)
> At that time Mahāpajāpatī Gotamī approached the Buddha, paid homage with her head at the Buddha's feet, stood back to one side, and said: "Blessed One, can women attain the fourth fruit of recluseship? For that reason, can women leave the home out of faith and become homeless to train in the path in this right teaching and discipline?" The Blessed One replied: "Wait, wait, Gotamī, do not have this thought, that women leave the home out of faith and become homeless to train in the path in this right teaching and discipline. Gotamī, you

> shave off your hair like this, put on monastic robes, and for your whole life practice the holy life in purity."
>
> (*Second Chinese version*:)
> At that time Mahāpajāpatī Gotamī approached the Blessed One. Having arrived, she paid homage with her head at the Blessed One's feet and stood back to one side. Standing back to one side, Mahāpajāpatī Gotamī said to the Blessed One: "Blessed One, would it be possible for women to attain the four fruits of recluseship? Will you not let women go forth in this teaching and discipline out of serene faith, becoming homeless to train in the path?" [The Buddha replied]: "Wait, Gotamī, do not [think like] this. Women do not obtain the going forth in this teaching and discipline out of serene faith, becoming homeless to train in the path. Gotamī, you can always shave your hair, put on ochre robes, and until the end [of your life] practice the pure holy life."

In the Pāli counterpart, Mahāpajāpatī Gotamī does not refer to the spiritual potential of women and only petitions for permission to be granted for women to go forth.[11] In this account, it is instead the Buddha's attendant Ānanda who, intervening later on behalf of Mahāpajāpatī Gotamī and her followers, brings up the topic of women's ability to awaken, which the Buddha confirms in the following words:[12]

> "Having gone forth from home to homelessness in the teaching and discipline made known by the Tathāgata, women are capable of realizing the fruit of stream-entry, the fruit of once-return, the fruit of nonreturn, and the fruit of arahantship."

The important indication given in the above passage reflects the inclusiveness underpinning the Buddha's teaching activities, whose main scope was precisely to enable others to reach these four fruits of recluseship. Bhikkhunī Dhammanandā (2010, 153) comments that it was "because of this equal spiritual ability that the Buddha allowed women to join the sangha, and the statement should be [an] encouragement for Buddhist women everywhere."

In the ancient Indian setting, a monastic lifestyle was generally considered the most appropriate avenue for progress to awakening. In addition, from the perspective of early Buddhist thought, it seems as if someone who attains the highest of these four and becomes an arahant will be unable to continue to live the lay life and would therefore soon go forth, if that had not already happened (see also below p. 100).[13] This point relates to a minor difference between the two versions translated above, as in the first Chinese version Mahāpajāpatī Gotamī inquires whether women can reach the *fourth* fruit of recluseship, whereas in the second her query is about all four fruits. Needless to say, if they can reach the fourth fruit, the other three are implicitly covered. But by highlighting the fourth fruit in particular, her inquiry could be read to convey at the same time the implicit question: What does the Buddha expect to happen if a lay woman successfully implements his teachings and becomes an arahant, thereby becoming unable to continue living as a lay person. Should there not be some provision for such a case?

Whether this was indeed meant to be implicit in the formulation adopted in the first version translated above or not, another and particularly important difference emerges with the Buddha's reply: In the Pāli version he simply denies her request, without offering her any alternative. In the two discourse versions translated above, however, he allows Mahāpajāpatī Gotamī to live like a monastic, in the sense of shaving her hair and wearing robes, but without going forth as a wandering mendicant. This difference changes a flat refusal to grant ordination to women into what can be read to reflect a concern for their protection.

Embarking on the life of a wandering mendicant at a time when the Buddhist monastic order was still in its formative stages would have involved hardships and dangers for women that may have made it appear advisable to postpone such a step. In the ancient Indian setting, a woman who had gone forth risked being perceived by others to be without the protection of what in those times were considered to be her rightful guardians—her father, husband, or son—and thus potentially being considered by some males as an easily available commodity to satisfy their sexual urges. In such a situation, it would indeed make sense to be circumspect so as to prevent Mahāpajāpatī Gotamī and her followers from being exposed to abuse. Wendy Garling (2016, 242) reasons on the Buddha's attitude:

> establishing a separate order of nuns at that time [may have] appeared as a logistical challenge, one for which he was yet unprepared. In this scenario, his hesitation would have arisen out of a concern for his charges, not bias. Creating and managing a monastic community of men was one thing, but now hundreds of women were also asking to put their future in his hands. Too much, too soon ... Requiring more than just a system of religious guidance and discipline, his suppliants all needed food, clothing, and shelter. Now living outside the patriarchal social structure, the women would also require a measure of protection ... this was no doubt more than he had bargained for, and as a leader it simply could have been more than he felt he could responsibly handle.

The alternative proposed by the Buddha in the two discourse versions translated above, by permitting them to shave their heads and wear monastic robes but for the time being live the holy life in a protected environment rather than as wandering mendicants, could have been meant to address such concerns. Even though such a suggestion is not found in the Pāli discourse, the same version does record that Mahāpajāpatī Gotamī and her followers shaved off their hair and put on monastic robes:[14]

> Then Mahāpajāpatī Gotamī had her hair cut off and put on monastic robes. Together with many Sakyan women, she left for Vesālī.

The Pāli discourse continues by reporting that they encountered Ānanda, who noticed their travel-worn physical condition without making even a passing comment on the circumstance that they had shaved off their hair and were wearing robes. For Mahāpajāpatī Gotamī and her followers to do so of their own accord would have been an act of open defiance, something which would have merited a comment if not criticism by Ānanda and later by the Buddha, on being informed of what had happened. The absence of any such reaction makes it fair to propose that some earlier permission by the Buddha also stands in the background of the Pāli account, even though it is no longer found explicitly.

The Gift of a Robe

The story line of how the order of nuns came into existence appears to be the result of considerable textual developments, unfortunately heavily influenced by reciters who were not particularly well disposed toward the nuns. One of these developments takes the form of some overlap, and ensuing mixing up, of textual portions from the above story of Mahāpajāpatī Gotamī's request to become a nun and another request by her, made on a different occasion, that the Buddha accept a robe she had made for him. This request takes the following form in two discourses extant in Chinese, presented one after the other:[15]

> (*First Chinese version*:)
> At that time Mahāpajāpatī Gotamī approached the Buddha, holding a new robe of yellow color made of thread with a golden [hue]. Having paid homage with her head at the Buddha's feet, she stood back to one side and said: "Blessed One, I have myself made this new robe out of yellow-colored thread with a golden [hue] for the Blessed One. May you deign to accept it, out of compassion for me."
>
> (*Second Chinese version*:)
> At that time there was a nun called Mahāpajāpatī Gotamī, who approached the Buddha holding a new cotton robe. Having reached the Buddha and paid homage with her head at the Buddha's feet, she stood back to one side and said to the Buddha: "Blessed One, I made this new cotton robe with my

> own hands and offer it to the Blessed One. I only wish that you would accept it, causing me to gain great benefit and happiness for a long time."

The two versions agree with their Pāli counterpart that the Buddha refused and suggested instead an alternative, namely offering the robe to the entire monastic community.[16] According to Buddhist doctrine, such an offering would be more meritorious than giving the robe just to an individual, even if this individual should be the Buddha himself.

According to her statement in the Pāli version, she had spun and woven a pair of robes, which requires considerably more effort than *making* a robe, as that would just involve sewing together existing cloth. In all versions, Ānanda intervened on her behalf, reminding the Buddha of his debt of gratitude to Mahāpajāpatī Gotamī. When his mother had passed away soon after his birth, her sister Mahāpajāpatī Gotamī nursed the infant Buddha with her own milk. In reply, the Buddha clarified that he had already settled his debt of gratitude by establishing Mahāpajāpatī Gotamī in the attainment of stream-entry. This episode reflects the early Buddhist attitude of granting superiority to progress to awakening over family bonds and affections. The need to fulfill one's obligations to one's parents is a recurrent theme in the early discourses, so the point is not to encourage an ignoring or even denying of one's debt of gratitude. But the debt of gratitude incurred toward one's spiritual parent, in the sense of the teacher who enables one to reach one of the four fruits or levels of awakening, carries more weight.

A noteworthy difference between the two passages translated above is that only the second Chinese version qualifies Mahāpajāpatī Gotamī as a nun. In the other two versions, she could well be still a lay woman. However, this would create an inner inconsistency, as in the same discourse the Buddha eventually gives an exposition on the meritoriousness of gifts toward various recipients, one of which is the order of nuns, which implies that this order was already in existence. This inconsistency in the first Chinese version translated above as well as in the Pāli discourse could be the result of joining together originally different textual pieces during oral transmission, due to which the episode translated above came to be connected to an exposition on the meritoriousness of various offerings.[17] The same type of pattern is in fact also evident elsewhere, showing the apparent attraction among Buddhist reciters and narrators of the episode of Mahāpajāpatī Gotamī's offering the Buddha a robe (or a pair of robes). This attraction appears to have been responsible for some elements from this tale migrating to and interacting with the account of how the order of nuns came into existence or with some other stories.[18]

Ordination

Returning to the beginnings of the order of nuns, the parallel versions agree in reporting that the Buddha promulgated eight specific regulations whose acceptance would count as Mahāpajāpatī Gotamī's ordination. The two discourse versions extant in Chinese report that she accepted this happily:[19]

> (*First Chinese version*:)
> Venerable Ānanda, listen to me speaking a simile. On hearing a simile, the wise will understand its meaning. Venerable Ānanda, it is like a warrior girl, or a brahmin [girl], or a householder [girl], or a worker[-class] girl, handsome and beautiful, who bathes so as to be totally clean, applies perfume to her body, puts on bright clean clothes, and adorns herself with various ornaments. Suppose there is, furthermore, someone who thinks of that girl, who seeks her benefit and well-being, who seeks her happiness and ease. He takes a head wreath made of lotuses,[20] or a head wreath of champak flowers, or a head wreath of jasmine flowers, or a head wreath of [another type of] jasmine flowers, or a head wreath of lilies,[21] and gives it to that girl. With great joy, that girl accepts it with both hands and adorns her head with it. Venerable Ānanda, in the same way, these eight guiding principles to be respected, which the Blessed One has set forth for women, I receive on my head and uphold for my whole life.

(*Second Chinese version:*)
Venerable Ānanda, it is like this. You may listen to my simile; on hearing a simile the wise will understand its meaning. Venerable Ānanda, it is just as if a warrior girl, or a brahmin girl, or a skilled artisan[-class] girl, or a girl from among common people, washes and perfumes herself well, putting on bright and clean clothes. Suppose there were a person who thinks of her and sympathizes with her, desiring her benefit and desiring her well-being. [This person] takes a head wreath made of lotuses, or a head wreath made of champak flowers, or a head wreath made of jasmine flowers, or a head wreath made of lilies, and gives it to her. She accepts it by receiving it with both hands and places it on her head. Venerable Ānanda, in the same way I shall receive on my head for my whole life these eight weighty principles that the Blessed One has set forth.

The Pāli version differs in so far as the person who receives the flower garland could alternatively be a male who is similarly fond of ornaments and has just bathed.[22] This helps to clarify that the simile is quite probably just meant to be a positive expression of joy and happiness, rather than portraying behavior specific to women.

The depiction of such joyful acceptance raises the question if perhaps this was, as suggested by Wendy Garling (2021, 159), in response "to a different, more affirmative list of eight rules—rules that were later altered that we have never seen?" At the very least, the above passage makes it quite clear that Mahāpajāpatī Gotamī was very happy with the final outcome of her petition and joyfully took on the eight rules that served as her ordination. Regarding the report that the Buddha promulgated such a set of eight rules,[23] Alice Collett (2021, 32) reasons:

> It is quite possible that, initially, the eight rules were put in place to protect nuns ... Women were expected to be under the guardianship of men. If they were not, they were viewed as sexually available. Therefore, in order to make clear that nuns were not sexually available to any man who sought to

> gratify himself, the community needed to make clear to villagers, townsfolk, city dwellers, and all inhabitants of north India that the nuns who followed the Buddha were under the guardianship of the monks. If monks are seen to be overseeing the activities of the nuns, the status of monks as the guardians of the nuns is established. Then the nuns are considered to "belong" to the monks and thereby unavailable to other men. If this is the case, there was no malfeasance; the rules were not originally put in place to cast nuns in a lower status to monks, but to safeguard them from sexual assault.

Such a reading would resonate with the impression conveyed by the above-surveyed reports, according to which the Buddha had offered Mahāpajāpatī Gotamī and her followers the option of shaving their heads and wearing monastic robes but living the holy life in a protected environment rather than as wandering mendicants. In this way, taking into account the ancient Indian setting can help to put into perspective what otherwise can appear to spring from a rather negative attitude toward women and their spiritual aspirations.

In sum, although comparative study shows that a story of success, namely Mahāpajāpatī Gotamī's petitioning the Buddha to start an order of nuns, over centuries of transmission developed in ways that became considerably less positive, it nevertheless remains a story of success. Perhaps this is the most important part to be taken away from this narrative. In the words of Shobha Rani Dash (2008, 154 and 162):

> Mahāpajāpatī, the first bhikkhunī and the foster mother of the Buddha, added a new chapter not only in the history of Buddhism but in the history of womenfolk too … The legacy of Mahāpajāpatī bhikkhunī has been transmitted from generation to generation and is still well preserved, despite various ups and downs, by hundreds and thousands of women worldwide following in her footsteps out of deep respect for her, the mother of the Buddha as well as of the bhikkhunī saṅgha.

Wendy Garling (2016, 260) adds:

> Mahaprajapati's story of leadership and liberation is as needed and relevant today as it was twenty-five hundred years ago. With Buddhist women continuing to struggle for gender equality in a faith system that continues to be broken by androcentrism, her spirit persists as a steady, guiding light ... Mahaprajapati commands an incomparable place of honor not just in the Buddha's life story, but in the story of Buddhism.

Freedom and Gratitude

Although centuries of transmission have left a negative impact on Mahāpajāpatī Gotamī's story of success, the same oral transmission has also preserved a collection of poems by ancient Indian nuns, extant in Pāli as the *Therīgāthā*. This collection includes a poem by Mahāpajāpatī Gotamī herself, presented here by alternating between translation of the Pāli verses and my own explanatory comments:[24]

> "Homage be to you, Buddha and hero,
> Supreme among sentient beings,
> Who freed me from *dukkha*
> As well as many other people."

The verses begin with an expression of respect and gratitude to the one who helped Mahāpajāpatī Gotamī to find freedom from *dukkha*. Notably, her compassionate disposition seems to become evident when she immediately brings in also the many others that have similarly benefitted. Such helping others to find freedom, after having found it oneself, is what indeed makes one a hero in the Buddhist sense.

> "*Dukkha* has been entirely understood,
> Its cause in craving has been dried up,
> The eightfold path has been cultivated,[25]
> Cessation has been experienced by me."

In this verse, Mahāpajāpatī Gotamī proclaims her own accomplishment, thereby confirming that women are indeed able to reach the fourth fruit of recluseship. She has personally experienced the cessation of Nirvana, thereby coming to understand *dukkha* fully and drying up craving for good. Such accomplishment is based on having cultivated the eightfold path, the first topic in the first sermon given, according to tradition, by the Buddha, in which he presented the noble eightfold path as the middle way aloof from the two extremes of sensual indulgence and ascetic self-mortification.

> "Formerly I was a mother and a son,
> A father, a brother, and a grandmother;
> Not understanding it as it really is,
> Without resting I cycled on in *saṃsāra*."

As a fully awakened one, Mahāpajāpatī Gotamī no longer identifies with her role as a mother, which from the lofty perspective of her consummate achievement becomes just another instance in a series of family roles she had in former lives.[26] Due to not understanding, a reference perhaps intending a lack of realizing the predicament inherent in such roles, she kept on cycling in *saṃsāra*. The present instance thereby is in line with a tendency noted by Ranjini Obeyesekere (2001, 18), in that several of the "early poems of the nuns (included in the Buddhist canon) reveal the sense of freedom that came from being able to escape their traditional female roles."

> "I have truly 'seen' that Blessed One:
> This is my last body,
> Birth and *saṃsāra* are finished,
> There is now no more renewed existence."

Mahāpajāpatī Gotamī has truly "seen" the Buddha, as it is by seeing the Dharma that one really sees him.[27] With such vision gained, faring on in *saṃsāra* is over and the present body is her last, as there will not be another rebirth for her.

"Behold the disciples in concord,
With energy aroused and resolute
Always making a strong effort:
This is paying homage to Buddhas."

In this verse, Mahāpajāpatī Gotamī again seems to manifest her compassionate disposition, already evident in the first verse by immediately bringing in others, which in the present case takes the form of turning to the disciples of the Buddha in general. Perhaps with the intention to provide a source of inspiration for future generations, she points out that energetic dedication to the Buddha's teachings is the way to pay homage.

"Surely for the benefit of many
Did Māyā give birth to Gotama,
The dispeller of the mass of *dukkha*
Of those struck by disease and death."

Mahāpajāpatī Gotamī's final verse refers to her sister Māyā, who gave birth to the Buddha, in recognition of the manifold benefits that his coming into the world has produced. This is what really counts, namely showing a way out to those who are oppressed by disease and death.

A Spectacular Passing Away

The topic of death continues with the next and final episode related to Mahāpajāpatī Gotamī, which reports her own passing away. The text translated below stems from the *Ekottarikāgama* extant in Chinese, which has Pāli counterparts in comparatively late collections, namely in the *Apadāna* and the commentary on the *Therīgāthā*. The present case is one of several instances where the *Ekottarikāgama* collection shows signs of having remained open to the addition of later material for a considerably longer time than other discourse collections extant in Pāli and Chinese translation. This is not to say that the *Ekottarikāgama* is late throughout. Some of its discourses can be quite early and even help to correct errors that appear to have occurred in the course of the transmission of their Pāli discourse parallels. But at other times, such as in the present instance, the presentation in an *Ekottarikāgama* discourse reflects a type of thought that is no longer representative of early Buddhism only. Since the version translated below is a discourse found in the *Āgama* collections, however, it falls within the scope of my present survey.

A sign of lateness is the description in the discourse below of Mahāpajāpatī Gotamī performing supernormal feats by levitating, a performance then repeated by five hundred of her nun followers. Closer inspection of descriptions of levitation in the early discourses in general gives the impression that several such feats appear to have originally been intended as actions performed with a mental body, while the physical body remains seated in meditation.[28] Literalism, a pervasive tendency at work in Buddhist texts, seems to have led at a subsequent stage to a growing tendency for depictions of levitation to be performed with the physical body, as is the case for the narrative below. Another feature of lateness is the performance of the twin miracle, the simultaneous manifestation of water and fire, which is not attested in Pāli discourses. Due to the length of the narrative of Mahāpajāpatī Gotamī's passing away, I present the translation interspersed with comments:[29]

> Thus have I heard. At one time the Buddha was staying at Vesālī in the communal hall, being in the company of a great group of five hundred monks. At that time Mahāpajāpatī was dwelling in the Kūṭāgārasālā in Vesālī, being in the company of a great group of five hundred nuns, all of whom were arahants with their influxes eradicated.

The opening of the discourse follows a standard pattern of announcing the whereabouts of the Buddha and his company of five hundred monks, a number with a somewhat symbolical function that usually serves to convey the idea of a rather large group.[30] Of further interest, however, is the application of the same description to Mahāpajāpatī Gotamī's dwelling in the company of five hundred nuns. These are additionally qualified as arahants who had eradicated their influxes, the latter being the term most often used in the early discourses to refer to the complete freedom from defilements reached with full awakening. Since no such specification is made about the monks, the introductory narration presents Mahāpajāpatī Gotamī's company in a more favorable light than the Buddha's company. A comparable indication recurs in the Pāli counterparts, which explicitly qualify the five hundred nuns to be "liberated."[31] Since the Pāli versions do not mention the company of the Buddha at all, however, no implicit comparison results from this indication.

> Then Mahāpajāpatī heard the monks saying: "The Tathāgata will soon enter complete extinction, within three months and between the twin Sal trees at Kusinārā." Then Mahāpajāpatī in turn thought: "I cannot stand seeing the Tathāgata enter complete extinction and I also cannot stand seeing Ānanda enter complete extinction. It is proper that I should now enter complete extinction first." Then Mahāpajāpatī in turn approached the Blessed One, paid respect with her head at his feet, and sat to one side. Then Mahāpajāpatī said in front of the Buddha: "I heard that the Blessed One will soon enter complete extinction, within three months from now, between the twin Sal trees at Kusinārā. Now I cannot stand seeing the Blessed One and Ānanda enter complete extinction. I only wish that the Blessed One would permit me to enter complete extinction first." Then the Blessed One approved it by remaining silent.

In addition to a reference to Ānanda's passing away, according to the Pāli parallels Mahāpajāpatī Gotamī also did not want to witness the passing away of the two chief disciples Sāriputta and Mahāmoggallāna, as well as of Rāhula and Nanda.[32]

Expressing the wish to enter Nirvana is a recurrent trope in Buddhist texts, whose application is not confined to female protagonists. As already pointed out by Liz Wilson (2011, 142), "Gotami is not alone in responding to the immanent [sic] death of the Buddha by orchestrating her own death. She is only one of many saints who made this choice." For example, the Sanskrit *Mahāparinirvāṇasūtra* and several of its Chinese parallels report that the last convert made by the Buddha also decided to enter final Nirvana before the Buddha's impending passing away.[33] A discourse in the *Udāna* relates, in agreement with two parallels extant in Chinese, that the monk Dabba told the Buddha that the time for his entry into final Nirvana had come, followed by performing miracles in front of the Buddha and then passing away.[34] According to another discourse in the *Ekottarikāgama*, Sāriputta also wanted to pass away, since he could not stand seeing the Buddha enter final Nirvana.[35]

It seems that the idea of not wanting to witness the Buddha's passing away is best read as a polite way of expressing one's own wish to precede him in this respect, rather than as an indication that an arahant can still be overwhelmed by grief. The wish to enter final Nirvana as such, moreover, is in line with the overarching soteriological orientation of early Buddhist thought. A discourse to be taken up later distinguishes between the Nirvana element with a residue and the Nirvana element without a residue (see p. 214). The former stands for the total mental freedom achieved by arahants and the Buddha, who still live in the world. The latter stands for what Mahāpajāpatī Gotamī in the present narrative episode felt ready to enter.

> Then Mahāpajāpatī further said to the Buddha: "From now on, I only wish the Blessed One would grant that the nuns recite the rules [without me]." The Buddha said: "I now permit that the nuns in turn grant [other] nuns the reciting of the precepts,[36] just as I originally promulgated the precepts, without causing any deviation."
>
> Then Mahāpajāpatī went forward to pay respect at the Buddha's feet and stood in front of the Buddha. Then Mahāpajāpatī further said to the Buddha: "Now I will no longer see the Tathāgata's face, and I will also not see future Buddhas. I will not take birth in a womb, but forever abide in the unconditioned. Today I depart and will never again see the noble one's complexion."
>
> Then Mahāpajāpatī circumambulated the Buddha seven times and she also circumambulated Ānanda seven times.[37] She completed circumambulating the community of monks,

withdrew and left. Returning to be among the community of nuns, she said to the nuns: "I now wish to enter into the unconditioned element of Nirvana. The reason is that the Tathāgata will soon enter complete extinction. You should each act according to what is suitable at this time."[38]

At that time the nun Khemā, the nun Uppalavaṇṇā, the nun Kisā[gotamī], the nun Sakulā, the nun Sāmā, the nun Paṭācārā, the nun *Bhaddacālā, the nun [Bhaddā] Kaccānā, the nun [Vi]jayā, and five hundred nuns approached the Blessed One and stood to one side.[39] Then the five hundred nuns, with the nun Khemā at their head, said to the Buddha: "We all heard that the Tathāgata will soon enter complete extinction. We cannot stand seeing the Blessed One and Ānanda enter complete extinction first. We only wish that the Blessed One would permit us to enter complete extinction first. We would now enter Nirvana, this being proper and suitable." Then the Blessed One approved it by remaining silent. When the nun Khemā and the five hundred nuns saw that the Blessed One had approved it by remaining silent, they came forward to pay respect at the Buddha's feet, circumambulated him three times, withdrew, and in turn left to return to their former dwellings.

The discussion about the precepts conveys the impression that, up to that time, Mahāpajāpatī Gotamī had been the one to recite the precepts at the fortnightly observance ceremony. This concords with her role as the most senior nun, mentioned in the listing of outstanding nuns in the *Ekottarikāgama*, taken up at the outset of this chapter. In addition to speaking of the Buddha as the "Blessed One," she also refers to him with the term "Tathāgata," which could be translated as "Thus Gone One." This term does not invariably refer to the Buddha but in other contexts can also stand for arahants in general.

The circumstance that her following of nuns adopts the same decision of entering Nirvana shows that taking this decision was not motivated by the impending loss of close relatives, as the nuns mentioned by name in the above passage were not necessarily relatives of the Buddha and

Ānanda. In fact, the present episode has no relationship to the Indian custom of a married woman reacting to the death of her husband (or on rare occasions to the death of other male family members) by committing suicide.[40] Due to having gone forth as nuns, Mahāpajāpatī Gotamī and her followers had already stepped out of the traditional framework of male guardianship by close family members and no longer needed to avoid the role of the surplus woman without male guardianship.[41]

> Then Mahāpajāpatī closed the door of the oration hall, hit the gong, put down her sitting cloth in an open place, and soared up into the empty sky. [While] sitting, lying down, standing, and walking in the empty sky, [from her body] burning flames came out; from her lower body smoke came out; from her upper body fire came out; from her lower body water came out; from her upper body smoke came out; her whole body released flames; her whole body released smoke; from the left side of her upper body water came out; from the right side of her upper body fire came out; from the right side of her upper body water came out; from the left side of her upper body fire came out;[42] from the front [of her body] fire came out; from the back [of her body] water came out; from the front [of her body] water came out; from the back [of her body] fire came out; from her whole body fire came out; and from her whole body water came out.

The above is a description of the "twin miracle," the simultaneous manifestation of complete control over the two elements of water and fire. Narratives of the performance of this type of miracle tend to occur in later texts, with the difference that Theravāda literature limits this type of feat to the Buddha only, whereas other traditions envisage that disciples of the Buddha can also perform the twin miracle.[43] Mahāpajāpatī Gotamī's miracle in the Pāli counterparts does include the manifestation of fire and smoke, as well as raining down water,[44] but these fall short of being a performance of the twin miracle, as they do not occur simultaneously.

The same Pāli versions report that the Buddha had explicitly asked her to perform supernormal feats to dispel the doubts of the foolish regarding the ability of women to gain realization in his teaching.[45] In this way, her performance of miracles is enhanced by being done in compliance with a personal invitation by the Buddha, combined with an explicit reference to the need to counter the foolish belief that women are not as capable as men in matters of meditative realization. This reference explains the purpose of such a public manifestation of supernormal abilities, which due to being done on the verge of passing away could not give rise to the mistaken impression of being tainted by the wish to motivate an increase of offerings to the performant.

> When Mahāpajāpatī had performed many transformations, she returned to her original seat to sit down cross-legged with straight body and straight mind, collecting mindfulness in front. She entered the first absorption. Rising from the first absorption, she entered the second absorption. Rising from the second absorption, she entered the third absorption. Rising from the third absorption, she entered the fourth absorption. Rising from the fourth absorption, she entered the sphere of [infinite] space. Rising from the sphere of [infinite] space, she entered the sphere of [infinite] consciousness. Rising from the sphere of [infinite] consciousness, she entered the sphere of nothingness. Rising from the sphere of nothingness, she entered the sphere of neither-perception-nor-nonperception. Rising from the sphere of neither-perception-nor-nonperception, she entered the cessation of perception and knowing.
>
> Rising from the cessation of perception and knowing, she returned to enter the sphere of neither-perception-nor-nonperception. Rising from the sphere of neither-perception-nor-nonperception, she returned to enter the sphere of nothingness.[46] Rising from the sphere of nothingness, she returned to enter the sphere of [infinite] consciousness. Rising from the sphere of [infinite] consciousness, she returned to enter the sphere of [infinite] space. Rising from the sphere of [infinite] space, she returned to enter the fourth absorption. Rising from the fourth absorption, she returned to enter the third absorption. Rising

> from the third absorption, she returned to enter the second absorption. Rising from the second absorption, she returned to enter the first absorption. Rising from the first absorption, she returned to enter the second absorption. Rising from the second absorption, she returned to enter the third absorption. Rising from the third absorption, she returned to enter the fourth absorption. Having entered the fourth absorption, she in turn entered complete extinction.
>
> At that time there was a great earthquake in the world. The east rose up and the west sank down, the west rose up and the east sank down. The four sides rose up and the center sank down, and on all four sides a cool breeze arose. [Some] celestials in the sky danced and made music. [Some] celestials of the sensual sphere were crying in grief, which was like timely rain that falls from the sky in a month of the spring season. The sublime celestials scattered various lotus fragrances and various [kinds of] sandalwood powder on her [body].

The above description of Mahāpajāpatī Gotamī's meditative tour corresponds to a similar meditative tour performed, according to a range of sources, by the Buddha on the eve of his own passing away.[47] This meditative tour proceeds through the four levels of absorption and the four formless spheres, culminating in the superb attainment of cessation. Being able to execute this entire series in forward and backward order functions as a mark of exceptional meditative mastery in the early discourses. Having completed this tour, the final part of the meditative journey then involves proceeding from the first to the fourth absorption in order to use the latter as the most appropriate platform for entering Nirvana. The Pāli parallels to the above description differ by not including her attainment of cessation in an otherwise similar meditative tour.[48]

Before turning to the part of the *Ekottarikāgama* version that reports how Mahāpajāpatī Gotamī's followers performed the same feats before passing away, it needs to be noted that neither the Pāli versions nor the above description imply that she has become a female Buddha of sorts.[49] In early Buddhist thought, being a Buddha implies that one has discovered the path to awakening on one's own and then teaches it to others. This is clearly not the role taken by Mahāpajāpatī Gotamī.[50] Nor does an earlier portion of one of the two relevant Pāli texts present Mahāpajāpatī Gotamī in the role of a universal monarch.[51] With all her impressive attainments and abilities, Mahāpajāpatī Gotamī remains a disciple of the Buddha and could not herself have become a universal monarch or a Buddha.

> At that time the nun Khemā, the nun Uppalavaṇṇā, the nun Kisāgotamī, the nun Sakulā, the nun Sāmā, the nun Paṭācārā, the nun [Bhaddā] Kaccānā, the nun [Vi]jayā, being at the head of five hundred nuns, each put down their sitting cloths in an open place and soared up into the empty sky. [While] sitting, lying down, standing, and walking in the empty sky, they performed eighteen transformations ... *up to* ... they entered into the cessation of perception and knowing ... and each of them entered complete extinction.

The text abbreviates and just refers to "eighteen transformations" and the attainment of cessation, which implies that the full account given earlier for Mahāpajāpatī Gotamī should be supplemented. In other words, all of her five hundred followers also performed the twin miracle and did a meditative tour in forward and backward order of the four absorptions and the four formless spheres, up to cessation, before entering Nirvana.

The Pāli parallels make a point of explicitly stating that Mahāpajāpatī Gotamī's passing away was, on the whole, more remarkable than that of the Buddha.[52] Miranda Shaw (2006/2007, 151) points out that "her achievements exceeded those of Shakyamuni in one area, for the Buddha was not followed into parinirvāṇa by any of his disciples, whereas five hundred of Gotamī's congregation of nuns ... accompanied her on her final journey." The overall impression conveyed by this episode, as noted by Susan Murcott (1991, 18), is that "the early sangha judged Pajapati to have been a remarkable person."

The importance attributed in later tradition to the above episode can be seen in the circumstance that the seventh-century Chinese pilgrim

Xuanzang refers to the *stūpa* at the site where Mahāpajāpatī and her nuns were held to have passed away.[53] Miranda Shaw (2006/2007, 149) comments on the same episode:

> The inclusion of a large congregation of female disciples in Gotamī's story forecloses on the inference that she is a uniquely accomplished woman and makes it clear that she is not an anomaly, token, or isolated case. The writers of this text offer an unambiguous portrait of women's capabilities and deliver their proclamation in clarion, victorious tones that would surely encourage others to emulate the lofty example they set forth.

Khemā

> The foremost of those nuns who are wise and intelligent is the nun called Khemā.[54]

IN THE ACCOUNT of Mahāpajāpatī Gotamī's spectacular passing away, taken up in the previous chapter, Khemā was at the head of the group of nuns who approached the Buddha to request permission to enter final Nirvana. This conveys the impression that she was of such renown as to take the leading position in Mahāpajāpatī Gotamī's absence (in this particular case due to the fact that Mahāpajāpatī Gotamī had already made such a request on her own).

The above statement from the listing of eminent nuns in the *Ekottarikāgama* considers her to be outstanding in wisdom and intelligence, a role similarly accorded to her in the Pāli parallel, which more specifically speaks of her "great wisdom."[55] A later text, the *Avadānaśataka*, repeats the same qualification and adds to this her "great eloquence."[56]

On the Nature of the Tathāgata

A testimony to Khemā's outstanding wisdom and eloquence can be found in a Pāli discourse of which no parallel is known.[57] Such absence of a parallel is not in itself a sign of lateness. Often this can just be the result of the circumstance that a full set of discourse collections is only extant from the Theravāda tradition. Combined with the differing distribution of discourses over the four main collections in other reciter traditions, the net result is that parallel versions to a Pāli discourse are at times simply no longer extant.[58] This may well apply to the present instance, which does not show any evident sign of lateness, unlike the episode of Mahāpajāpatī Gotamī's spectacular passing away.

According to the introductory narration that precedes the part translated below, King Pasenadi had asked one of his attendants to find out if there was some religious teacher whom he could visit. Having scoured the area, this attendant recommended the nun Khemā as the most appropriate choice for the king's visit, reporting that she was renowned for her wisdom, capability, intelligence, learnedness, exceptional speaking ability, and eloquence. This thereby conveys the message that in the whole area in which the king was staying at that time the nun Khemā was the religious teacher most worth a visit. The suggested worthiness of paying her a visit turned out to be true, as can be seen from the powerful and profound exposition found below, which I present alternating between translations and my comments.

> Then Pasenadi, the king of Kosala, approached the nun Khemā. Having approached and paid respect to the nun Khemā, he sat to one side. Sitting to one side, Pasenadi, the king of Kosala, said this to the nun Khemā:
>
> "Revered lady, how is it, does a Tathāgata exist after death?"
>
> "Great King, the Blessed One has not declared that a Tathāgata exists after death."
>
> "Then, revered lady, how is it, does a Tathāgata not exist after death?"
>
> "Great King, the Blessed One has also not declared that a Tathāgata does not exist after death."
>
> "Revered lady, how is it, does a Tathāgata exist and not exist after death?"
>
> "Great King, the Blessed One has not declared that a Tathāgata exists and does not exist after death."
>
> "Revered lady, how is it, does a Tathāgata neither exist nor not exist after death?"
>
> "Great King, the Blessed One has also not declared that a Tathāgata neither exists nor does not exist after death."

The above exchange relies on an ancient Indian mode of thought, the tetralemma, differing from the twofold logic known in Western thought.[59] Simply said, in addition to affirmation and denial, this alternative model recognizes the possibility that both affirmation and denial could be appropriate, or both could be irrelevant. Expressed in terms of colors, instead of distinguishing merely between what is black and what is white, the fourfold presentation recognizes that something could be both white and black, namely gray, or neither white nor black, namely colors like blue, etc. The fourfold mode of reasoning as such was generally accepted in the ancient Indian setting and can be seen to underlie a range of the teachings attributed to the Buddha himself.

In the above case, however, as Khemā rightly makes clear, the Buddha was on record for having consistently refused to take up any of the four possibilities in relation to the postmortem destiny of a Tathāgata, a term which here refers to an arahant in general. This term appears to have been in general usage in ancient India to designate someone who has reached the acme of spiritual perfection. Combining the fourfold mode of reasoning with the issue of what happens to a fully realized one at death seems to have been a standard way of ascertaining the type of teachings proclaimed by another religious practitioner, serving at the same time as a succinct way of inquiring about the type of goal the practitioner aspired to. Said simply: Does your form of religious practice lead to eternal life? Or does it lead to the opposite? Does it lead to a combination of the two? Or does your conception of the final goal not fit either of these two options?

The Pāli discourse continues with the king repeating the questions he had posed and the replies he had received. Although in itself a natural procedure in an oral setting, in order to ensure that one has correctly understood, the repetition can at times serve as an expression of some exasperation. This could well be the case here, as the king next inquires why the Buddha had not taken up anyone of the four possible alternatives:

> "Revered lady, what is the reason, what is the cause why the Blessed One has not declared this?"
>
> "Now then, Great King, I will ask you in return about this very matter, and you may reply as you see fit. What do you

think, Great King, do you have an accountant or calculator or mathematician who is able to count the [grains of] sand in the Ganges: 'There are so many [grains of] sand,' or 'There are so many hundreds of [grains of] sand,' or 'There are so many thousands of [grains of] sand,' or 'There are so many hundreds of thousands of [grains of] sand'?"

"No, revered lady."

"Do you have an accountant or calculator or mathematician who can count the water in the great ocean: 'There are so many gallons of water,' or 'There are so many hundreds of gallons of water,' or 'There are so many thousands of gallons of water,' or 'There are so many hundreds of thousands of gallons of water'?"

"No, revered lady. Why is that? Great is the ocean, revered lady, deep, immeasurable, difficult to fathom."

The early discourses time and again show the Buddha's contemporaries being puzzled and even vexed by his persistent refusal to adopt any of the four possibilities of envisaging the destiny of an accomplished one after death. One discourse even reports that a Buddhist monk threatened to disrobe unless the Buddha took a definite stance on one of these positions.[60] Another Pāli discourse reports that a different Buddhist monk, finding himself in basically the same situation as the nun Khemā of having to explain the Buddha's position to others, tried to deal with the issue by claiming that there was still another way of making a statement on the matter. Since in ancient Indian thought the fourfold mode of reasoning exhausts the possible ways of taking a position, this reply earned him the ridicule of his visitors.[61] Yet another monk just opted for the second of the four alternatives by proclaiming that a Tathāgata will be annihilated at death,[62] a mistaken view he had to relinquish on receiving a teaching from Sāriputta.

In stark contrast to these monks, Khemā handles the situation very skillfully. In order to drive home the fact that some questions cannot really be answered in a straightforward manner, she brings the matter at hand right into the sphere of personal experience for the king, who must have had some accountants assisting him in overseeing his affairs. Yet, however much these would have been apt at counting the king's revenue or other things, they would not have been able to count the grains of sand in the Ganges or the gallons of water in the great ocean. In this way, Khemā illustrates the situation with examples taken from the material world in a way that is directly comprehensible by the king. Other Pāli discourses attribute both similes to the Buddha but never to any of his other disciples.[63] Khemā not only stands out for being the only disciple to employ these similes, she also presents them together in a manner that leads the king to the assessment that the ocean is deep and immeasurable, thereby in a way preparing the ground for what she will expound next. Based on having delivered these two similes, Khemā clarifies the situation in the following manner:

> "In the same way, Great King, that bodily form by which, [in an attempt at] defining, one may define a Tathāgata, that bodily form has been abandoned by a Tathāgata, cut off at the root, made like a palm-tree stump, made something that does not become, being of the nature not to arise again in the future. Great King, a Tathāgata is freed from being reckoned in terms of bodily form, being deep, immeasurable, and difficult to fathom, just like the great ocean.
>
> "'A Tathāgata exists after death' does not apply, 'a Tathāgata does not exist after death' also does not apply, 'a Tathāgata exists and does not exist after death' also does not apply, 'a Tathāgata neither exists nor does not exist after death' also does not apply."

Khemā continues by applying the same explanation to the remaining four aggregates of feeling tone (*vedanā*, often also translated as "feeling" or as "sensation"), perception, volitional formations, and consciousness.[64] In each case, the four alternatives of predicating the destiny of a Tathāgata after death do not apply, because such predications involve a mistaken notion of the nature of a Tathāgata while still alive. The point is that such mistaken notions are based on reifying a self as a substantial entity, which in turn is grounded in clinging to one or another of the aggregates. Yet, since someone who is truly a Tathāgata has gone beyond clinging to any of the five aggregates, the basis for such self-notions has been thoroughly abandoned, leaving no room for postulations that have these very self-notions as their premise.[65]

The clarification offered by Khemā in this way, based on comparing the nature of the Tathāgata to that of the great ocean, is yet another instance of her being the only disciple in Pāli discourses to explain matters in the same way as the Buddha reportedly did on another occasion.[66]

The above discourse continues by reporting that King Pasenadi was delighted at the explanation he had received. On a later occasion, when he had a chance to meet the Buddha and pose the same question, he reportedly received exactly the same reply. This in turn serves as a seal of authentication for the remarkable exposition given by Khemā. Gisela Krey (2010, 30) comments:

> Khemā's answer skillfully combines two didactic methods: ... she asks a counterquestion (*paṭipucchā*) to King Pasenadi, and by doing so, she employs a double simile [about] trying to fathom the *Tathāgata*'s unfathomableness: grains of sand and the deep ocean. Thereby the *sutta* is enriched with an element of poetic style.

Dispassion Toward Sensuality

In addition to the above discourse, the voice of Khemā has also been preserved in a set of verses to rebuff Māra, who had vainly tried to tempt her with sensual indulgence. His challenge takes the following form:[67]

> "You are young and beautiful,
> I am also young and in my prime.
> Come, Khemā, let us enjoy ourselves
> With the fivefold music."

The reference to fivefold music appears to intend traditional Indian music performed with five different instruments, comprising percussion instruments, stringed instruments, and wind instruments.[68] Metaphorically the same reference evokes the enjoyment of sensual pleasures by way of the five senses. The invitation to sensual indulgence is voiced by Māra, who features as the tempter in early Buddhist discourse, in the sense of at times personifying external challenges and even potential threats by outsiders.[69] In other words, the depiction of Māra inviting Khemā to indulge does not carry any implication that she has not yet overcome the attractions of sensuality, as she in fact makes quite clear in her reply:

> "This foul body,
> Sickly and perishable,
> Disgusts and distresses me.
> Craving for sensuality has been rooted out.
>
> Sensual pleasures are like the blade of a sword
> And the aggregates like its chopping block.
> What you call the delight of sensuality,
> For me now is no delight [at all]."

The reference to being disgusted and distressed in the first of the above two verses employs rather strong terminology, which seems somewhat out of place for one who has been completely liberated. The same verse recurs in the *Saṃyuttanikāya*,[70] here attributed to the nun Vijayā (on which see below p. 55). The corresponding verses in two parallels preserved in Chinese translation do not have any reference to being disgusted with one's own body.[71] The *Saṃyuttanikāya* version presents Vijayā as a fully awakened one (as do the parallels), by indicating that she had gone beyond sensual desire and was free from ignorance in relation to the form and formless realms. This makes her case similar to that of Khemā, as in both instances a reference to a pronouncedly negative attitude toward their own bodies seems out of place for fully awakened ones. Judging from the parallels, it seems probable that an error in transmission has occurred.

The remainder of Khemā's poem is unproblematic, as it just shows her conveying in no uncertain terms a total disinterest in sensuality and a lack of infatuation with her own body. Regarding the issue of infatuation with one's own body, according to the commentary she had formerly been quite obsessed with her own beauty.[72] Ria Kloppenborg (1995, 159) considers the reference to the body being "sickly" (*ātura*) to be probably a wordplay on the reference to "music" (*turiya*) in Māra's challenge. The comparison of sensual indulgence to the blade of a sword occurs elsewhere in the Pāli discourses with the same function of illustrating the dangers of sensual indulgence.[73] The final line succinctly sums up the matter: What Māra (and with him most people in the world in general) considers to be a source of delight, from the viewpoint of a fully liberated one is the very opposite.

> "[Sensual] enjoyment has been destroyed in every way,
> The mass of darkness has been shattered.
> Know this, Bad One:
> You are defeated, End-Maker."

With this verse, Khemā confirms what is already evident in the final lines of the two previous verses, according to which craving for sensuality has been rooted out and sensual delight has become nondelight. Such transformation is a matter of wisdom, hence the mass of darkness, representing ignorance, has been shattered.

The reference to darkness is in this context best not taken too literally. It does not imply that the realization of awakening involves experiencing some form of light. In fact, had that been intended, the verse would quite probably not speak of darkness having been "shattered," a choice of terminology that does not fit the dispelling of darkness by light. Of further relevance here would be a verse in the *Udāna*, which in evident reference to the realization of Nirvana indicates that, although there is no light of the sun, the moon, or the stars, there is also no darkness.[74] In other words, the experience of Nirvana goes beyond both light and darkness.

Having shattered the darkness of ignorance for good and with full confidence in her own inner freedom, Khemā announces her victory over

Māra, who is also called the "end-maker" in the sense of standing representative of death. Khemā has realized the deathless, which is another term for Nirvana, thereby leaving Māra completely defeated.

> "You honor the constellations,
> [Ritually] tending fire in the forest,
> Not knowing as it really is,
> Fools, you do not consider [true] purity.
>
> But worshipping [instead]
> The Buddha, the supreme of humans,
> Undertaking the teacher's teaching
> Freed I am from all *dukkha*."

Khemā's final verses provide a contrast between practices considered to be purifying in the ancient Indian setting, such as offering oblations to fire tended in a forest, and her own successful progress to complete inner purification. From the viewpoint of the superb liberation she had reached, any worship should best be directed to the Buddha, since putting into practice his instructions is what leads to freedom from *dukkha*.

Uppalavaṇṇā

> The foremost of those nuns who excel in psychic powers, being able to summon divine beings, is the nun called Uppalavaṇṇā.[75]

THE ABOVE QUOTE from the *Ekottarikāgama* agrees with the Pāli list of outstanding nuns that Uppalavaṇṇā was foremost in psychic powers, although the latter comes without a reference to summoning divine beings. Early Buddhist thought clearly acknowledges the possibility of acquiring supernormal abilities through dedicated meditation practice, namely by cultivating the deep levels of mental tranquility that were believed to yield psychic powers. The notion of such powers is an integral part of early Buddhist thought, together with descriptions of supernormal events and celestial realms, so that it would not be doing justice to the actual textual evidence to pretend that these are just later accretions. At the same time, however, there is a discernible increase in emphasis on such phenomena, combined with a more literal understanding of their implications, in later texts. As already mentioned earlier in relation to Mahāpajāpatī Gotamī's passing away, the idea of physical levitation appears to become more and more prominent in later times. Nevertheless, levitating mentally to visit celestial realms and interact with their inhabitants is clearly present already in the earliest textual testimonies of Buddhist thought still extant.

Role Models for Nuns

The inspiration to be gained from those who, through their meditation practice, have gained psychic powers or cultivated wisdom finds explicit expression in a discourse extant in Chinese, which has several Pāli parallels. The parallels agree in presenting Khemā and Uppalavaṇṇā as role models for women who have chosen to go forth:[76]

> If a woman wants to shave off her hair ... and don the three monastic robes to go forth and train in the path,[77] she should be like the nun Khemā and the nun Uppalavaṇṇā. The reason is that this is the measure, this is the standard,[78] namely the nun Khemā and the nun Uppalavaṇṇā.

In this way, as noted by Alice Collett (2016, 207), "Uppalavaṇṇā is declared ... someone who[m] the other nuns could look to emulate." By serving as role models for other nuns, Khemā and Uppalavaṇṇā become the female counterparts to the two chief monk disciples of the Buddha, Sāriputta and Mahāmoggallāna, who similarly excelled in wisdom and psychic powers, respectively. From this perspective, then, Khemā can be seen as a female complement to Sāriputta just as Uppalavaṇṇā was a female complement to Mahāmoggallāna.

This balanced mode of presentation reflects a stance of soteriological inclusiveness in contrast to ancient Indian patterns of discrimination against women. The same inclusiveness was already evident in the first chapter on Mahāpajāpatī Gotamī's going forth, taking the form of the explicit indication that women can reach all four levels of awakening. The motif of serving as role models for other monastics, however, at the same time also points to another type of inclusiveness. In a study of Uppalavaṇṇā in a Sinhala Buddhist text, Ranjini Obeyesekere (2001, 109) reasons: "Since the rank of second chief disciple, whether male or female, had to be filled by one of dark complexion, she was born as dark skinned." She adds that the significance of the notion that one in each of the two pairs of chief disciples (Sāriputta and Mahāmoggallāna as well as Khemā and Uppalavaṇṇā) should be of dark skin color "was perhaps to emphasize the all-embracing inclusiveness of the Doctrine in the context of the varied people and castes" in ancient India (2001, 109n3).

The explicit recognition of certain disciples as role models indeed reflects the importance of having an inspiring exemplar to look up to and emulate, making it natural to ensure that such inspiration takes as inclusive a form as possible. In the present case this happens by complementing a pair of males with a pair of females (the same holds for lay disciples, see p. 207). On the above reasoning presented by Ranjini Obeyesekere, then, this inspirational function is further enhanced by each pair of monastics consisting of a member with lighter skin (Khemā/Sāriputta) and another member with darker skin (Uppalavaṇṇā/Mahāmoggallāna).

Defeating Māra

The *Saṃyuttanikāya* and its Chinese parallels, in the form of two *Saṃyuktāgama* collections, dedicate an entire section to teachings given by nuns. This section presents a series of encounters between various nuns and Māra. Here is the first part of the encounter between Uppalavaṇṇā and Māra, as reported in one of the two *Saṃyuktāgama* collections (T 99):[79]

> Thus have I heard. At one time the Buddha was staying at Sāvatthī in Jeta's Grove, Anāthapiṇḍika's Park. At that time the nun Uppalavaṇṇā was staying in a community of nuns in the Rājakārāma in Sāvatthī. In the morning, she put on her robes, took her bowl, and entered Sāvatthī to beg for alms. Having finished her meal, she returned to the monastery, put away her robe and bowl, finished washing her feet, took her sitting mat, placed it over her shoulder, entered the Andhavana Grove, and sat down under a tree for the day's abiding.

The above introductory narrative recurs in the same way for a range of other encounters between individual nuns and Māra, to be explored in the following chapters. This element of repetition, which from now on I will avoid by not translating the full introductory narration for the other nuns, is additionally strengthened by the fact that each discourse continues by repeating the whole description (except for "thus have I heard") as a reflection made by Māra. After having completed that reflection, Māra thinks:

> "I shall now approach and disturb her." He transformed himself into a youth of handsome appearance, approached the nun Uppalavaṇṇā, and said in verse:
>
> "What a beautiful flowering Sal tree
> Under which you have come to stay,
> Alone, without a companion,
> Are you not afraid of wicked men?"

The Sal tree (*shorea robusta*) is a majestic tree that can grow to considerable height and girth, thus offering ample protection against the weather for someone sitting outside in nature to meditate. In its flowering season, such a tree will be beautifully covered with pale yellow flowers, a visual delight that was evidently not lost on Māra.

The second part of his challenge carries an underlying current of threat and sexual aggression. Serinity Young (2004, 193) summarizes the gist of the episode as being "Māra's attempt to distract her from meditating by reminding her that solitary women in lonely places could easily be raped." Yet, as will become clear soon, Uppalavaṇṇā was not to be perturbed by such malicious threats.

> Then the nun Uppalavaṇṇā thought: "Who is this person, wanting to frighten me? Is he a human or is he a nonhuman? Is this person scheming to seduce me?" Having considered it in this way, she realized: "This is certainly the wicked Māra. The Bad One wants to confound me." She spoke in verse:
>
> "Even if there were a hundred thousand men
> All scheming to seduce me,
> Just like you, wicked Māra,
> Coming to where I am,

They could not stir a hair of mine.
I am not afraid of you, wicked Māra."

This direct and self-confident response by Uppalavaṇṇā is all the more remarkable in view of the report in the Pāli *Vinaya* that she had endured the horrible experience of being raped.[80] The rapist had hidden in her hut and, when she returned from her daily begging round, attacked and raped her. On the assumption that this event happened before the present encounter, her composed and calm reaction reported in the above passage conveys the message that a fully awakened one will not be traumatized even by the atrocious experience of rape. With complete self-confidence, she is able to proclaim that a sexual threat will not stir a single hair of hers and not cause her to have any fear at all.

Māra spoke again in verse:

"I will now enter your belly,
And stay hidden inside,
Or stay between your eyebrows,
You will not be able to see me."

A substantial difference occurs in the Pāli version at this juncture, as according to its report it is Uppalavaṇṇā who threatens to get into Māra's belly.[81] Another discourse parallel extant in Chinese translation, however, supports the above presentation that this idea was a threat made by Māra.[82] In fact, it is not clear if Māra was believed to have a digestive system at all. Moreover, it seems rather odd for a nun to threaten to enter someone else's belly. In contrast, for Māra such an action would be more easily conceivable, from the viewpoint of the ancient setting, as another discourse reports that Māra indeed got into the belly of an arahant monk.[83] In view of these indications, it seems reasonable to propose that the Pāli version has suffered an error in transmission, and that the original sense was indeed that Māra threatened to get into Uppalavaṇṇā's belly.

The proposed attribution of the threat to Māra also accords better with the overall attitude maintained by other arahant nuns on being challenged by him, to be explored in subsequent chapters, as they do not respond to his threats with counter-threats and instead remain equanimous and unimpressed by Māra's ruses. It also fits the present denouement of events, where Māra's first attempt to unsettle Uppalavaṇṇā by threatening rape has been unsuccessful, and she has right away recognized that the youth of handsome appearance is none other than Māra. His identity being recognized, it makes sense for him to issue another threat that is in line with the various types of mischief that the early discourses associate with Māra.

> Then the nun Uppalavaṇṇā spoke again in verse:
>
> "My mind has great might,
> Having well cultivated the psychic powers.
> Being liberated from the great bondage,
> I do not fear you, wicked Māra."

Māra's new threat leaves Uppalavaṇṇā just as unimpressed as his earlier tactic regarding the danger of sexual assault. Her excellence in psychic powers is well beyond whatever Māra might try to do, hence Uppalavaṇṇā does not fear him at all.

> "I have vomited out the three stains,
> Which are the root of fear.
> Being established in the state of fearlessness,
> I am not afraid of Māra's army."

This verse, together with the ensuing and final one, is without a counterpart in the Pāli version, although comparable verses do occur in the other version extant in Chinese.[84] The reference to the three stains intends the root defilements of greed/lust, anger/hatred, and delusion.[85] Once these are eradicated, all fear and anxiety, including even just restlessness, are also left behind for good.

"In regard to all craving and rejoicing,
I am entirely separated from darkness,
Having realized the quietude of extinction;
I dwell in peace, established in the eradication of the influxes.
I recognized you, wicked Māra,
You should make yourself disappear and go!"

Then Māra, the Bad One, thought: "The nun Uppalavaṇṇā has understood my intentions." Harboring sadness and worry within, he vanished and was seen no more.

Having earlier declared her supernormal abilities and proclaimed her utter fearlessness, Uppalavaṇṇā now proceeds by giving further details on her successful gaining of freedom from defilements. Liberated from craving and the darkness of ignorance, she has realized Nirvana. With the extinction of the influxes, she is completely at peace within.

The poem concludes with Uppalavaṇṇā telling Māra in no unclear terms to leave, as he has been recognized for who he is, and his intention to upset her mind has been seen through. Aware of his complete failure to achieve what he had set out to do, Māra is forced to leave in distress.

In this way, relying on her superb meditative mastery, which has endowed her with supernormal potency and, even more importantly, with complete freedom from defilements, Uppalavaṇṇā can remain completely unperturbed in the face of Māra's challenges.

Mastery of the Mind

The Pāli version of Uppalavaṇṇā's words spoken when thoroughly defeating Māra recur as part of a long poem in the *Therīgāthā*.[86] According to the Pāli commentary, the first three verses of this poem refer to the pre-ordination experiences of another nun,[87] concluding with the indication in the third verse that "*she* went forth in Rājagaha from the home life to homelessness."[88] The use of the third person singular ("she") in this verse would concord with the commentarial indication that this part should not be considered an autobiographical report of Uppalavaṇṇā's own experiences. The part of the poem that appears to be indeed concerned with Uppalavaṇṇā herself sets in by depicting her superb accomplishments in the following way:

> "I know my former lives,
> The divine eye has been purified,
> There is knowledge of the minds of others,
> And the [divine] ear element has been purified.
>
> I also realized psychic powers,
> And reached the destruction of the influxes.
> The six supernormal knowledges have been realized:
> The Buddha's teaching has been done."

In early Buddhist thought, recollection of one's former lives has its counterpart in the "divine eye," which enables directly witnessing the passing away and being reborn of other sentient beings in accordance with their former deeds. These are the first two of the three higher knowledges which, according to the traditional account, the Buddha realized on the night of his awakening.[89] Uppalavaṇṇā has attained these as well as the telepathic ability to know what is going on in the minds of others. She has achieved the divine ear, understood to enable extending one's hearing far beyond the normal range of the physical ear to include sounds that manifest in both human and celestial realms. Together with psychic powers and the destruction of the influxes, these are the six supernormal knowledges that according to early Buddhist thought can be reached through dedicated meditative practice. As one who has mastered all of these, Uppalavaṇṇā is indeed in the position to proclaim that she has put into practice the Buddha's teaching.

> "By psychic power I created
> A four-horsed chariot,
> I worshiped the Buddha's feet:
> The such-like protector of the world."[90]

The Pāli commentary relates this verse to an occasion when the Buddha performed the twin miracle (of simultaneously manifesting water and fire) in a contest with non-Buddhist practitioners.[91] According to the Pāli commentaries, Uppalavaṇṇā had magically created a chariot and offered to defeat non-Buddhist practitioners on behalf of the Buddha, which the latter declined.[92] Taking this story to stand in the background of the above verse is not entirely compelling, as a mere offer that is subsequently declined by the Buddha would hardly merit explicit mention as a stanza in its own right, alongside the other highly remarkable achievements of Uppalavaṇṇā taken up in her poem.

It seems thus perhaps more likely that the reference is to a tale known in a range of Buddhist traditions, according to which she had transformed herself into giving the impression of being a wheel-turning king in order to drive easily to the front of a large crowd and receive the Buddha, who was returning from a long sojourn in heaven.[93] This tale should probably be read in light of the proclamation that women by nature cannot fulfill the position of a wheel-turning king.[94] In fact, according to a later treatise, her motivation for performing this supernormal feat was precisely "wishing to get rid of the bad reputation of women."[95]

Whatever may be the final word on the tale in the background of the preceding verse, her next verses clearly refer to her encounter with Māra, already discussed above. Due to such overlap, here and with several other nuns to be taken up subsequently, my survey will move through the basically same episode twice: once as part of my study of the *Saṃyuktāgama* account and again when exploring the verses attributed to the same nun in the *Therīgāthā*. This affords the opportunity to review the same exchange with closer attention to some variations. The *Therīgāthā* version of Uppalavaṇṇā's encounter with Māra begins by reporting his challenge:

> "Having gone to a Sal tree in full bloom,
> You are staying alone at its root
> And without any companion.
> Foolish one, are you not afraid of rogues?"

This verse by Māra is the counterpart to his challenge taken up above, the main difference being that in the present version Māra calls her a foolish one. According to the Pāli commentary, the third line could be read in two alternative ways. It could be stating that she is without a second in the sense of having no companion or carry the meaning that she is without a second in the sense that her beauty is unrivalled.[96] The *Saṃyuttanikāya* version of this line has a different Pāli term that indeed conveys the sense that her beauty is unrivalled.[97] Caroline Rhys Davids (1917/1979, 164–65n5) reasons that, given that the previous line had already mentioned that she is alone, it would have been "redundant to add anything as to her want of a chaperone." This is indeed the case, although it needs to be kept in mind that such redundancy is not uncommon in early Buddhist poetry. Moreover, the corresponding line in the Chinese version translated above (of which Caroline Rhys Davids could of course not have been aware) refers to her being without a companion, and the same holds for the other Chinese version.[98] In view of the resultant ambiguity, perhaps the line could be read as a double entendre? In a way, precisely her unrivalled beauty is what makes her being alone more dangerous in a setting infested with lecherous males.[99]

> "Even if a hundred thousand rogues
> Like you were to come together,
> Not a hair will be stirred nor tremble.
> What could you alone do to me, Māra?"

Her corresponding fearless reply in the Chinese version, translated above, makes the implied sexual threat more explicit by referring to the hundred thousand as "all scheming to seduce me."

> "I will disappear,
> Or enter your belly,
> I will stand between your eyebrows;
> You will not see me standing there."

As mentioned above, the impression that this verse should be attributed to Uppalavaṇṇā is unconvincing for several reasons. It would therefore quite probably do more justice to its intended import to read it as a threat issued by Māra. The motivation for such a threat would be his realization that his earlier sexual threat had been unsuccessful in arousing fear in Uppalavaṇṇā, who had seen through his disguise and realized that she was facing Māra.

> "I have gained mastery over the mind,
> The bases of success have been well developed.
> The six supernormal knowledges have been realized:
> The Buddha's teaching has been done."

The verse refers to the "four bases of success" (Pāli: *iddhipāda*; Sanskrit: *ṛddhipāda*), sometimes also translated as the "four roads to psychic power." Simply said, these are modes of arriving at concentrative mastery of the mind by relying on either (wholesome) desire, energy, (a natural inclination of the) mind, or investigation.[100]

> "Sensual pleasures are like the blade of a sword
> And the aggregates like its chopping block.
> What you call the delight of sensuality,
> For me now is no delight [at all].
>
> [Sensual] enjoyment has been destroyed in every way,
> The mass of darkness has been shattered.
> Know this, Bad One:
> You are defeated, End-Maker."

These two verses correspond to verses spoken by Khemā, discussed above (see pp. 31 and 32). Although these verses recur also in the poems of other nuns, the correspondence established in this way between Khemā and Uppalavaṇṇā offers me an occasion to revisit the recommendation, translated at the outset of this chapter. According to this recommendation, these two nuns should be taken as role models by other women who decide to go forth and embark on the monastic life, living the life of renunciation that has become possible thanks to Mahāpajāpatī Gotamī's petitioning the Buddha to start on order of nuns. Their superb achievements and abilities make such a recommendation deeply meaningful; Khemā and Uppalavaṇṇā indeed provide an inspiring example for all generations of nuns, from the distant past into the future.

Kisāgotamī

> The foremost of those nuns who undertake ascetic practices,
> the eleven restraints, is the nun called Kisāgotamī.[101]

THE ABOVE PROCLAMATION from the listing of outstanding nuns speaks of Kisāgotamī's eminence in terms of eleven types of ascetic practices. Within the same discourse collection, the *Ekottarikāgama*, the count of ascetic practices tends to differ between eleven and twelve observances of this type.[102] Such listings of ascetic practices in general tend to show some variations, with the Theravāda tradition presenting a list of thirteen.[103] By way of illustration of what such practices could comprise, the listing of thirteen ascetic observances in the *Visuddhimagga* could be relied on.[104] Before turning to this list, however, it needs to be noted that not all of these thirteen practices are suitable for nuns. Sleeping out in the open, for example, would have been too dangerous an undertaking for any woman in the ancient setting, due to the high probability of leading to sexual abuse and related bodily and mental harm.

The practices listed in the *Visuddhimagga* comprise having only three robes, which additionally can be restricted to robes made of rags, as well as relying only on food obtained by begging (instead of going to invitations), with an additional practice of not skipping any house along the chosen path in anticipation of receiving only food of low quality or even none. Other such practices are taking just a single meal per day, putting all the food in a single bowl (so that it gets mixed), and refusing additional food that is offered subsequently. Ascetic practices can also have a bearing on where one dwells, which could be in a forest, at the root of a tree, out in the open, or in a cemetery. Two more practices are to accept whatever bed one is assigned and to sit up even throughout the night without lying down.

In the Pāli listing of outstanding nuns, Kisāgotamī's eminence concerns a single practice, which is the wearing of coarse robes.[105] This does not precisely correspond to any of the set of thirteen summarized above, although having robes made from rags would quite probably result in wearing rather coarse robes.

No Need for a Man or Children

Unlike Khemā and Uppalavaṇṇā, Kisāgotamī does not appear to have been of exceptional beauty and we may picture her to have been quite lean and, in keeping with the above indication, dressed in coarse robes.

She pertains to the group of nuns known for having successfully faced an encounter with Māra. The *Saṃyuktāgama* version of this encounter begins by describing in detail where she stayed, how she went begging, and that after the meal she went to sit under a tree to meditate, a description then repeated by Māra. As mentioned in the previous chapter, here and elsewhere I do not provide a full translation of this standardized description and instead turn directly to the last part of Māra's reflection:[106]

> [Māra thought:] "The nun Kisāgotamī ... has entered the Andhavana Grove and sat down cross-legged under a tree for the day's abiding. I shall now approach and disturb her." He transformed himself into a youth of handsome appearance and went to the nun Kisāgotamī. He said in verse:
>
> "Why are you, having lost your child,
> Weeping and, with sad and worried face,
> Sitting alone under a tree?
> Are you searching for a man?"

Similar to the case of Uppalavaṇṇā, Māra's challenge involves a barely veiled sexual threat. Another similarity is that, in his attempt to unsettle the meditating nuns, he somewhat cruelly brings up a particularly painful experience from their past. Whereas in the case of Uppalavaṇṇā the challenge appears to be connected to her having been raped, with Kisāgotamī the reference to "having lost your child" seems to relate to her extreme grief, when still a married woman, at the unexpected death of her only child.

According to the commentary on the *Therīgāthā*, having been born in a poor family, she had married into a wealthy family, where she was treated with contempt.[107] The situation changed substantially when she gave birth to a son, in line with the prevalent view in the ancient setting that the main function of a woman was precisely to give birth to sons. When the child died unexpectedly, she was overwhelmed with grief and went from house to house in town, carrying the dead child on her hip, to ask for some medicine for her son. Eventually she met the Buddha, whom she also solicited for a cure. Whereas previously others had just treated her with scorn, the Buddha met her exactly where she was by telling her where to find the required remedy. This medicine was a mustard seed that she should get from a household where so far nobody had passed away.

Glad to have finally found someone willing to help her, Kisāgotamī started touring the town to get the mustard seed. Yet, even though people were in principle quite willing to give her such a seed, which is after all an item of hardly any value, the households she visited did not fulfill the required qualification, because people had died in every one of them.

Made in this way to realize the universality of death, Kisāgotamī regained her senses and brought her dead child to the cemetery. She returned to the Buddha with the message that no such mustard seed could be found. He gave her a teaching during which she realized stream-entry, after which she decided to go forth.

Her dramatic story and transformation from bereaved mother to Buddhist nun would presumably have become public knowledge. In the present episode, apparently aware of the traumatic experience she had endured, Māra seems to try to take advantage of that to unsettle her.

> Then the nun Kisāgotamī thought: "Who is this, [trying] to frighten me? Is he a human or is he a nonhuman? Is he scheming to seduce me?" Having considered it in this way, certainty

of knowledge arose in her: "Māra, the Bad One, has come [trying] to flirt with me." She spoke in verse:

"Without limit are the sons,
Who all have died and been lost.
This, then, is the end of men [for me];
I have gone beyond [the attraction of] men's external appearance."

The reference to countless sons who have died, which places her personal tragedy within a wider frame of endless births and deaths, is not found in this way in the parallel versions. These nevertheless agree that Kisāgotamī no longer had any desire for children. Her lack of concern for fulfilling the ancient Indian expectation that a woman should bear children (ideally male ones) stands in contrast to what earlier had completely preoccupied her mind. This lack of concern comes conjoined with a disinterest in men. In this way, having rebuffed Māra's attempt to trigger her traumatic past experience, Kisāgotamī expresses her complete disinterest in what male company could offer.

"Not troubled, not sad or worried,
I have done what should be done in the Buddha's dispensation.
Separated from all craving and *dukkha*,
Having entirely relinquished darkness,
I have realized cessation.

I dwell in peace and at ease,
With the influxes eradicated.
I recognize you, wicked Māra,
Now make yourself disappear and go!"

Then Māra, the Bad One, thought: "The nun Kisāgotamī has understood my intentions." Being worried and sad, afflicted and annoyed, he vanished and was seen no more.

Contrary to Māra's malicious insinuation, Kisāgotamī is definitely not sad or worried. Having overcome craving and relinquished the darkness of ignorance, she has fully put into practice the teachings of the Buddha. With the experience of cessation, probably a reference to Nirvana, she dwells in the peace and ease that come from having eradicated all defilements. Endowed with complete self-confidence in her superb accomplishment, Kisāgotamī dispatches Māra, who has to leave distressed and annoyed.

The Wisdom of Release

Besides featuring in the above encounter with Māra, Kisāgotamī is also one of the nuns whose verses have been preserved in the *Therīgāthā*:[108]

"The Sage has praised, in regard to the world,
The condition of having a spiritual friend.
Associating with a spiritual friend,
Even a fool may become wise.

Worthy people should be associated with;
Wisdom increases for those who associate in this way.
On associating with worthy people,
One may even find release from all *dukkha*."

The highlight placed in Kisāgotamī's first two verses on the role of spiritual friends or worthy people is probably best read in the light of the story summarized above, according to which the Buddha's skillful and compassionate intervention led to a substantial increase of her wisdom and helped her to find release from *dukkha*.

"One should understand *dukkha*,
The arising and the cessation of *dukkha*,
And the eightfold path as well;
In all,[109] the four noble truths."

This verse appears to refer to Kisāgotamī's attainment of stream-entry, with which one gains an understanding of the arising and cessation of *dukkha* and of the import of the four noble truths, the fourth of which corresponds to the eightfold path. According to the Pāli commentary, the next two verses are not spoken by her,[110] and four ensuing verses seem to refer to experiences undergone by the nun Paṭācārā before going forth. My translation therefore leaves these out and continues directly with the final two verses by Kisāgotamī. Before turning to these two verses, however, I first summarize the story of Paṭācārā, whose pre-ordination experiences are even more dramatic than those of Kisāgotamī. In fact, had there been a record of some teaching given by her, Paṭācārā would have merited a chapter on her own in my present study.

The basic storyline, according to the commentary on the *Therīgāthā*, is as follows:[111] Paṭācārā fell in love with a servant in her family's household. Finding out that her family planned to marry her to someone else, she escaped to live with him together elsewhere. Becoming pregnant, she wished to be with her family, but her partner tried to delay her return, apparently out of apprehension at the reception he would receive from her family. She eventually set out on her own but then gave birth on the road and decided to return to the place where she had been living with her partner, who had followed and by then caught up with her. Later, when Paṭācārā became pregnant a second time, the same pattern happened. She again gave birth on the road, this time during a great storm. She asked her partner to find some shelter for her. While doing her bidding, he was bitten by a poisonous snake and died. Not knowing why he did not return to help her, she spent the night at the mercy of the weather, on her knees and hands to protect her children. In the morning, Paṭācārā found that her partner was dead.

Continuing her journey crying and desolate, she arrived at a river whose waters were high due to the recent rain. Exhausted from her previous trials, she felt unable to carry both children across at the same time. Leaving the elder child on the riverbank, she crossed over carrying the recently born infant. Having placed the infant on the ground, Paṭācārā was on her way back to get the other child when a bird of prey swooped down and carried away the infant. Seeing what was happening, she tried to chase away the bird by waving her hands and shouting. The other child, trying to watch closely what she was doing in the belief that she was signaling him, fell into the river and was carried away by the water. Overwhelmed with grief, Paṭācārā continued toward her family home, only to be told by another traveler that the same storm had caused her family's home to collapse, killing all its members. On hearing this news, she became insane.

Chancing on an assembly listening to the Buddha, she heard him teach, recovered her senses, and attained stream-entry. At the end of the Buddha's discourse, she requested the going forth and in due time became an arahant.

The listing of eminent nuns in the *Ekottarikāgama* agrees with its Pāli parallel in considering Paṭācārā to have been foremost in upholding the monastic discipline:[112]

> The foremost of those nuns who respectfully uphold the disciplinary rules without infraction is the nun called Paṭācārā.

Upholding the monastic rules is a quality that naturally calls forth high esteem by other monastics and lay supporters. This stands in stark contrast to the contempt with which she was treated by others earlier, at the time when she had become insane due to her overwhelming grief.

In view of the similar transformation from a deeply traumatized woman into an exemplary female saint, it is perhaps not surprising that the verses by Paṭācārā and Kisāgotamī could have gotten mixed up during the course of oral transmission. Both were treated by others as hopelessly deranged, yet the Buddha was able to meet each just where they were and not only help them to regain their senses but even facilitate their attainment of the fruits of the path. Such sublime attainment is the theme of the final two verses by Kisāgotamī:

> "I have cultivated the path,
> The noble eightfold one that leads to the deathless.
> Nirvana has been realized,
> I have looked into the mirror of the teaching.

I am one who has cut out the dart,
Laid down the burden, and done what had to be done indeed.
The Therī Kisāgotamī
Said this with her mind released.[113]

The expression "mirror of the teaching" (*dhammādāsa*) refers to the firm inner confidence gained by a stream-enterer regarding the Buddha, his teaching, and the community of awakened beings, together with unwavering dedication to the basics of ethical conduct. Having looked into this mirror, so to say, through the realization of stream-entry, according to early Buddhist thought one is certain of progress to full awakening without ever being reborn in lower realms of existence.[114]

On this understanding, Kisāgotamī's first verse still refers to her attainment of stream-entry. The second verse, however, is rather a declaration of having become an arahant. It is only with full awakening attained that the dart of craving has been cut out, the burden of clinging (to the five aggregates in particular) has indeed been laid down, and what had to be done has indeed been done. This is the sublime achievement realized by Kisāgotamī, involving a transformation from a mother traumatized by desperate sorrow to an arahant with a mind that is completely released.

Vijayā

> The foremost of those nuns who have attained the four analytical knowledges, being without timidity in the heart, is the nun called Vijayā.[115]

THE ABOVE EXTRACT from the listing of eminent nuns in the *Ekottarikāgama* is without a counterpart in the corresponding Pāli list. Vijayā's eminence in regard to the four analytical knowledges (*paṭisambhidā*) implies the ability to know the meaning or sense of things and the principle that underlies them, as well as knowing the (proper use of) language, and having eloquence in regard to these. Possession of these four analytical knowledges appears to have been held in high esteem among the disciples of the Buddha.[116] The Pāli listing of outstanding monks agrees with its *Ekottarikāgama* parallel in presenting Mahākoṭṭhita as outstanding in this respect.[117] The passage translated above thereby presents Vijayā as the female counterpart to Mahākoṭṭhita, with the additional indication that she was free of timidity.

Meditation Instead of Entertainment

Vijayā pertains to the nuns having an encounter with Māra, which in the *Saṃyuktāgama* takes the following form (I abbreviate the introductory narration):[118]

> [Māra thought:] "The nun Vijayā ... has entered the Andhavana Grove and sat down under a tree for the day's abiding. I shall now approach and disturb her." He transformed himself

> into a youth of handsome appearance, went into her presence, and said in verse:
>
> "Now you are young,
> I am also young.
> Let us, in this place,
> Perform the five types of music,
> And enjoy ourselves together!
> Of what use is this meditative musing?"

The invitation to enjoy the five types of music already came up in the verses attributed to Khemā, in which she reports her own encounter with Māra. In the present case, such a reference stands in explicit contrast to meditating. Although not openly mentioned in the parallel versions, the contrast made in this way is quite meaningful and can safely be assumed to be implicit in all instances when Māra approaches a meditating nun and tries to tempt her with enjoyment or music. In the corresponding line in the other version extant in Chinese translation, Māra queries why she is sitting there alone instead of being with him,[119] which in a similar way attempts to dismiss the value of meditative solitude, especially for women.

> Then the nun Vijayā thought: "Who is this person, wanting to frighten me? Is he a human or is he a nonhuman? Is this person scheming to seduce me?" Having considered it in this way, she gained the realization: "This is Māra, the Bad One, wanting to confound me." She spoke in verse:
>
> "Singing, dancing, doing various kinds of performances,
> All sorts of enjoyments,
> I now grant them all to you,
> I have no need of them.
>
> With the quietude of extinction attained,
> I take the five sense pleasures of even celestials, or of humans,

And give them all [to you];
I have no need of them."

What men in the world tend to consider a source of enjoyment particularly when being in female company, namely singing and dancing, is something for which Vijayā has no need at all. Even celestial pleasures of the senses, held to be superbly gratifying in the ancient Indian cultural setting, are something of no relevance at all to a woman who has attained the quietude of extinction, the peace of Nirvana.

"Having relinquished all rejoicing and delight,
I am entirely separated from darkness.
By having realized the quietude of extinction,
I dwell in peace, established in the eradication of the influxes.
I recognize you, wicked Māra,
You should make yourself disappear and go!"

Then Māra, the Bad One, thought: "The nun Vijayā has understood my intentions." Harboring sadness and sorrow within, he vanished and was seen no more.

The reference to relinquishing all rejoicing and delight intends those of a sensual type. As will become evident from Vijayā's verses, taken up below, her very realization of the quietude of extinction, through which her influxes were eradicated and she was separated from the darkness of ignorance, had been such a powerful source of joy that she sat cross-legged continuously for seven days without getting up. In other words, the final goal of meditation practice in early Buddhist soteriology is considered to offer a wellspring of joy and happiness; what should be left behind to be able to progress to that are only the sensual types of enjoyment.

From Restlessness to Liberation

A set of verses attributed to the nun Vijayā is extant from the *Therīgāthā*.[120] These describe in detail how she was able to reach liberation, thereby conveying information that is of considerable relevance to other meditators. This holds true in particular for the need to keep the mind balanced and for the potential impact of key elements of the teachings on progress to liberation.

"Four times, five times,
I went out of my dwelling,
Not having gained peace of mind,
Being without mastery of the mind."

The reference to leaving their dwelling "four times, five times" recurs in verses by two other nuns.[121] In relation to the first of these two cases, the commentary offers an explanation.[122] This explanation conveys the impression that what led to such going out of the dwelling was excessive application of energy. Although motivated by the sincere wish to gain liberation, overexertion can just result in restlessness. This is indeed an obstruction, as it interferes with mental tranquility and prevents gaining the inner balance needed for proper progress.

A convenient illustration for such balance is the simile of the lute, reportedly delivered by the Buddha to a former musician who had become a monk and was on the verge of disrobing as he had not made any progress.[123] Yet, his lack of progress appears to have been precisely due to excessive striving. Just as the strings of a lute need to be neither too tight nor too lax in order to produce harmonious sound, in the same way there is a need for balanced application of effort to progress on the path.

"Having approached a nun,
I paid respect and questioned her.
She instructed me with teachings
On the elements and sense spheres,

On the four noble truths,
The faculties and powers,
The awakening factors, and the eightfold path
For attaining the supreme goal."

According to the commentary on Vijayā's verses, the nun she approached was none other than Khemā.[124] In this way, the present set of verses contains yet another pointer at Khemā's remarkable wisdom. Perhaps in an attempt to redirect Vijayā's apparently somewhat restless pushing for the breakthrough, Khemā gave her a comprehensive overview of the teachings. The idea could be that her excessive energy needed to be redirected by engaging her in different perspectives on the teachings.

Besides giving her something to do, several of these teachings point to the need for inner balance. This holds in particular for the five faculties or powers, which involve a balancing of confidence with wisdom and energy with concentration, based on the key quality of mindfulness. The same holds for the seven awakening factors, of which three are more energizing and three are more calming. Here, too, mindfulness plays a foundational role, being the one out of the set of seven that is commendable at all times.[125] Such pointers at the need to balance the mind, together with the inspiration that can be gained by reflecting on the deep teachings that Khemā had expounded to her, would have facilitated gaining the peace of mind Vijayā had so far been unable to gain.

> "Having heard her utterance,
> I followed her advice.
> In the first part of the night
> I recollected my past births;
>
> In the middle part of the night,
> I purified the divine eye;
> In the last part of the night,
> I shattered the mass of darkness."

Khemā's wise and skillful teachings bore ample fruit. Following her advice, Vijaya was able to shatter the darkness of ignorance. She did so by meditatively following in the Buddha's footsteps, namely by proceeding from recollection of her own past lives to witnessing the passing away and being reborn of others in the first two watches of the night of her full awakening.

> "And I dwelt suffusing the body
> At that time with joy and happiness;
> On the seventh day I stretched out my feet,
> Having shattered the mass of darkness."

The bliss of liberation suffused her body to such an extent that she remained seated cross-legged in meditation for seven days. This confirms that her reference to having relinquished all rejoicing and delight, made in her rebuttal to Māra, was concerned with sensual types of rejoicing only. Leaving these behind, the doors are flung wide open to the possibility of gaining spiritual types of joy and happiness. This is what Vijayā had been able to accomplish, thanks to the wise teaching she had received from Khemā.

Cālā

Transcending Birth

Although the nun Cālā is not mentioned in the list of foremost nuns either in the *Ekottarikāgama* or in its Pāli parallel, her outstanding capabilities become quite evident in the record of how she dispatched Māra in the *Saṃyuktāgama*, whose Pāli counterpart recurs also in the *Therīgāthā*. In this way, whereas my survey of previous nuns involves various episodes, the present case is based on a single episode: how Cālā faced Māra. As earlier, I abbreviate the introductory narration in the *Saṃyuktāgama* account:[126]

> [Māra thought:] "The nun Cālā ... has entered the Andhavana Grove and sat down under a tree for the day's abiding. I shall now approach and disturb her." He transformed himself into a youth of handsome appearance, went into the presence of the nun Cālā, and said in verse:
>
> "Understand that to experience birth is delightful,
> Being born one partakes of the five sense pleasures.
> Who taught you,[127]
> Making you weary of birth?"

The present challenge by Māra revolves around the ancient Indian conception of rebirth and the aspiration to transcend such rebirth as a key element of early Buddhist soteriology. In fact, the notion of rebirth as such is an integral part of Buddhist thought. A closer study makes it clear that to pretend that the historical Buddha did not really teach rebirth or even that he merely accommodated current beliefs fails to do justice to the textual evidence. This does not mean that in order to become a Buddhist or even to adopt Buddhist meditation practices one needs to affirm rebirth. It only means that the centrality of rebirth needs to be acknowledged and kept in mind in any attempt to understand early Buddhist thought.[128]

> Then the nun Cālā thought: "Who is this person, wanting to make me become frightened? Is he a human or is he a nonhuman? Is this person scheming to seduce me?" [She understood: "This is the wicked Māra],[129] who has come here wanting to make me become confounded." She spoke in verse:
>
> "For those who are born, there certainly will be death,
> To be born is thus just to experience all [kinds] of *dukkha*.
> It is being whipped by vexations and *dukkha*,
> All of which exists in dependence on birth.
> One should eradicate all *dukkha*
> and transcend all births."

With this poetic statement, Cālā expresses the chief motivation that informed the Buddha's own quest for awakening and his subsequent teaching. The inevitability of death (and aging) for those who are born corresponds to the last link in the standard exposition of dependent arising (*paṭicca samuppāda*), which identifies the specific conditions on which *dukkha* depends.[130] The predicament of mortality has birth as its antecedent condition, in the sense that birth is required for death to manifest. The same holds for disease, aging, and various other vexing experiences that human beings have to undergo. Hence, freedom from *dukkha* requires transcendence of birth and with it the transcendence of all the links in dependent arising that lead from the root cause of ignorance to the predicament of being subject to birth.

"With the eye of wisdom contemplate the noble truths.
This is the teaching that has been proclaimed by the Sage:
The affliction of *dukkha*, the arising of *dukkha*,
Its cessation by being separated from all *dukkha*,
Cultivation of the eightfold right path
To peace and ease, destined to Nirvana.

The impartial teaching of the great teacher,
In that teaching I delight.
Because I understand that teaching,
I no longer delight in experiencing birth."

Cālā has gained the eye of wisdom through insight into the four noble truths, the key teaching that according to tradition the recently awakened Buddha disclosed to those who were to become his first disciples.[131]

The reference to delighting in the Buddha's teaching is of further significance, since it provides a reply to part of Māra's challenge in the Pāli version. According to the *Saṃyuttanikāya* account, their exchange started off with Māra inquiring what Cālā approves of.[132] In the ancient Indian setting, this would have been a way of finding out what type of teaching or doctrine someone else followed. Cālā's short reply is that she does not approve of birth. This then leads to Māra inquiring why she does not approve of birth, the source of sensual pleasure, followed by querying who had persuaded her to take such a position. Perhaps some such exchange should also be considered to stand in the background of the *Saṃyuktāgama* version, which would fit her statement "in that teaching I delight."

Her final verses then describe her sublime attainment, gained on following that teaching, and her dispatching of Māra:

"Being separated from all craving and [deluded] rejoicing,
Having entirely relinquished darkness,
By having realized the quietude of extinction,
I dwell in peace, established in the eradication of the influxes.

> I recognize you, wicked Māra,
> You should make yourself disappear and go!"
>
> Then Māra, the Bad One, thought: "The nun Cālā knows my intention." Harboring sadness and sorrow within, he vanished and was seen no more.

The final part of Cālā's self-confident reply to Māra is similar to Vijayā's response. One who has reached the highest and gone beyond the darkness of ignorance, the first and foundational link in dependent arising, can easily send Māra off in this way, leaving him sad and sorrowful at his lack of success.

The Misery of Birth

A Pāli version of the above encounter between Cālā and Māra, besides being found in the *Saṃyuttanikāya*, also recurs in the *Therīgāthā*. Notably, the verses in question are instead attributed to her sister Upacālā. According to the commentary on the *Therīgāthā*, Cālā and Upacālā, as well as Sīsupacālā, were all sisters of Sāriputta.[133] The similarity in the names of these sisters appears to have led to some confusion in the course of oral transmission. Since the *Saṃyuttanikāya* report of Cālā's encounter with Māra agrees with its Chinese parallels that the main issue at hand was birth, it seems fair to assume that the verses of Cālā have been mistakenly assigned to Upacālā in the *Therīgāthā*. On the assumption that these fit the case of Cālā, it is the verses attributed in this work to Upacālā that I translate below.[134]

> "Endowed with mindfulness and endowed with vision,
> Being a nun with cultivated faculties,
> I penetrated the state of peace,
> Resorted to by the lofty."

The commentary relates her vision, mentioned in the first line, to the eye of wisdom that sees the arising and vanishing of phenomena, which in turn leads to disenchantment.[135] Her ability to penetrate the state of peace, which is a reference to Nirvana, relies on her having cultivated the five spiritual faculties of confidence, energy, mindfulness, concentration, and wisdom. The elevating nature of the realization of Nirvana then finds expression in the indication that this is not resorted to by lowly people. The next verse reports the challenge by Māra:

> "How is it that you do not approve of birth?
> On being born, one partakes of sensual pleasures.
> Partake of the delight of sensuality,
> Lest you later have regrets!"

In the *Saṃyuttanikāya* account, the second part of Māra's challenge to Cālā differs. Instead of taking up the topic of regrets due to forgoing sensual indulgence, he inquires who had persuaded her to disapprove of birth.[136] The verses below provide a reply to both topics, the first one explaining why she disapproves of birth and the second one revealing the identity of her teacher.

> "For those who are born there is death,
> Hands and feet being cut off,
> Killing, bondage, and misery.
> One who is born, undergoes pain."

Cutting off hands and feet appears to have been a typical punishment in the ancient Indian setting. The references in the next line to killing, being put in bondage, and other types of misery could also intend types of punishment. Besides being regularly inflicted on criminals, at times innocent persons could also be subjected to such pains by despotic rulers. By referring to such extremely painful experiences, the verse provides a stark contrast to sensual pleasures, perhaps with an implied hint at the fact that the pursuit of sensual indulgence often stands in the background of criminal activities.

"The unvanquished Buddha,
Who was born in the Sakyan clan,
Proclaimed to me the teaching,
That transcends birth:

Dukkha, the arising of *dukkha*,
The transcendence of *dukkha*,
And the noble eightfold path
That leads to the stilling of *dukkha*."

The two verses provide an answer to the second query posed by Māra in the *Saṃyuttanikāya*, regarding the identity of her teacher. The reply comes with a subtle touch of humor, as it is the one who was *born* in the Sakyan clan who teaches how to transcend being *born* again. In other words, rather than viewing birth as a welcome occasion for sensual indulgence, the same instead serves as an opportunity to transcend birth and teach others how to achieve the same.

"Having heard his utterance,
I dwelled delighting in his teaching.
The three knowledges have been attained:
The Buddha's teaching has been done.

[Sensual] enjoyment has been destroyed in every way,
The mass of darkness has been shattered.
Know this, Bad One:
You are defeated, End-Maker."

The *Saṃyuttanikāya* account of Cālā's verses instead indicates that beings of the realms of form and formlessness come back to existence due to not having understood cessation.[137] One way or the other, Cālā has definitely defeated Māra, who has no choice but to leave in utter dismay.

Upacālā

> The foremost of those nuns who delight in empty and secluded places, not in being among people, is the nun called Upacālā.[138]

THE *EKOTTARIKĀGAMA'S* HIGHLIGHT on the nun Upacālā is without a counterpart in the corresponding Pāli list of eminent nuns.

Her delight in seclusion, reported in the above passage, shows her to be foremost in a quality held in high esteem in early Buddhist thought. The discourses repeatedly show the Buddha recommending seclusion and withdrawal from company and socialization. One of the eight thoughts of a great person highlights that the Buddha's teaching is for one who delights in seclusion rather than being fond of company.[139] The introductory narration of the *Mahāsuññatasutta*, the Greater Discourse on Emptiness, reports the Buddha admonishing his attendant Ānanda for excessive socialization, pointing out that one who delights in company will not be able to make full progress on the meditative path.[140] In view of these assessments, for Upacālā to be considered outstanding for delighting in empty and secluded places puts a spotlight on an important requirement for successful meditation practice. At the same time, it also undermines the popular but misguided assumption that women always want to be in company.

No Interest in Heaven

Besides not having a longing for human company, Upacālā was also not at all interested in any heavenly form of company, birth, or realm, as becomes evident from her encounter with Māra.[141]

> [Māra thought:] "The nun Upacālā ... has entered the Andhavana Grove and sat down under a tree for the day's abiding. I shall now approach and disturb her." He transformed himself into a youth of handsome appearance, went to the nun Upacālā, and said in verse:
>
> "In the upper Heavens of the Thirty-Three,
> Of Yāma and of Tusita,
> Of the Nimmānaratī and the Paranimmitavasavattī,
> Aspire to attain rebirth there!"

Māra's challenge involves several celestial realms recognized in ancient Indian cosmology. The Heaven of the Thirty-Three is the realm ruled over by Sakka, the Buddhist counterpart to the Indian warrior god Indra. More refined is the heavenly realm of Yāma, and still more elevated is the Tusita realm, where according to tradition the Buddha spent his previous life. The next two realms, still more refined, are the heavens of those who delight in creating and of those who wield power over the creations of others. All of these celestial realms belong to the sense sphere and thereby fall within the sphere of Māra's control. Beyond the realms of the sense sphere are the celestial realms of form and formlessness, cosmological counterparts to the attainments of the four absorptions and the four formless spheres.

Similar to the topic of rebirth as such, taken up in the previous chapter, these celestial realms are an integral part of early Buddhist thought. At the same time, celestial realms and corresponding meditative experience stand in a continuum.[142] A map of different heavens is also a map of the equivalent mental states, and the other way round. In other words, a meaningful engagement with the early Buddhist teachings can approach such aspects of ancient Indian cosmology as maps of possible mental experiences, as long as this does not lead to a wholesale dismissal of the other side of the coin, the idea of actually existing celestial realms, as an alternative and valid interpretation.

> The nun Upacālā thought: "Who is this person, wanting to frighten me? Is he a human or is he a nonhuman? Is this per-

son scheming to seduce me?" Considering on her own she realized: "This is certainly the wicked Māra, wanting to make me become confounded." She spoke in verse:

"In the heavenly realms of the Thirty-Three,
Of Yāma and of Tusita,
Of the Nimmānaratī and the Paranimmitavasavattī,
All these types of heavenly realms,
Are not separated from being a product of formations.[143]
Therefore, they are in Māra's power."

The Pāli parallel indicates that all the celestial beings in these heavenly realms are still bound by the bondage of sensuality.[144] Although differing in formulation, the main import is the same, insofar as Māra represents the bondage of sensuality.

The other version extant in Chinese translation offers a different perspective, noting that the inhabitants of these celestial realms have not yet separated themselves from the view of self and for this reason are certainly in bondage to Māra.[145] Now, a stream-enterer could in principle be reborn in any of these celestial realms. Since a stream-enterer has left behind the view of self (although conceit and subtle forms of selfing still have to be eradicated), the presentation in the other Chinese parallel would more specifically apply to the predicament of worldlings being reborn in these realms. In contrast, being a product of formations or bound by the bondage of sensuality would apply to everyone in these heavenly worlds. For this reason, the presentations in the version translated above and in its Pāli parallel seem to offer a more straightforward reply to Māra's challenge.

"The whole world is entirely a collection of various formations.
The whole world is entirely of a shakable nature.
The whole world is afflicted by fire, constantly ablaze.
The whole world has become entirely enveloped in smoke and dust.

The imperturbable and unshakable,
Which is not approached by worldlings

And which does not accord with Māra's inclinations,
This is the place to be enjoyed."

From having assessed the nature of the celestial realms of the sensual sphere, Upacālā turns to extend her assessment to the whole world, comprising any realm, noting that all of this is merely a product of formations. In fact, the whole world is shakable and ablaze, a reference that according to the Pāli commentary intends to highlight the condition of being afflicted by defilements.[146] This indication concords with a statement in another discourse that identifies three types of fire, which are the three root defilements of greed/lust, anger/hatred, and delusion.[147] The resultant perspective is as applicable in contemporary times as it was in ancient India. A brief look at the latest news from around the world will easily identify the smoke and dust created by the blazing fires of defilements, leading to so much unnecessary harm and pain.

In contrast to the shakable and blazing nature of the world under the influence of defilements stands the imperturbable and unshakable nature of freedom from defilements. This is directly opposed to what Māra advocates. Such freedom is the one place that can and should indeed be enjoyed.

"Being separated from all craving and *dukkha*,
Having entirely relinquished darkness,
By having realized the quietude of extinction,
I dwell in peace, established in the eradication of the influxes.
I recognize you, wicked Māra,
Therefore, make yourself disappear and go!"

Then Māra, the Bad One, thought: "The nun Upacālā has understood my intentions." Being sad and sorrowful within, he vanished and was seen no more.

Beyond the World

The apparent confusion between the three sisters of Sāriputta, mentioned in the previous chapter, also affects the present case. The verses that, judging from their content, should be attributed to Upacālā, occur instead under the name of Sīsupacālā. My procedure here is the same as earlier, in that in this chapter on Upacālā I translate the verses that appear to fit her case.[148]

"A nun endowed with morality,
With sense faculties well controlled,
May attain the state of peace,
Which is insatiably nourishing."[149]

According to the Pāli commentary, the indication that the state of peace is of a nourishing nature conveys the sense that Nirvana allays the disease of defilements.[150] The next verse reports Māra's challenge:

"To the celestials of the Thirty-Three,
Of Yāma and of Tusita,
To the Nimmānaratī celestials,
And those [Paranimmita]vasavattī celestials,
Direct your mind there,
Where you lived in the past."

The last line of the corresponding verse in the *Saṃyuttanikāya* version instead promises that she will experience delight.[151] This provides a more generally applicable sense, since in the ancient Indian setting to direct one's mind to rebirth in any of these celestial realms would have been motivated by the wish to experience delight, quite independent of whether or not one recollects having lived in such a realm at some time in the past. That such directing the mind to a heavenly rebirth is not the way out becomes clear in the reply to Māra provided in the next two verses:

"The celestials of the Thirty-Three,
Of Yāma and Tusita,
The Nimmānaratī celestials,
And those [Paranimmita]vasavattī celestials,

Time and again, life after life,
Are under the sway of [a reified sense of] identity.
Not transcending [a reified sense of] identity,
They pursue birth and death."

The term rendered above as "[a reified sense of] identity" is usually translated as just "identity" or else "personality." The relevant Pāli term (*sakkāya*) combines a reference to what "exists" or is "real" with the term "group," which here represents the five aggregates of clinging (bodily form, feeling tone, perception, volitional formations, and consciousness). My rendering as "[reified sense of] identity" is meant to prevent potential misunderstandings due to the connotations carried by the terms "identity" and "personality" in general usage. An arahant still has individual subjective experiences. She knows who she is (= her "identity"), and she still has particular character traits (= her "personality"). But an arahant is free from any notions of selfhood or any clinging in relation to the five aggregates, in other words free from reifying identity or personality. From the perspective of such freedom, the following assessment of the world emerges:

"The whole world is burning;
The whole world is aflame;
The whole world is ablaze;
The whole world is shaking.

The unshakable and incomparable teaching,
Proclaimed to me by the Buddha,[152]
Which is not resorted to by worldlings,
Of that my mind is fond."

In regard to the second of these verses a difference emerges in the *Saṃyuttanikāya* account of Upacālā's reply to Māra, in the form of the indication that this unshakable and incomparable teaching (not resorted to by worldlings and of which Upacālā is fond) is beyond Māra's reach.[153] The indication in the above verse that this teaching was proclaimed by the

Buddha fits well with the next verse, which continues with the topic of the Buddha's teachings:

> "Having heard his utterance,
> I dwelled delighting in his teaching.
> The three knowledges have been attained:
> The Buddha's teaching has been done.
>
> [Sensual] enjoyment has been destroyed in every way,
> The mass of darkness has been shattered.
> Know this, Bad One:
> You are defeated, End-Maker."

Sīsupacālā

THE LAST OF the three sisters of Sāriputta, Sīsupacālā, does not feature in the list of outstanding nuns, hence I turn directly to her encounter with Māra.

BEYOND VIEWS

Sīsupacālā's encounter with Māra takes the following form in the *Saṃyuktāgama*:[154]

> [Māra thought:] "The nun Sīsupacālā ... has entered the Andhavana Grove and sat down under a tree for the day's abiding. I shall now go and disturb her." He transformed himself into a youth of handsome appearance, went to the nun Sīsupacālā, and said:
>
> "Lady, in what method do you delight?"
>
> The nun replied: "I do not delight in anything!"
>
> Then Māra, the Bad One, said in verse:
>
> "What counsel did you receive,
> That you shaved your head and became a recluse?
> You wear yellow robes on your body
> And have the marks of one who has gone forth,
> [Yet] you do not delight in any method,
> You dwell [just] preserving your stupidity!"

In the *Saṃyuttanikāya* parallel, Māra begins the exchange by asking which doctrine meets with her approval.[155] In the other Chinese parallel, he instead wants to know in which one out of the "ninety-six methods" she delights.[156] According to later exegesis, the count of ninety-six relates to six teachers that were contemporaries of the Buddha. These six teachers occur in the introductory narration of the Discourse on the Fruits of Recluseship (*Sāmaññaphalasutta*), in which a king reports to the Buddha his earlier visits to each of these well-known and reputed teachers:[157] Pūraṇa Kassapa, Makkhali Gosāla, Ajita Kesakambalī, Pakudha Kaccāyana, Nigaṇṭha Nātaputta, and Sañjaya Belaṭṭhiputta. In this discourse and elsewhere, these six teachers stand representative for what from an early Buddhist perspective are mistaken tenets and doctrines.[158] These include annihilationism, the denial of karma, equivocation, as well as the attempt to expiate karma in the Jain tradition, whose leader Mahāvīra is known in Buddhist discourse under the name of Nigaṇṭha Nātaputta.

The count of ninety-six derives from the idea that the students of each of these six teachers dissented from their teachers and furthermore broke up into fifteen different traditions in each case, as a result of which there came to be six times fifteen new tenets, plus the original six tenets by the above teachers, amounting to altogether ninety-six.[159] The number ninety-six thereby serves to represent the diversity of such teachings and views held in the ancient Indian setting, none of which met with Sīsupacālā's approval.

> Then the nun Sīsupacālā thought: "Who is this person, wanting to frighten me? Is he a human or is he a nonhuman? Is this person scheming to seduce me?" Having considered it in this way, she realized: "Māra, the Bad One, wants to make me become confounded." She spoke in verse:
>
> "All paths outside of this teaching,
> Are entangled in views.
> Being bound by any view,
> One is always under Māra's power."

Sīsupacālā explains why she does not approve of or delight in any of the tenets, namely because each of these are entangled in views that do not lead beyond Māra's power. The qualification provided of those views is significant, since following the early Buddhist teachings also involves having a view. In fact, right view is the first and foundational factor of the noble eightfold path, providing the required directional input for the other path factors.[160] Yet, such right view (in the form of an initial appreciation of the four noble truths, to be deepened as one progresses on the path) transcends the entanglement of views and leads beyond Māra's power. This is the ingenious discovery made according to tradition by the Buddha, to whom Sīsupacālā now turns:

"Yet, there has arisen, in the Sakyan clan,
A naturally endowed and incomparable great teacher,
Who is able to subdue all of Māra's enmity
And who will not be subdued by him.

Purified and entirely liberated,
With the eye of the path, he contemplated it all.
The supreme victor who is separated from all influxes,
He knew it all with complete knowledge.

He, then, is my great teacher,
I delight only in his teaching.
Having entered his teaching,
I attained the aloofness of the quietude of cessation."

The reference to the Buddha's complete knowledge could be taken as implying omniscience. Such a reading, however, would not find support in the parallels. In fact, the idea that the Buddha was omniscient is a later development and at times in conflict with how the early discourses portray him.[161] In view of this, it seems preferable to view the above line simply as an expression of the comprehensive insight of the Buddha.

"Being separated from all craving and rejoicing,
Having entirely relinquished darkness,

By having realized the quietude of extinction,
I dwell in peace, established in the eradication of the influxes.
I recognize you, wicked Māra,
Thus make yourself disappear and go!"

Then Māra, the Bad One, thought: "The nun Sīsupacālā has understood my intentions." Harboring sadness and sorrow within, he vanished and was seen no more.

The Vision That Frees

As already mentioned in the previous two chapters, there appears to be some confusion of names in the *Therīgāthā* among the sisters of Sāriputta. In what follows I translate the set of verses attributed in this collection to Cālā, on the assumption that these should rather be considered Sīsupacālā's poem:[162]

"Having established mindfulness,
Being a nun with cultivated faculties,
I penetrated the state of peace,
The happiness of the stilling of formations."

According to the commentary, the first line refers to the practice of the four establishments of mindfulness in such a way that the four mistaken modes of perception are overcome.[163] These four mistaken modes see what in reality is unattractive as beautiful, what is unsatisfactory as a source of happiness, what is impermanent as everlasting, and what is empty as being a self (in the sense of a substantial entity). The second line in turn should, according to the same commentary, be understood to intend the five spiritual faculties. These five faculties were also part of the teaching given by Khemā to Vijayā, discussed in a previous chapter (see above p. 58). Balancing these faculties is a key requirement for progress to penetration of the state of peace. In other words, the verse can be understood to delineate key elements of meditative progress to the superb happiness of Nirvana, the stilling of all formations. Having in this way provided a succinct overview of the practice required to reach the highest accomplishment, the next verse turns to the encounter with Māra, reporting his challenge:

> "On account of whom have you shaved your head?
> You look like a recluse,
> Yet you do not approve of a doctrine;
> Why do you wander as if lost?"

The challenge issued by Māra here, closely similar to the one in the *Saṃyuktāgama* translated above, queries after her doctrinal affiliation. Although she looks like a recluse, having a shaven head and wearing robes, she does not adopt any of the various doctrines usually upheld by recluses. Hence, the suggestion that she does not know what she is doing. Her reply clarifies that she knows what she is doing much better than the one who tries to challenge her:

> "Doctrines outside of this
> Rely on their views;
> They do not understand the Dharma,
> They are not skilled in the Dharma."

The implication is that those who rely on mistaken views for this very reason do not understand the Dharma, which here could be taken to convey nuances of "truth" and "the nature of reality."[164]

> "The peerless Buddha,
> Who was born in the Sakyan clan,
> Proclaimed to me the teaching
> That transcends views:
>
> *Dukkha*, the arising of *dukkha*,
> The transcendence of *dukkha*,
> And the noble eightfold path
> That leads to the stilling of *dukkha*.

Having heard his utterance,
I dwelled delighting in his teaching.
The three knowledges have been attained:
The Buddha's teaching has been done.

[Sensual] enjoyment has been destroyed in every way,
The mass of darkness has been shattered.
Know this, Bad One:
You are defeated, End-Maker."

The *Saṃyuttanikāya* account of Sīsupacālā's reply to Māra proceeds with some differences. It has no reference to the four noble truths and instead expands on qualities of the Buddha, noting that he is the one who subdued Māra.[165] The final verse then proclaims her reaching of the goal, expressed in terms of having attained the end of karma. Her poem concludes with the clarification that she does approve of the Buddha's teaching.

Vīrā

VĪRĀ ALSO DOES not feature in the list of outstanding nuns, hence I turn directly to her encounter with Māra.

Dismantling Reification

The encounter between Vīrā and Māra involves a topic of considerable relevance for early Buddhist thought, as it relates directly to the doctrine of not self. Being certainly one of the most significant departures from the type of teachings otherwise prevalent in the ancient Indian setting, the need to avoid the type of reification that underlies self-notions is a recurrent and pervasive topic in the early discourses. This already came up with the nun Khemā and the different possible ways of conceiving the nature of a fully accomplished one. The same comes up as a challenge posed by Māra in the episode below.[166]

> [Māra thought:] "The nun Vīrā ... has entered the Andhavana Grove and sat down under a tree for the day's abiding. I shall approach and disturb her." He transformed himself into a youth of handsome appearance, approached the nun Vīrā, and said in verse:
>
> "How has this bodily shape been created?
> Who is its creator?
> Whence has this bodily shape arisen?
> Where will this bodily shape go?"

The slightly cryptic reference to the "bodily shape" in the above version has as its Pāli counterpart the term "puppet" or "image" (*bimba*), which the commentary glosses as a reference to individual existence (*atta-bhāva*).[167] In other words, the reference to the "bodily shape" in the passage translated above is best taken to carry connotations of a substantial self. In the present case, these appear to come together with a veiled sexual threat, as Māra's inquiry after the supposedly existing self speaks either of her bodily shape, drawing attention to her female attractiveness, or else treats her as a puppet, presumably something a male can just pick up and use as he pleases.

Another difference, compared to the Pāli version, is the name of the nun who faced this particular challenge. Whereas the previous three chapters noted disagreements between texts transmitted within the same Theravāda tradition on which set of verses should be attributed to each of the three sisters of Sāriputta, in the present case the disagreement is between different reciter traditions. The above version and the other parallel extant in Chinese speak of Vīrā, whereas their Pāli counterpart instead refers to Selā. The matter does not end here, as the nun to be taken up in the next chapter is Selā in the Chinese versions but Vajirā in the Pāli tradition.[168]

Such confusion of names is not at all uncommon in an oral tradition and not restricted to the identification of nuns. The same can happen even with otherwise well-known monk disciples of the Buddha.[169] From the viewpoint of the early generations of reciters, what counted was apparently mainly the teaching itself and less the identity of whoever spoke it.

> The nun Vīrā thought: "Who is this person, coming to frighten me? Is he a human or is he a nonhuman? Is this person scheming to seduce me?" Considering in this way, she gained the realization: "This is the wicked Māra. The Bad One wants to confound me." She spoke in verse:
>
> "This bodily shape is not self-created,
> Nor is it created by another.

It has arisen through the conjunction of conditions
And will be obliterated by the dissolution of conditions.

In her reply, Vīrā aptly conveys the early Buddhist position, which avoids taking the stance that everything is entirely wrought by oneself or else that it is completely determined by others. Instead, anything existing is the product of a conjunction of conditions. Her reply shifts the discourse from thinking in terms of entities to viewing everything as processes. From this viewpoint, the inquiry after a creator is misconceived. There is no creator, as whatever manifests is the result of a range of conditions. Moreover, with the dissolution of these conditions, what has come into existence will come to an end. Vīrā thereby exhibits her profound insight into the teachings on conditionality and dependent arising, which is but the other side of the coin of not self or emptiness.

Next Vīrā illustrates her understanding with an example taken from nature:

"Just as any seed in the world
Grows in dependence on the great earth,
In dependence on earth, water, fire, and wind,
So it is also with the aggregates, elements, and sense-spheres:
Through the coming together of conditions they arise,
Being separated from those conditions they will be obliterated."

Having earlier delineated the early Buddhist doctrinal position, Vīrā complements this with a simile. Out of the whole set of four elements listed by her, the Pāli version focuses in particular on earth and water (the latter in the form of moisture).[170] Although these are indeed key requirements for the growth of a seed, the other two elements also have their contribution to offer: the fire element in particular in the form of sunshine and the wind element, representative of motion, as the basic principle behind any growth. At the same time, the Pāli version's emphasis on earth and moisture facilitates relating the above imagery to another discourse, according to which karma is the field, consciousness the seed, and craving the moisture responsible for the continuous faring on of sentient beings in the cycle of birth and death.[171]

Vīrā's employment of the example of a seed appositely drives home the need to shift to process-oriented thinking, which helps us understand how a large tree could result from a small seed. Rather than involving some immutable tree or seed entity, the growth of a tree is a process, which takes place through the conjunction of the needed conditions. The same applies to a human being, be it conceived in terms of the five aggregates, the six sense-spheres of experience (the five physical senses and the mind as sixth) or the six elements (the four material elements, space, and consciousness). Each of these analytical perspectives points to the composite nature of what can mistakenly appear as if it were a unit or an entity. Yet, closer inspection shows it to be a composite, which depends on conditions to exist and without those conditions does not exist. This undermines the basis for any reification, be it of trees or of human beings, as unchanging entities. Such understanding leads out of the darkness of ignorance and results in transcending craving and *dukkha*.

> "I have relinquished all craving and *dukkha*,
> I am entirely separated from darkness,
> Having realized the quietude of extinction,
> I dwell in peace, established in the eradication of the influxes.
> Wicked Māra, I know you,
> Make yourself disappear and go!"

> Then Māra, the Bad One, thought: "The nun Vīrā has understood my intentions." Great sadness and sorrow arose [in him], he vanished and was seen no more.

An Excellent Field of Merit

In addition to the above record of her powerful rebuttal to Māra—dismantling the reification underlying his challenge by directing attention to the composite and conditioned nature of all aspects of existence—Vīrā also features in another discourse as an outstanding field of merit. The introductory narration reports that she was dwelling at Rājagaha, whose inhabitants did not supply her with the needed monastic requisites. This is often a problem for monastics dedicated to a more secluded life, but is all the more challenging for nuns, who often find it additionally difficult to gain material support, compared to monks. Vīrā's predicament motivates a sprite to tour the town and alert people to her status as an excellent field of merit. This takes the following form in the *Saṃyuktāgama* version:[172]

> "People in the town of Rājagaha,
> [Must be] drunken, confused, or asleep,
> As nobody is making offerings
> To the nun Vīrā.
>
> The nun Vīrā
> Is brave and has cultivated all the faculties.
> She aptly teaches about seclusion from pollution,
> About Nirvana, the cool state.
>
> You should all follow what is taught by her,
> And for the whole day you will be delighted without becoming weary.
> She conveys those who hear her teachings on wisdom,
> To gaining the transcendence of the stream of births and deaths."

The entertaining assumption that people must be drunk, confused, or asleep avoids confronting the probably underlying androcentrism head on and instead tries to sober, clarify, and awake people to the great opportunity to make merits that they are missing. This procedure had its effect:

> At that time, one lay disciple took a robe and offered it to the nun Vīrā and another lay disciple offered her food. That sprite said in verse:

"Wise lay disciple
You have now gained much merit
Through a robe offering to one who has cut off all bondage:
The nun Vīrā.

Wise lay disciple
You have now gained much merit
Through a food offering to the nun Vīrā,
Who intentionally remains secluded from all company."

Then, having spoken these verses, that sprite vanished and was seen no more.

The present episode provides a welcome contrast to Māra, who has nothing better to do than trying to disturb meditating nuns. Here, a sprite does the very opposite by ensuring that an outstanding nun, who due to her secluded lifestyle has apparently not been recognized by potential donors for the remarkable field of merit she is, receives the needed support with monastic requisites, in particular robes and food.

The *Saṃyuktāgama* and its Chinese parallel collection report a closely similar episode for the nun Sukkā,[173] thereby confirming the impression that nuns regularly encountered difficulties in getting sufficient supplies. The Chinese discourses concerned with Vīrā and Sukkā have three Pāli parallels. The first of these reports the praise of Sukkā's qualities and encouragement of people to listen to her teachings, the second has the rejoicing in the gift of food to Sukkā, and the third the rejoicing in the gift of a robe to Vīrā.[174] This could be the result of some accident in transmission, resulting in a loss of the storyline leading from at first eulogizing the nun and then, when this has inspired someone to make an offering, rejoicing in the merit accrued in this way. Such an assumption would find support in the fact that a *Vinaya* text extant in Sanskrit also presents both episodes together.[175]

A Heroine

A single stanza attributed to Vīrā occurs in the *Therīgāthā*.[176] This stanza puns on her name, Vīrā, which means "heroine."

> "Through your heroic qualities, heroine (Vīrā),
> Being a nun with cultivated faculties,
> Bear your last body,
> Having conquered Māra and his retinue!"

Selā

A Teaching on Emptiness

As mentioned in the previous chapter, a confusion of names during the course of oral transmission has led to a disagreement between different reciter traditions, resulting in the Pāli version attributing to Selā the words spoken, according to the parallel traditions, by Vīrā. This in turn affects the present case, where three parallel versions attribute the present teaching, given in an encounter with Māra, to Selā, whereas according to the Pāli version it should rather be attributed to Vajirā .[177]

> [Māra thought:] "The nun Selā ... has entered the Andhavana Grove and sat down under a tree for the day's abiding. I shall now approach and disturb her." He transformed himself into a youth of handsome appearance and went to the nun Selā. He said in verse:
>
> "How has this sentient being been born?
> Who is its creator?
> Whence has this sentient being arisen?
> Where will it go?"

The challenge voiced by Māra here is comparable to the one he presented to Vīrā, taken up in the previous chapter, in that it involves a reification of subjective existence into a self as a persisting entity.

> The nun Selā thought: "Who is this person, wanting to frighten me? Is he a human or is he a nonhuman? Is this person scheming to seduce me?" Having considered it, the realization arose: "This is the wicked Māra, wanting to confound me." She spoke in verse:
>
> "Your speaking of the existence of a sentient being:
> This, then, is wicked Māra's view.
> There is only a collection of empty aggregates;
> There is no sentient being [as such]."

Instead of referring to the aggregates, the parallel versions speak of "formations."[178] This difference in terminology does not substantially affect the meaning, as the main point remains that an essentialized view of a sentient being, reified as an entity, needs to be replaced by insight into the composite and conditioned nature of all aspects of subjective experience. Such subjective experience is indeed empty, in the sense of being empty of anything that could correspond to a substantial self or a "sentient being" in the sense of an unchanging entity. Whereas Vīrā illustrated the matter with the example of the growth of a seed, Selā accomplishes the same with the example of a chariot:

> "Just as when the various parts are assembled,
> The world calls it 'a chariot,'
> [So,] in dependence on the combination of the aggregates,
> There is the appellation: 'It is a sentient being.'"

The significance of this famous simile has not always remained clear in later tradition, examples of which I explore in the next subsection of this chapter. First of all, however, it needs to be noted that this simile is unique in the early discourses. In other words, had it not been for the superb and dexterous wisdom of Selā, this simile would quite probably be unheard of in the Buddhist traditions.

The point she intends to make is simply that the appellation of a "sentient being" refers to something composite, namely a combination of the five aggregates. The same holds for the term "chariot." Taking up an example from daily life experiences in ancient India that would have been as familiar to everyone as the growth of a seed, she highlights its composite nature. This must have been self-evident to anyone living at her time, given that chariots need to be constructed in the first place and later can break down and then need to be repaired. That is, it can reasonably be expected that members of an ancient Indian audience would have had a personal understanding that a chariot is not an independent and self-existing entity, due to at some time having seen its disjointed parts. This understanding should now be similarly applied to a sentient being. Note that the terms used for such composites are not in themselves problematic, as long as those who use the term "chariot" or "sentient being" do so in awareness of the conditioned and composite nature of what they are referring to.

> "The arising of that [sentient being] is [just] the arising of
> *dukkha*;
> Its persistence is also [just] the persistence of *dukkha*.
> Nothing else arises but *dukkha*;
> *Dukkha* arises and *dukkha* itself ceases."

Having offered a penetrative teaching on emptiness with her delivery of the chariot simile, Selā now turns to an assessment of the nature of the sentient being. This may well be motivated by the fact that the reification inherent in Māra's inquiry needs to be countered not only on the cognitive level, by combining a doctrinal clarification with an illustrative simile, but also on the affective level. The sentient being that Māra wishes to celebrate turns out on proper inspection to be just *dukkha*. Just *dukkha* arises and *dukkha* ceases, nothing more.

> "Having relinquished all craving and *dukkha*,
> I am entirely separated from darkness.
> Having realized the quietude of extinction,
> I dwell in peace, established in the eradication of the influxes.
> I recognize you, wicked Māra,
> Therefore, make yourself disappear and go!"

> Then Māra, the Bad One, thought: "The nun Selā has understood my intentions." Harboring sadness and sorrow within, he then vanished and was seen no more.

The Chariot Simile

The chariot simile, indubitably a major contribution made by the nun Selā to Buddhist thought past, present, and future, has served as a prominent illustration of emptiness in later tradition. A well-known instance is a debate between a Bactrian king by the name of Milinda and the Buddhist monk Nāgasena, records of which are extant in Pāli and Chinese. Nāgasena employs the chariot simile during their encounter; according to the Pāli version he explicitly referred to the exposition given by Selā (that is, Vajirā).[179] This employment reflects the importance of this dexterous illustration, originally devised by a nun, as Nāgasena was tasked with debating King Milinda and converting him to Buddhism. The introductory narration leading up to their actual encounter shows that this was no mean task; in fact, King Milinda had up to that point been successful in defeating others, including a respected Buddhist monk, through his debating skills. For Nāgasena to rely on the simile originally devised by Selā in his first rebuttal of King Milinda throws into relief the power of her illustration.

In a debate in the ancient Indian setting, reducing the other to silence spells victory.[180] For this reason, the deconstruction of the chariot fits the context well, aptly expressing the key Buddhist insight into the composite nature of phenomena. A somewhat different perspective emerges, however, in the Pāli version of this exchange, which in general appears to be more developed and later than the version of the encounter between Nāgasena and Milinda extant in Chinese.[181] In the Pāli version, Nāgasena introduces the quote from the exposition by Selā (or Vajirā) by stating that in the ultimate sense no person can be found.[182] The same type of argument recurs in the *Visuddhimagga*, where Buddhaghosa draws on the simile by Selā (or Vajirā) to support the position that "there is no being and no person," since the simile supposedly shows that "in the ultimate sense, when each single part is examined, there is indeed no chariot."[183]

Yet, this is not the point made by Selā. She was not denying the existence of a chariot or a sentient being. Her point was that these terms refer to composites and not to entities. By taking a chariot apart, that which makes it a chariot has been demolished. A chariot refers to a functional assemblage of parts that can be used to drive. None of the single parts of a chariot can fulfill this purpose on their own, nor is it possible to drive with the different parts spread out on the ground. The very taking apart has undone the chariot, and its individual parts are now just individual parts. It is a misunderstanding to believe that, because the individual parts are not a chariot, there is no chariot in some supposedly ultimate sense. After the chariot has been destroyed by being taken apart, it is hardly surprising that one is no longer able to find a chariot. As explained by Bhikkhunī Dhammadinnā (2020, 13):

> the point of *bhikṣuṇī* Śailā's illustration is not a denial of the conditioned existence of a chariot or a self, but a calling into question [of] the shift from concept to ontology evident in Māra's pressing her on the characteristics of a 'being' ... The use of the notions or terms 'chariot' and 'being' are not problematized as such. Nor does Śailā make a metaphysical affirmation of their conventional existence but ultimate or absolute nonexistence, unlike the type of arguments that developed in later Buddhist tradition.

The apparently perplexing nature which the chariot simile came to acquire in the course of time could be seen in a reference found in a collection of Chan teachings, the *Gateless Barrier*, in which the presumably puzzling situation resulting from a chariot taken apart features as a *kōan*.[184] Yet, it can safely be assumed that Selā would have had no difficulties in "solving" this *kōan* on the spot.

Freedom from Sensuality

The *Therīgāthā* has preserved a set of three stanzas attributed to Selā.[185] Due to the confusion of names, discussed above, from the viewpoint of the Pāli tradition these verses would belong to the nun taken up in the previous chapter. The actual verses have no relationship to either the simile of a seed or that of a chariot, which are central to the two powerful expositions examined in the last and in the present chapter. Instead, they revolve around the recurrent theme of Māra tempting a nun to indulge in sensuality:

> "There is no escape from the world!
> What will you accomplish through seclusion?
> Partake of the delight of sensuality,
> Lest you later have regrets!"

In line with the rebuttal of Māra spoken by Uppalavaṇṇā, Selā proclaims her complete disinterest in sensuality:

> "Sensual pleasures are like the blade of a sword
> And the aggregates like its chopping block.
> What you call the delight of sensuality,
> For me now is no delight [at all].
>
> [Sensual] enjoyment has been destroyed in every way,
> The mass of darkness has been shattered.
> Know this, Bad One:
> You are defeated, End-Maker."

Somā

> The foremost of those nuns who have compassion for living beings that have not yet reached the path is the nun called Somā.[186]

THE NUN SOMĀ does not feature in the Pāli list of outstanding nuns. Her excellence in the above quote from the *Ekottarikāgama* takes up an interesting quality, namely compassion for worldlings. A way of reading this qualification would be to relate it to her encounter with Māra, to be taken up below, in which she clarifies that women are as capable of progressing in meditation and reaching awakening as men. Such a clarification would indeed be particularly relevant for women who "have not yet reached the path," as those who have reached it of course know for certain that awakening is not a prerogative of males.

WOMEN'S ABILITIES

Somā's encounter with Māra takes the following form in the *Saṃyuktāgama*:[187]

> [Māra thought:] "The nun Somā ... has entered the Andhavana Grove to sit in meditation. I shall now approach and disturb her." He transformed himself into a youth of handsome appearance, went to the nun Somā, and asked her: "Lady, where do you want to go?"
>
> She replied: "Friend, I wish to go to a secluded place."
>
> Then Māra, the Bad One, spoke in verse:

> "The state wherein the seers dwell,
> This state is very difficult to attain.
> One with [just] a two-fingers' wit
> Is unable to attain that state."

The Pāli version does not precede the above verse with an exchange between the two, so that in its presentation Māra directly comes out with his challenge to women's ability.[188] The other Chinese version, however, does have such an exchange before presenting its version of Māra's challenge.[189]

His derogatory remark about a woman's two-fingers' wit appears to be a pun on women's use of two fingers when doing household chores. According to the commentary on the *Therīgāthā*, when cooking rice ancient Indian women would take out a grain of rice with a spoon and then press it between two fingers to know if it is cooked.[190] This would then refer to the use of two fingers as a way to feel with precision the degree of softness of a cooked rice grain.

An alternative explanation in the commentary on the *Saṃyuttanikāya* describes women cutting a thread from a cotton ball by holding it up with two fingers.[191] The idea could be that, since one hand holds the scissors or knife, in order to cut the thread, there is a need to distance it from the cotton ball, presumably kept in the palm of the hand. This can be accomplished by having the thread between two fingers and stretching these out. However, the verb used in this description can alternatively refer to spinning. On adopting this sense, one hand holds the spindle with the cotton, and two fingers of the other hand are employed in the actual spinning. Since in spinning the two fingers are used to gauge the thickness of the yarn as it is being spun in order to keep it uniform, this would involve a type of sensory discernment similar in type to the testing of a cooked rice grain.

Whatever the exact implications, the reference to the two-fingers' wit of women appears to have been a popular saying, as it recurs elsewhere.[192] As explained by Alice Collett (2009b, 99n7), "the broad inference of the term is clear: women's 'intelligence' is confined to the domestic sphere." Bhikkhunī Dhammadinnā (2018, 277) adds that, in this way, "Māra is shown to extrapolate from a societal norm (confinement to the domestic sphere) to arrive at a statement on the nature of women (inability to attain a spiritual goal)." Somā meets such foolish extrapolation head on, as evident in what follows:

> Then the nun Somā thought: "Who is this, wanting to frighten me? Is he a human or is he a nonhuman? Is this person scheming to seduce me?" Having considered it, certainty of knowledge arose in her and she knew: "This is the wicked Māra who has come wanting to confound me." She spoke in verse:
>
> "[Once] the mind has entered a [meditative] attainment,
> What has a female appearance to do with that?
> If knowledge has arisen,
> The unsurpassable state will be reached."

Somā's reply appositely rebuts Māra's challenge. Meditative attainments depend on cultivating the mind; they do not depend on characteristics of one's body. The requirement for reaching the state of seers, to use Māra's own expression, is arousing knowledge within. As Susan Jootla (1988, 44) points out, when "one is really developing morality, concentration and wisdom, it does not matter whether one was born male or female." In short, the gaining of insight "is completely irrespective of superficial distinctions of sex, race, caste, etc." Ria Kloppenborg (1995, 155) notes that Somā's "reply emphasizes the Buddhist position that the way towards liberation is a mental and spiritual process, which has nothing to do with the physical or social state of a person." Alice Collett (2009b, 99) sums up: "Somā is essentially saying that the notion of a female nature and the question of definitions by sex and gender are irrelevant to those who are truly practicing." Having offered this clarification, Somā turns to an analysis of the misguided viewpoint that stands behind Māra's challenge:

> "If the mind has not reached complete separation
> From the perception of being a 'man' or a 'woman,'

> Then such a one will speak like you, Māra,
> You should go and speak to such a one!"

In other words, the very idea that there is a substantial difference in soteriological potential between males and females just reflects the poor level of understanding of the speaker. Someone who refers to a woman's two-fingers' wit must have a mind completely caught up in the dualistic contrast between men and women. This is the category to which Māra belongs himself. If he wishes to engage in such talk, he should go and find others who are similarly caught up in such silly ideas. In contrast, as noted by Elizabeth Harris (1999, 61), "true spiritual progress leads to a point where beings are beyond male and female."

> "Separated from all *dukkha*,
> Having entirely relinquished darkness,
> Having attained and realized cessation,
> I dwell in peace, established in the eradication of the influxes.
> I recognize you, wicked Māra,
> Make yourself disappear and go!"
>
> Then Māra, the Bad One, thought: "The nun Somā has understood my intentions." Harboring sadness and regret within, he vanished and was seen no more.

Female Saints

Somā's self-confident rebuffing of Māra has been quoted repeatedly in writings about the role of women in early Buddhism.[193] Since Māra's challenges are sometimes misunderstood to reflect the inner thoughts of those he accosts, however, and perhaps also because in the Pāli version Somā's status as an arahant is not as explicit as in the Chinese parallels, the significance of Somā's exchange with Māra has not always been fully appreciated. The prejudice voiced by Māra does not imply that Somā had any doubt about a woman's ability to gain awakening. Instead of reflecting Somā's uncertainties, the point made by the present episode is that, from an early Buddhist perspective, doubting women's ability to reach awakening can only be the work of Māra.[194]

Confirmation of women's ability in matters of realization could be garnered from another discourse, which reports a meeting between the Buddha and a non-Buddhist wanderer. This is one in a whole series of such encounters between these two, with the present episode standing out for resulting in the conversion of this wanderer, who decides to go forth as a Buddhist monk. Whereas various earlier explanations of doctrinal issue did not achieve such a conversion, this finally happened when the Buddha replied to this wanderer's query regarding the levels of realization reached by disciples. The wanderer takes care to inquire about the ability of a monk, a nun, a male, and a female lay disciple respectively. For the case of nuns and female lay disciples, the Buddha's reply takes the following form in the *Saṃyuktāgama*:[195]

> "Not only one, two, or three nuns, or up to five hundred, [but] there are many [more] nuns who in this teaching and discipline have eradicated the influxes and, with the influx-free liberation of the mind and liberation by wisdom, here and now personally have understood and realized that 'birth for us has been eradicated, the holy life has been established, what had to be done has been done, we ourselves know that there will be no receiving of any further existence.'"

Parallels extant in Pāli and Chinese agree that well over five hundred nuns had reached the final goal. As already mentioned earlier (see p. 16), the number five hundred carries a symbolic sense in its use in the early discourses. However, the present instance differs from the standard procedure of just referring to five hundred, as such instances do not involve a counting up from one to five hundred. Such counting up does convey the impression of an additional emphasis on the large number of accomplished practitioners. Perhaps even more important is that the depiction of the ability of monks employs the same number. This confirms the position taken by Somā: being female or male has no bearing on spiritual ability. The same discourse also offers a pronouncement on the ability of female lay disciples:

> "Not only one, two, or three female lay disciples, or up to five hundred, [but] there are indeed many [more] female lay disciples who in this teaching and discipline have abandoned the five lower fetters and attained nonreturn, who will be of spontaneous rebirth there, no longer returning to be reborn here."

The reference to being reborn "there" intends the Pure Abodes, celestial realms in which only nonreturners are reborn. Becoming such a nonreturner requires the complete removal of the five lower fetters, which comprise belief in (a reified sense of) identity, (skeptical) doubt, clinging to rules and observances (as self-sufficient for awakening), sensual desire, and ill will. According to early Buddhist thought, these five lower fetters bind sentient beings to rebirth in the sense sphere realms.[196]

By not mentioning lay arahants, the present passage implicitly takes a position on the existence of lay arahants (the same holds for male lay disciples). As mentioned in the first chapter on Mahāpajāpatī Gotamī (see above p. 6), in the thought-world of early Buddhism a lay person can become an arahant but thereby becomes unable to continue to live the lay life and will soon ordain.

Freedom of the Mind

The key elements from the encounter between Māra and Somā recur in her verses in the *Therīgāthā*, beginning with Māra's challenge:[197]

> "What is to be attained by sages,
> That place is difficult to achieve;
> With her two-fingers' wit
> A woman is unable to attain it."

Next comes the stanza with Somā's rebuttal:

> "What could being a woman do to us,
> When the mind is well composed,
> When knowledge continues,
> On rightly seeing the Dharma with insight?"

The *Saṃyuttanikāya* counterpart to the above verses continues with a stanza inviting Māra to talk to those still caught up in identification with being a woman or a man, similar to the *Saṃyuktāgama* report translated above. This part of her reply has not been included in the *Therīgāthā*, which instead continues directly with her declaration of liberation:

> "[Sensual] enjoyment has been destroyed in every way,
> The mass of darkness has been shattered.
> Know this, Bad One:
> You are defeated, End-Maker."

The above stanza thereby forms a counterpart to the final verse in the *Saṃyuktāgama* version and its Chinese parallel, although such a verse is not found in the *Saṃyuttanikāya* version. In this way, the present *Therīgāthā* stanza supports the presentation in the Chinese versions, where Somā and the other nuns conclude with a verse proclaiming their attainment of the supreme. This indeed forms a fitting conclusion to each of their encounters with Māra, as it is precisely their consummate achievement that enables them to dispatch Māra so easily. In a comment on Somā's verses, Isaline Horner (1930/1990, 165) reasons:

> Women as well as men can explore and make discovery in the remoter but none the less close, in the less used but none the less malleable processes of their own minds. There is nothing in their nature to prevent them from willing and from attaining. That a woman could be represented as making such an utterance is a proof that the old life of Hinduism in which

women were regarded merely as child-bearers and as commodities was, if not suffering a decline, at least not passing entirely unquestioned.

Āḷavikā

An Escape from the World

The encounter between the nun Āḷavikā and Māra is the last of this type of episode to be explored in the present book. The *Saṃyuktāgama* report of Māra's challenge and Āḷavikā's reply takes the following form:[198]

> [Māra thought:] "The nun Āḷavikā ... has entered the Andhavana Grove to sit in meditation. I shall now approach and disturb her." He transformed himself into a youth of handsome appearance and went to that nun. He said to the nun: "Lady, where do you want to go?"
>
> The nun replied: "Friend, I am going to a secluded place."
>
> Then Māra, the Bad One, spoke in verse:
>
> "In the world there is no escape.
> Of what use is searching for seclusion?
> Return to partake of and consume the five sense pleasures,
> So that you do not later come to have regrets!"

The Pāli parallel does not report an initial exchange on where Āḷavikā wants to go and thus sets in directly with Māra's challenge.

In a way, this challenge can be seen as reflecting central trends underpinning the suggestions made by Māra in the episodes studied in previous chapters, as it combines an assertion of the uselessness of a woman's spiritual endeavor with the invitation to indulge in sensuality.

> Then the nun Āḷavikā thought: "Who is this, wanting to frighten me? Is he a human or is he a nonhuman? Is this person scheming to seduce me?" She had [this] thought in her mind: "This certainly is the wicked Māra wanting to confound me." Having realized this, she spoke in verse:
>
> "In the world there is an escape,
> I have come to know it for myself.
> Mean and wicked Māra,
> You do not know that path."

Similar to Somā, who dispatches Māra by pointing out that his voicing of doubts about women's spiritual abilities simply reflects the degree to which he is caught up in male identity, Āḷavikā clarifies that Māra's belief that there is no escape from the world simply shows that he does not know the path that leads to such an escape. His doubts in both cases are just an expression of his ignorance. In this way, both Somā and Āḷavikā dexterously return the challenge to Māra, disclosing the underlying rationale for his silly presumptions to be his own patterns of identification and ignorance.

Next, Āḷavikā turns to his attempt to attract her to sensual indulgence:

> "Just like being harmed by sharp knives,
> Like that are the five sense pleasures.
> Just like flesh-cutting torture,[199]
> Such is the *dukkha* of the aggregates of clinging.
>
> Such is what you just spoke about:
> Partaking of and delighting in the five sense pleasures.
> Therefore, I cannot delight in that condition,
> Which is to be much dreaded."

Instead of fear (also mentioned in the other Chinese version), in the Pāli parallel she just speaks of her lack of delight (*arati*).[200] One way or another, Āḷavikā unmistakably expresses her complete disinterest in sensuality, which from the lofty viewpoint of her inner freedom is similar to being stabbed by sharp knives. She then further broadens the scope of the strong imagery called up in this way by viewing the very clinging to the five aggregates in a similar way. In this way, grounded in her realization of the supreme, she is ready to dispatch Māra:

> "Separated from all rejoicing and delight,
> Having relinquished all the great darkness
> By having realized cessation,
> I dwell in peace, established in seclusion from the influxes.
> I recognize you, wicked Māra;
> You have been discovered, make yourself disappear and go!"

> Then Māra, the Bad One, thought: "That nun Āḷavikā has understood my intentions." Worried, sad, and unhappy, he vanished and was seen no more.

The Nuns and Māra

This last instance of nuns defeating Māra completes my survey of their impressive self-confidence when facing his challenges. A particularly prominent theme among these challenges is sensuality. In fact, some form of sexual threat constitutes an undercurrent throughout these episodes in which a man approaches a nun who is alone in a forest. In the passages translated above, this undercurrent finds reflection in each nun wondering whether the speaker might be scheming to seduce her.

It is noteworthy that the present set of discourses from the *Saṃyuttanikāya* and *Saṃyuktāgama* collections contains several instances where Māra overtly acts as a sexual aggressor, insinuating that withdrawal into solitude implies looking for a man (Kisāgotamī), inviting a nun to enjoy herself with him (Vijayā), and in one instance even apparently insinuating rape (Uppalavaṇṇā). This sets a contrast to sexual aggression by Māra's daughters, who on one occasion in the *Saṃyuttanikāya* and *Saṃyuktāgama* collections unsuccessfully try to tempt the recently awakened Buddha.[201] In the present set of discourses, it is the male Māra (and by definition only a male can be Māra) who stands for sensual temptation and sexual aggression.[202] In contrast, those who are disinterested in sex are females.

In the episodes surveyed above, as noted by Alice Collett (2009a, 111–12), "far from women being themselves the snare of Māra, instead, Māra is himself attempting to ensnare them." In this way, "Māra is representative of male sexuality, which is positioned as a potential danger for the women he approaches."

Notably, in another discourse extant in Pāli and Chinese, Māra approaches a group of monks with the challenge that they should enjoy sensual pleasures instead of living the life of one gone forth.[203] In this case, the advance and its rebuttal are both given by males, corroborating that there is no unilateral bias against women as the sole agents of sexual temptation. Māra, his daughters, and his baits simply stand for sensual desire in general, independent of gender.

Overall, the majority of actual challenges by Māra occur in the *Saṃyuttanikāya* and *Saṃyuktāgama* collections. On surveying such instances, another feature worthy of note emerges in that each nun facing such a challenge instantly recognizes Māra and sends him away. A telling juxtaposition emerges once this is compared to cases in the same collections where Māra challenges monks. Reports of such challenges involve several monks unable to recognize Māra and in need of the Buddha's personal intervention to deal with the situation.[204] In this way, these monks are shown to have been incapable of handling Māra on their own in the way their monastic sisters did. In contrast, not a single nun is on record for having failed to recognize Māra or for having been unable to dispatch him singlehandedly with a self-confident rebuttal. This of course reflects the circumstance that these nuns were arahants, whereas some of their male colleagues had not yet reached the same level of spiritual perfection. Nevertheless, it is worthy of note that reports of challenges by Māra in the *Saṃyuttanikāya* and *Saṃyuktāgama* collections end up presenting the nuns in a considerably more favorable light than their male counterparts.

Dhammadinnā

> The foremost of those nuns who analyze the meaning and widely discourse on divisions and parts [of the Dharma] is the nun called Dhammadinnā.[205]

THE PĀLI VERSION of the listing of outstanding nuns considers Dhammadinnā foremost among those who give teachings, literally of those who are "speakers on the Dharma."[206] Although using slightly different terminology, the two versions agree in meaning. That she was indeed an exceptional and outstanding teacher, based on having gained deep meditative realization, can be seen in the discourse below.

THE DISCOURSE BY DHAMMADINNĀ

The discourse given by Dhammadinnā takes the form of a question-and-answer exchange with a visitor, in the course of which she clarifies a range of different and at times quite profound aspects of the Buddha's teaching. This discourse is extant in Pāli, Chinese, and Tibetan. In what follows I translate the Tibetan version section by section.[207]

The Pāli commentary provides some background to this encounter.[208] According to its report, the husband of Dhammadinnā, the merchant Visākha, had as a lay disciple of the Buddha progressed to the level of nonreturn. Having thereby left behind sensual desires for good, he was unable to continue his marital relationship as before. Hence, he offered Dhammadinnā wealth and the freedom to do whatever she felt appropriate, upon which she decided to go forth. After having gone forth, she left the monastery in town to seek seclusion and practice intensively. Within a short time, she became an arahant, after which she returned to town. Hearing that she had come back to town so soon from seclusion, her former husband decided to visit her, to find out the reasons for her unexpectedly quick return.

According to the commentarial account, the questions posed by the nonreturner Visākha would have the purpose of testing out Dhammadinnā's wisdom. That is, he would want to discover if she has reached realization, or if she has just been unable to adapt to the living conditions in seclusion.

The Mūlasarvāstivāda *Vinaya* differs from this account, as it reports that the two were never even wed. Instead, with considerable struggle, she managed to get ordained on the eve of their scheduled wedding.[209] Whether the setting of the discourse is seen from the perspective of the Pāli commentary or from that of the Mūlasarvāstivāda *Vinaya*, some degree of challenge and assessment of Dhammadinnā's understanding and depth of realization during the question-and-answer session with her former (or would-be) husband is evident in each of the extant discourse versions.

Clarifications on Selfing

After the standard initial indication of the whereabouts of the Buddha, the introductory narration describes how Visākha approached Dhammadinnā, paid respect to her, and asked for permission to put some questions, which she readily granted.[210] The actual exchange then begins right away with a topic that stands at the heart of the early Buddhist teachings: the mistaken belief in a self in relation to the five aggregates of clinging.

> [Visākha asked:] "Noble lady, [a reified sense of] identity has been expounded, the arising of [a reified sense of] identity has been expounded, and the cessation of [a reified sense of] identity has been expounded. What is [a reified sense of] identity, what is the arising of [a reified sense of] identity, and what is the cessation of [a reified sense of] identity?"

[Dhammadinnā replied:] "Honorable Visākha, the five aggregates of clinging are reckoned [a reified sense of] identity in the excellent teachings of the noble Dharma. What are the five? The bodily form aggregate of clinging, the feeling tone ... perception ... volitional formations ... and the consciousness aggregate of clinging. The arising of [a reified sense of] identity is [due to] delight and attachment in relation to future becoming,[211] together with craving that relishes here and there.[212] The cessation of [a reified sense of] identity is accomplished through the removal of delight and attachment in relation to future becoming, together with [the removal of] craving that relishes here and there; through their complete renunciation, exhaustion, fading away, cessation, and pacification."

[Visākha asked:] "Noble lady, how does the view of [a reified sense of] identity arise?"

[Dhammadinnā replied:] "Honorable Visākha, an immature ordinary person, who is not learned, regards bodily form as truly being the self, or bodily form as possessing the self, or bodily form as being in the self, or regards the self as truly abiding in bodily form. Likewise, they regard feeling tone ... perception ... volitional formations ... consciousness as truly being the self, or consciousness as possessing the self, or consciousness as being in the self, or the self as abiding in consciousness. Thus, the view of [a reified sense of] identity arises."

[Visākha asked:] "Noble lady, how does the view of [a reified sense of] identity not arise?"

[Dhammadinnā replied:] "Honorable Visākha, a noble disciple, who is learned, does not regard bodily form as truly the self, or bodily form as possessing the self, or bodily form as being in the self, or the self as abiding in bodily form. They do not regard feeling tone ... perception ... volitional formations ... consciousness as truly the self, or the self as possessing consciousness, or consciousness as being in the self, or the self as abiding in consciousness. Therefore, the view of [a reified sense of] identity does not arise."

> [Visākha asked:] "Noble lady, the aggregates and the aggregates of clinging have been expounded. Noble lady, how is it, are the aggregates the same as the aggregates of clinging, or else are the aggregates different from the aggregates of clinging?"
>
> [Dhammadinnā replied:] "Honorable Visākha, the aggregates of clinging are the very aggregates, [yet] the aggregates are not [necessarily] aggregates of clinging. How is it that the aggregates of clinging are the very aggregates, [yet] the aggregates are not [necessarily] aggregates of clinging? Honorable Visākha, bodily form that is with influxes and clinging, feeling tone ... perception ... volitional formations ... consciousness that is with influxes and clinging, these are aggregates as well as aggregates of clinging. Form that is without influxes and without clinging, feeling tone ... perception ... volitional formations ... consciousness that is without influxes and without clinging, these are aggregates, but they are not reckoned aggregates of clinging."

The above exchange explores the significance of a reified sense of identity, of the corresponding view, and of the relationship between the five aggregates and clinging. The third part of the present exchange turns in particular to the difference between the aggregates as such and the aggregates of clinging. An exploration of the above teaching can conveniently begin with this last topic.

The point explicated here by Dhammadinnā is that, in the case of a fully awakened one, these five aggregates still exist, yet all clinging to them is gone.[213] Hence, "these are aggregates, but they are not reckoned aggregates of clinging." Even though an arahant or the Buddha still has an identity in the sense that they are able to know who they are, and they also have a personality in the sense that some of their personality traits will still manifest, they no longer reify any aspect of subjective experience or cling to it. As Dhammadinnā points out, the whole issue revolves around getting out of the influxes and clinging.

The second part of the above discussion elucidates the topic of the view of a reified sense of identity. This concerns the belief that there is a self as a truly existing and permanent entity, which is then imagined standing in some relation to one or the other of the five aggregates of clinging. Taking the first of the five aggregates of clinging as an example, the idea could be that the body is the self, as a result of which one regards "bodily form as truly being the self." Alternatively, the body could be imagined to be related to the self through some form of ownership, on which reasoning one then regards "bodily form as possessing the self." Or else, the self is assumed to be in some way located inside of the body, that is, one regards "the self as truly abiding in bodily form." The opposite is also possible when, based on an idea of the self as something much larger than the body, one could posit that the body must be located inside of such a self, thereby regarding "bodily form as being in the self." The same four alternative modes of imagining a self can be applied to each of the other four aggregates, resulting in altogether twenty views that reify the sense of identity.[214]

Regarding the first case of identification with the body, its wide-ranging ramifications can be illustrated with the following comment by Lily de Silva (1984, 70–71):

> The identification with the physical self gets further fortified with the bonds of hereditary and cultural groups such as family, caste, class, nation and race. With these different forms of physical identification, one's exclusiveness gets further and further established. At [the] individual level, these identifications generate behaviour varying from extreme arrogance to abject humiliation, depending on whether the particular form of identification is socially esteemed or degraded ... when this identification spills beyond 'an average working level' and becomes fanatical, it can create very dangerous situations ... fanatism at a racial level was witnessed in the Nazi movement, infamous for its unbelievable crimes of horror and terror. Clear thinking, truly civilized human beings regard racism as a myth ... but in spite of being only a myth devoid of any reality, it has caused an indelible holocaust of stark grim reality.

The explanation presented by Lily de Silva helps to see the practical relevance of the analysis of a reified sense of identity provided by

Dhammadinnā, which is perhaps at first sight somewhat abstract. The contrast she makes between an ordinary person and a noble disciple points to the attainment of stream-entry as the decisive difference between these two. With the first experience of Nirvana at stream-entry,[215] noble disciples are beyond holding such views. The reason is that stream-enterers have had an experience completely devoid of any type of self-reference. Therefore, as Dhammadinnā points out, the view of a reified sense of identity no longer arises. However, the tendency to selfing as such, in the form of self-referentiality and conceit, still arises. This will only be overcome with full awakening; solely arahants (and Buddhas, of course) are completely free from ego and conceit.

In the Pāli counterpart to the above discussion, Dhammadinnā also points out the path that leads to overcoming this reified sense of identity, which is obviously the noble eightfold path.[216] The third parallel, extant in Chinese, does not take up the arising and cessation of a reified sense of identity, although a somewhat truncated reference gives the impression that a portion of text concerned with this topic could have been lost.[217] The same Chinese version also differs on the names of the two protagonists, as here the nun is called "Delight in Dharma," which could be a rendering of what in Pāli would be Dhammanandī or Dhammanandā,[218] and her interlocutor is the female lay disciple Visākhā. This appears to be the result of an error in transmission.[219]

Morality, Concentration, and Wisdom

> [Visākha asked:] "Noble lady, regarding [the relationship between] the three aggregates (which are the aggregate of morality, the aggregate of concentration, and the aggregate of wisdom) and the noble eightfold path: how is it, noble lady, is the noble eightfold path encompassed by the three aggregates, or else are the three aggregates encompassed by the noble eightfold path?"
>
> [Dhammadinnā replied:] "Honorable Visākha, the noble eightfold path is encompassed by the three aggregates; the three aggregates are not encompassed by the noble eightfold

> path. How is it that the noble eightfold path is encompassed by the three aggregates, [yet] the three aggregates are not encompassed by the noble eightfold path? Honorable Visākha, in this regard right speech, right action, and right livelihood have been assigned by the Blessed One to the aggregate of morality. Right mindfulness and right concentration have been assigned by the Blessed One to the aggregate of concentration. Right view, right intention, and right effort have been assigned by the Blessed One to the aggregate of wisdom. Honorable Visākha, therefore it should be understood that the noble eightfold path is encompassed by the three aggregates, whereas the three aggregates are not encompassed by the noble eightfold path."
>
> [Visākha asked:] "Noble lady, is the path conditioned or unconditioned?"
>
> [Dhammadinnā replied:] "Honorable Visākha, it is conditioned."
>
> [Visākha asked:] "Noble lady, is cessation of the same nature?"
>
> [Dhammadinnā replied:] "Honorable Visākha, it is not of the same nature."

The Pāli and Chinese versions precede the inquiry regarding the relationship between the eightfold path and the triad of morality, concentration, and wisdom by first providing a definition of this path.[220] It is a regular procedure in the early discourses to base a discussion on providing first a clear definition of the relevant item, so that the absence of such a definition in the Tibetan version could be a case of textual loss. At the same time, however, from the viewpoint of the background narration given in the Pāli commentarial tradition, such a definition would hardly be required in what appears to be a private discussion between a nonreturner and an arahant, as both must have been quite familiar with the path that led them to their lofty attainment.

Be that as it may, the inquiry regarding the relationship of the eightfold path to the threefold training takes up a rather intricate topic that, to the best of my knowledge, is not expounded in other early discourses.

This would imply that, comparable to Selā's dexterous simile of the chariot, Dhammadinnā here makes her own distinct contribution to Buddhist thought by explicitly clarifying that the noble eightfold path does not comprise the whole of the triple training. This is significant, since among the qualities pertinent to awakening, the noble eightfold path has precisely the function of providing a comprehensive framework.[221] Still, as Dhammadinnā points out, the compass of the threefold training is broader than that, as it can comprise forms of training that are not explicitly covered by the eightfold path.

Another aspect of considerable importance is the correlation between these two schemes, offered by Dhammadinnā. The parallel versions show some variation regarding the placing of right effort, which the Pāli version more convincingly relates to the aggregate of concentration.[222] They agree, however, that the foundational factor of right view belongs to the aggregate of wisdom. This indication runs counter to the usual sequence in which the three aggregates or types of training are enumerated, where morality invariably stands in first position. Practically speaking, this positioning in first place conveys the need to lay a foundation in moral conduct in order to be able to develop concentration, based on which wisdom can arise in turn.

Yet, there is a need to avoid turning this basic presentation into a rigid division.[223] This need is precisely what Dhammadinnā's clarification conveys, namely that some degree of wisdom is required from the outset. This takes the form of right view as the key reference point and guiding principle for a successful cultivation of the other factors of the noble eightfold path. In other words, yes, morality is the foundation, concentration builds on it, and wisdom relies on the other two. Nevertheless, even the foundation building in morality needs a minimal input of wisdom and some degree of mental collectedness. The gradual building up of these three dimensions of cultivation involves a flexible interrelation between them in actual practice. Central throughout, of course, is the guiding principle of right view.

Following this important clarification, Dhammadinnā also explains that the path to the unconditioned is itself conditioned. This is certainly not self-evident, as one might even wonder how the unconditioned can be reached with conditioned means.[224] Although the unconditioned is not the product of the path (as that would make it become conditioned), it can be experienced when the conditioned means of training in the path lead to a complete letting go, which can issue in the unpremeditated breakthrough to the unconstructed.[225] Against this background, the succinct explanation provided by Dhammadinnā that the path is conditioned can be seen to carry rather profound implications.

The Tibetan version continues with a brief exchange on cessation, indicating that this does not share the conditioned nature of the path. This exchange is not found in the Pāli version, although it does have a counterpart in the Chinese parallel.[226]

On Concentration

> [Visākha asked:] "Noble lady, how many factors does the first absorption possess?"
>
> [Dhammadinnā replied:] "Honorable Visākha, it possesses five factors: [directed] comprehension, [sustained] discernment, joy, happiness, and unification of the mind."[227]
>
> [Visākha asked:] "Noble lady, regarding concentration, the cause of concentration, the power of concentration, and the development of concentration: Noble lady, what is concentration, what is the cause of concentration, what is the power of concentration, and what is the development of concentration?"
>
> [Dhammadinnā replied:] "Honorable Visākha, wholesome unification of the mind is concentration; the four establishments of mindfulness are the cause of concentration; the four right efforts are the power of concentration; the undertaking of these very qualities, their full undertaking, the abiding in them, practicing and applying [oneself] to them is the development of concentration."

Unlike the remainder of the above exposition, the definition of the first absorption has a counterpart only in the Chinese version and is absent from the Pāli parallel.[228] A similar indication, however, is part of a question-and-answer exchange in the preceding discourse in the Pāli collection.[229] This is one of several instances giving the impression that, in the course of oral transmission, some shuffling of topics occurred between what in both the *Majjhimanikāya* and the *Madhyamāgama* are two adjacent discourses. For this reason, it is quite possible that the above discussion should indeed be allocated to the teachings given by Dhammadinnā.

The listing of five factors, which according to two out of the three parallel versions was given by Dhammadinnā, is of further significance as it explicitly indicates that already the first absorption is characterized by unification of the mind. The present passage thereby provides one of several indications that in the early discourses the first absorption features as already a deep meditative experience requiring considerable meditative expertise.[230]

The remainder of Dhammadinnā's exposition offers other helpful indications for meditation practice. She defines concentration as unification of the mind, further qualified as being "wholesome." The Chinese version also applies this qualification to unification of the mind, unlike the Pāli parallel.[231] In a way, the Pāli version has a point here, since concentration in general need not be wholesome. Yet, in the present context of a discussion between two highly advanced practitioners on subtle aspects of the practice, the point at stake is not so much concentration in general but concentration as an integral part of the path. Hence, to qualify unification of the mind as "wholesome" explicitly brings out this setting and thereby provides an important reference point for the whole complex relationship between cultivating certain meditation qualities and the need for the appropriate ethical foundation building. From an early Buddhist perspective, the cultivation of concentration (as well as of mindfulness) necessarily stands in an ethical framework; any such cultivation needs to be undertaken in such a way as to be wholesome.

This much does not yet exhaust the depth of Dhammadinnā's explanations. Another point worth noting is her clarification that the four establishments of mindfulness are the cause of concentration. This succinct formulation of the position taken in the early discourses is not found in this way elsewhere and thus is a unique contribution made by her. The indication presented by Dhammadinnā in this way points to a middle path position between the assumption that mindfulness is only a matter of insight and the belief that the primary purpose of the four establishments of mindfulness is to lead to absorption.[232] The explicitly stated purpose as well as the detailed exposition of the four establishments of mindfulness shows that the overarching purpose of such practice is to lead to the realization of Nirvana and is thus indeed a matter of insight. At the same time, however, mindfulness also furnishes an important support for tranquility meditation and is present in each of the four absorptions.[233] From this perspective, the four establishments of mindfulness are indeed "the cause" of concentration, as in combination with the four right efforts as the "power" of concentration they can lead to a natural deepening of concentration. The Chinese version adds to this the four bases of success as the "achievement" of concentration,[234] thereby providing an additional perspective on the collaboration of various qualities and practice related to the gaining of concentration.

The Three Formations

> [Visākha asked:] "Noble lady, regarding formations:[235] noble lady, what are these formations?"
>
> [Dhammadinnā replied:] "Honorable Visākha, there are bodily formations, verbal formations, and mental formations: these are the three."
>
> [Visākha asked:] "Noble lady, what are bodily formations, what are verbal formations, and what are mental formations?"
>
> [Dhammadinnā replied:] "Honorable Visākha, exhalation and inhalation are reckoned as bodily formations; [directed] comprehension and [sustained] discernment are reckoned as verbal formations; perception and intention are reckoned as mental formations."
>
> [Visākha asked:] "Noble lady, why are exhalation and inhalation reckoned as bodily formations, why are [directed] comprehension and [sustained] discernment reckoned as verbal formations, why are perception and intention reckoned as mental formations?"

> [Dhammadinnā replied:] "Honorable Visākha, exhalation and inhalation are bodily factors, they depend on the body, are related to the body, and depending on the body they enter its [domain]; therefore, exhalation and inhalation are reckoned as bodily formations. On having examined and discerned with [directed] comprehension and [sustained] discernment one speaks; therefore, [directed] comprehension and [sustained] discernment are reckoned as verbal formations. Perception and intention are factors arisen from the mind, go along with the mind, depend on the mind, are related to the mind, and depending on the mind they enter its [domain]; therefore, perception and intention are reckoned as mental formations."
>
> [Visākha asked:] "Noble lady, at the time when the body has been abandoned by these factors, when it is like a log, bereft of the mind, how many are the [other] factors that have been abandoned at that time?"
>
> "Honorable Visākha, life [force], heat, and consciousness, these are the three. At the time when life [force], heat, and consciousness have been abandoned, the body is like a log, bereft of the mind."

The definition of the three formations given here concerns the attainment of the cessation of perception and feeling tone, a deep meditative experience that requires a superb degree of mental mastery. Before exploring this attainment in more detail, however, by way of additional preparation, the discussion turns briefly to the condition of death. The progression in this part of the Tibetan discourse does not correspond to either of its parallels, as the discussion of the three formations is only found in the Pāli parallel and the exploration of the condition of death only in the Chinese parallel,[236] although a similar discussion is part of a question-and answer-exchange in the preceding Pāli discourse.[237] Another difference, found in the Pāli parallel to the discussion of the three formations, is that its definition of mental formations lists perception and feeling tone, rather than perception and intention.[238]

The present analysis into three formations is specific to the cessation attainment and not applicable to the case of formations as the second link in dependent arising.[239] The latter concerns intentions that are rooted in ignorance, whereas the three formations discussed here are basic functions of a human body and mind that are still operative in the case of an arahant. Unless, of course, the arahant enters cessation attainment. Dhammadinnā appears to have been one of those rare practitioners able to do so, as becomes evident from her dexterous exposition in the next part of the discourse.[240]

Cessation Attainment

> [Visākha asked:] "Noble lady, the occasion of passing away and dying and [the occasion] of entry into the meditative attainment of cessation: are these to be considered as distinct, are they different?"
>
> [Dhammadinnā replied:] "Honorable Visākha, the occasion of passing away and dying and [the occasion] of entry into the meditative attainment of cessation: these are considered as distinct; they have a number of differences. Honorable Visākha, on the occasion of passing away and dying, the bodily formations have ceased, the verbal formations [have ceased], and the mental formations have ceased. Honorable Visākha, the life [faculty] and heat leave [the body], the faculties become otherwise, and consciousness departs from the body.
>
> "On entering the meditative attainment of cessation, the bodily formations have ceased, the verbal formations [have ceased], and the mental formations have ceased. Yet, the life [faculty] and heat do not leave [the body], the faculties [do not] become otherwise, and consciousness does not depart from the body. Honorable Visākha, thus the occasion of passing away and dying and [the occasion] of entry into the meditative attainment of cessation are considered as distinct; they are different."

[Visākha asked:] "Noble lady, how does the attainment of cessation take place?"

[Dhammadinnā replied:] "Honorable Visākha, a monastic who enters the attainment of cessation does not think 'I enter the attainment of cessation.' Their mind has previously been developed in such a way that, having been developed in that way, they will stay in it accordingly."

[Visākha asked:] "Noble lady, how does the emergence from cessation take place?"

[Dhammadinnā replied:] "Honorable Visākha, a monastic who emerges from the attainment of cessation does not think 'I emerge from the attainment of cessation.' Yet, their mind has previously been developed in such a way that, having been developed in that way, they will emerge from it accordingly."

[Visākha asked:] "Noble lady, when a monastic enters the attainment of cessation, which factors will cease first: the bodily formations, the verbal formations, or the mental formations?"

[Dhammadinnā replied:] "Honorable Visākha, when a monastic enters the attainment of cessation, the verbal formations will cease first, then the bodily and mental formations."

[Visākha asked:] "Noble lady, when a monastic emerges from the attainment of cessation, which factors will arise first: the bodily formations, the verbal formations, or the mental formations?"

[Dhammadinnā replied:] "Honorable Visākha, when a monastic emerges from the attainment of cessation, the mental formations will arise first, then the bodily and verbal formations."

[Visākha asked:] "Noble lady, when a monastic emerges from the attainment of cessation, to where does their mind incline, to where does it flow, to where does it move?"

[Dhammadinnā replied:] "Honorable Visākha, when a monastic emerges from the attainment of cessation, the mind inclines toward seclusion, flows toward seclusion, moves

> toward seclusion; it inclines toward liberation, flows toward liberation, moves toward liberation; it inclines toward Nirvana, flows toward Nirvana, moves toward Nirvana."
>
> [Visākha asked:] "Noble lady, when a monastic comes out of the attainment of cessation, what contacts do they contact?"
>
> [Dhammadinnā replied:] "Honorable Visākha, [they contact] imperturbability, nothingness, and signlessness."
>
> [Visākha asked:] "Noble lady, to enter the attainment of cessation, how many factors does a monastic develop?"
>
> [Dhammadinnā replied:] "Honorable Visākha, this question should have been asked first. I will nevertheless reply to it now. To enter the attainment of cessation, a monastic develops two factors: tranquility and insight."

The preceding discussion of the three formations and the condition of death served as a preliminary for the present exploration of the attainment of the cessation of perception and feeling tone. One who is in such an attainment can appear as if dead from the outside, as evident from a tale in another discourse, according to which people saw a monk seated in this attainment and unsuccessfully tried to cremate him, mistakenly believing that he was dead.[241] Dhammadinnā clarifies the decisive difference between being dead and abiding in the attainment of cessation: The faculty of life continues in the latter, and the bodily heat and the sense faculties do not disintegrate. The Tibetan version stands alone in explicitly indicating that consciousness is still present during this attainment.[242]

With this basic clarification in place, Dhammadinnā provides a wealth of details on the actual attainment of cessation in a way that confirms the impression that she must be speaking from personal experience. The sequence in which the three formations cease on entry and arise again on emergence is similarly covered in the Pāli version but not in the Chinese parallel, as in this case the same topic is part of the adjacent discourse with a similar question-and-answer exchange.[243]

Regarding the inclination of the mind after emerging from the attainment of cessation, the parallels only mention seclusion.[244] The Tibetan version is more detailed here, as it adds being inclined toward liberation and Nirvana. Regarding the contacts experienced at this time, in the sense of what type of experience will take place when emerging, the Pāli version agrees on signless contact and in addition mentions emptiness and desireless contact, rather than nothingness and imperturbable contact.[245] The final exchange on the need for tranquility and insight to enter the attainment of cessation is not found in the parallels.

From having probed Dhammadinnā's expertise in relation to such intricate aspects of a deep meditation attainment, the discussion shifts to what at first sight may seem a rather simple topic, namely the different feeling tones. Yet, as the next part will show, here, too, Dhammadinnā is able to provide a deeper perspective that is of considerable practical relevance.

Feeling Tones and Underlying Tendencies

> [Visākha asked:] "Noble lady, how many feeling tones are there?"
>
> [Dhammadinnā replied:] "Honorable Visākha, there are three: pleasant, unpleasant, and neutral."
>
> [Visākha asked:] "Noble lady, what is pleasant feeling tone, what is unpleasant feeling tone, and what is neutral feeling tone?"
>
> [Dhammadinnā replied:] "Honorable Visākha, [whatever] bodily and mental pleasure or happiness that arises from contact experienced as pleasant is reckoned as pleasant feeling tone. Whatever bodily and mental displeasure or pain arises from contact experienced as unpleasant is reckoned as unpleasant feeling tone. Whatever bodily and mental neutral or equanimous experience arises from neutral contact is reckoned as neutral feeling tone."
>
> [Visākha asked:] "Noble lady, what increases with pleasant feeling tones, what increases with unpleasant feeling tones, what increases with neutral feeling tones?"

[Dhammadinnā replied:] "Honorable Visākha, desire increases with pleasant feeling tones, aversion increases with unpleasant feeling tones, and ignorance increases with neutral feeling tones."

[Visākha asked:] "Noble lady, do all pleasant feeling tones increase desire, do all unpleasant feeling tones increase aversion, and do all neutral feeling tones increase ignorance?"

[Dhammadinnā replied:] "Honorable Visākha, not all pleasant feeling tones increase desire, not all unpleasant feeling tones increase aversion, and not all neutral feeling tones increase ignorance. There are pleasant feeling tones that do not increase desire but [instead] abandon it; there are unpleasant feeling tones that do not increase aversion but [instead] abandon it; and there are neutral feeling tones that do not increase ignorance but [instead] abandon it."

[Visākha asked:] "Noble lady, what pleasant feeling tones do not increase desire but [instead] abandon it?"

[Dhammadinnā replied:] "Honorable Visākha, here a noble disciple, being free from sensual desire and free from bad and unwholesome states, with [directed] comprehension and [sustained] discernment, and with happiness and joy arisen from seclusion, dwells having attained the first absorption. With the stilling of [directed] comprehension and [sustained] discernment, with complete inner confidence and unification of the mind, free from [directed] comprehension and [sustained] discernment, with happiness and joy arisen from concentration, they dwell having attained the second absorption. With the fading away of joy, dwelling equanimous with mindfulness and comprehension, experiencing just happiness with the body, what the noble ones reckon an equanimous and mindful dwelling in happiness, they dwell having attained the third absorption. Such pleasant feeling tones do not increase desire but [instead] abandon it."

[Visākha asked:] "Noble lady, what unpleasant feeling tones do not increase aversion but [instead] abandon it?"

> [Dhammadinnā replied:] "Honorable Visākha, here a noble disciple generates an aspiration for supreme liberation: 'When shall I dwell realizing that sphere, which noble ones dwell having realized?' The mental displeasure and painful feeling tones [due to] that aspiration, that pursuit, and that longing do not increase aversion but [instead] abandon it."
>
> [Visākha asked:] "Noble lady, what neutral feeling tones do not increase ignorance but [instead] abandon it?"
>
> [Dhammadinnā replied:] "Honorable Visākha, here a noble disciple, leaving behind happiness and leaving behind pain, with the earlier disappearance of mental pleasure and displeasure, with neither happiness nor pain and with completely pure equanimity and mindfulness, dwells having attained the fourth absorption. Such neutral feeling tones do not increase ignorance but [instead] abandon it."
>
> [Visākha asked:] "Noble lady, what is pleasant, what is unpleasant, and what is the real shortcoming in regard to pleasant feeling tones? What is pleasant, what is unpleasant, and what is the real shortcoming in regard to unpleasant feeling tones? What is pleasant, what is unpleasant, and what is the real shortcoming in regard to neutral feeling tones?"
>
> [Dhammadinnā replied:] "Honorable Visākha, the arising of pleasant feeling tone and its abiding is pleasant; its transformation [into another feeling tone] is unpleasant. Upon [manifesting] its impermanence, because of that, [then] its real shortcoming [manifests]. The arising of unpleasant feeling tone and its abiding is unpleasant; its transformation [into another feeling tone] is pleasant. At the time when it [manifests] its impermanence, then its real shortcoming [manifests]. Being unaware of neutral feeling tone is unpleasant; the arising of awareness of it is pleasant. Whenever it [manifests its] impermanence, [then] its real shortcoming [manifests]."

Building on the basic distinction of feeling tones into three hedonic types, resulting from their corresponding contacts, Dhammadinnā clarifies their relation to mental tendencies. The Tibetan version here uses somewhat unexpected terminology with its reference to an "increase,"[246] which has its counterpart in references to an "underlying tendency" (*anusaya*) in the parallel versions. The important point to take away here is that, even though pleasant feeling tone tends to stimulate desire, unpleasant feeling tone aversion, and neutral feeling tone ignorance, this is not invariably the case.

Being in the first absorption furnishes an example for pleasant feeling tone that does not increase (sensual) desire or else stimulate the underlying tendency for lust. The Tibetan version stands alone in extending this indication to the second and third absorptions as well. All versions agree that the fourth absorption exemplifies the case of neutral feeling tone that does not stimulate ignorance.[247] For unpleasant feeling tone, the illustration in the parallel versions takes up the sadness of not yet having reached the goal of liberating the mind from defilements. It is noteworthy that in this way the yearning for freedom features as a commendable type of unpleasant experience. This is not to say that the position taken by Dhammadinnā intends recommending the arousing of spiritual frustration. The point is only that there is room for the unpleasant experience of witnessing one's own shortcomings as this serves to stir the mind to make an effort for progressing on the path.

The final part of Dhammadinnā's exposition on feeling tones takes up the topic of impermanence, which in itself is the chief shortcoming (literally "danger") of reacting to any feeling tone. Pleasant feeling tone is indeed pleasant when arising and persisting, but then its inevitable disappearance, sooner or later, will be unpleasant. Conversely, in the case of unpleasant feeling tone, an eventual change to a different feeling tone will provide the pleasure of relief. Yet, that, too, is impermanent. Clinging to either pleasant feeling tone or just to the absence of pain is shortsighted, since sooner or later the law of impermanence will make itself felt (pun intended), disclosing the inherent shortcoming of clinging to feeling tones. This type of observation is particularly relevant to meditation practice.[248] Once directly experienced, it provides a welcome support when having to face strong feeling tones, as these are much less able to unsettle a mind that knows they will sooner or later change.

This much being already a sufficient reason to engage in contemplation of feeling tones, additional inspiration for dedicating oneself to meditation can be gained from the knowledge that instances of the neutral category can become occasions for the experience of meditative joy, provided they are met with mindfulness and ideally in awareness of their impermanent nature. The presence of mindfulness is the key here, as neutral feeling tones tend to stimulate ignorance. Yet, when mindfulness is present and the occurrence of neutral feeling tones is noticed as simply a changing dimension of experience, this can lead to the subtle joy of being fully in the present moment and in possession of the clarity of understanding.

Counterparts

The three feeling tones also lend themselves to an examination of counterparts:

> [Visākha asked:] "Noble lady, what is the counterpart to pleasant feeling tone?"
>
> [Dhammadinnā replied:] "Unpleasant feeling tone."
>
> [Visākha asked:] "What is the counterpart to unpleasant feeling tone?"
>
> [Dhammadinnā replied:] "Pleasant feeling tone."
>
> [Visākha asked:] "What is the counterpart to pleasant and unpleasant feeling tone?"
>
> [Dhammadinnā replied:] "Neutral feeling tone."
>
> [Visākha asked:] "What is the counterpart to neutral feeling tone?"
>
> [Dhammadinnā replied:] "Ignorance."
>
> [Visākha asked:] "What is the counterpart to ignorance?"
>
> [Dhammadinnā replied:] "Knowledge."
>
> [Visākha asked:] "What is the counterpart to knowledge?
>
> [Dhammadinnā replied:] "Nirvana."
>
> [Visākha asked:] "Noble lady, what is the counterpart to Nirvana?"

> [Dhammadinnā replied:] "Honorable Visākha, you are going too far, you are really going too far, this is the end of it, it is not possible [to go further]. Following the Blessed One is for [the sake of] Nirvana; the final goal of the pure holy life is Nirvana, the eradication of *dukkha*."

The Pāli version does not inquire after the counterpart to both pleasant and unpleasant feeling tones as a lead over to neutral feeling tone.[249] Whereas up to this point the exposition involves contrasting what is pleasant to what is unpleasant, with neutral feeling tone the examination shifts toward a more explicitly soteriological perspective, when both versions identify the counterpart to neutral feeling tone to be ignorance. At this point the underlying thrust of the series of counterparts becomes fully apparent, showing that this is not just a doctrinal exercise but much rather meant to point to progress toward awakening.

From this perspective then, the basic contrast between the highs and lows of pleasant and unpleasant experiences has its middle ground in what is felt as neutral, and that has its counterpart, from the viewpoint of one dedicated to progress on the path, in ignorance. This in turn has its natural counterpart in knowledge, a simple statement that at the same time lays bare a crucial principle underlying the path to liberation. The topic of liberation comes up explicitly in the Pāli version, which proceeds from knowledge to liberation and from that to Nirvana.

In all versions, Dhammadinnā makes it clear that Visākha's attempt to push the line of inquiry beyond Nirvana is misguided. With all the meaningful indications that the series of counterparts can yield for progress to Nirvana, it needs to be recognized that its realization goes beyond any counterparts. Although the path is conditioned, the goal is unconditioned.[250] From this perspective, Nirvana is indeed the counterpart to knowledge (or liberation), but itself has in turn no counterpart.

A possible way of making practical sense of this presentation of counterparts could be the recommendation to face the arising of any type of strong feeling tone by briefly reminding oneself that this has a counterpart in the opposite type of feeling tone. When experiencing the peak of pleasure, for example, such a brief reminder, in the form of acknowledging that sooner or later there will be pain, can provide a grounding that prevents the mind being carried away. The same holds conversely for experiencing pain. Facing both of these feeling tones with composure in this way can lead to their counterpart in neutral feeling tones. Although becoming established in such a way is certainly commendable, it is not the final aim of the exercise. The point is not just to make sure one remains as much as possible established in hedonic neutrality. The problem is that behind neutral feeling tone lurks the potential counterpart of ignorance. This needs to be countered, quite literally, by cultivating knowledge in order to proceed toward liberation and Nirvana.

Authentication

> At that time, the lay follower Visākha rejoiced in the exposition given by the nun Dhammadinnā. He paid respect to the nun Dhammadinnā by prostrating and left. Not long after the lay follower Visākha had left, the nun Dhammadinnā approached the Blessed One. Having approached him she paid respect with her head at the feet of the Blessed One and sat down to one side. Sitting to one side, the nun Dhammadinnā reported to the Blessed One the whole conversation she had been having with the lay follower Visākha. The Blessed One said to the nun Dhammadinnā:
>
> "Well done, Dhammadinnā, well done! If the lay follower Visākha had asked me these matters in such words and with such expressions, I would have answered on these matters in just such words and expressions as you did, explaining it just like this."

The parallel versions agree that the Buddha expressed his full approval and authenticated Dhammadinnā's exposition by stating that he would have explained the matter in the same way. A difference in the Pāli version is that, instead of Dhammadinnā approaching him herself, here it is Visākha who reports the conversation.[251] The idea of approaching the Buddha for confirmation is a standard procedure in the discourses when expositions have been given by a disciple in the absence of the Buddha.

Looking back at the discourse as a whole, a recurrent pattern can be discerned that proceeds from relatively simple and innocuous questions to intricate and profound matters. This has already been noted by Caroline Foley (1894, 323) in an article written on the Pāli version of the present discourse before she married and became Caroline Rhys Davids:

> Visākha throughout the conversation is asking, not as a learner, but as an examiner and critic ... her swift and terse replies spur him on to test her with 'knot-questions' and by paradoxes to catch her tripping, whose wisdom and insight disclosed itself more and more as their talk went on. But Dhammadinnā evidently enjoyed dealing with a crux, and, like a daring player, let him lead her into the snare, only to slip through the noose in her own way.

A progression toward knotty questions can be seen, for example, when the topic of a reified sense of identity leads over to an inquiry about the precise relationship between clinging and the aggregates, a matter not easily explained unless the respondent has a very good level of understanding. Next comes the rather probing question regarding the relationship between the noble eightfold path and the three aggregates of morality, concentration, and wisdom: Which of these is the overarching category?[252] Another thorny question on the same topic concerns the conditioned nature of the noble eightfold path.

Once Dhammadinnā has settled each of these points, Visākha tests out her familiarity with mental tranquility as well, succinctly inquiring into the mental qualities and practices that are required to deepen concentration. This much ascertained, he proceeds further on the same track by tackling the attainment of cessation, an experience that requires a very high level of proficiency in insight and tranquility. Here, too, Dhammadinnā is able to prove her worth; in fact, in the Tibetan version translated above, this exchange ends with a little quip at Visākha for having asked a question out of the proper order, showing her self-confidence at this point in their discussion.

Visākha continues further, after having already ascertained Dhammadinnā's accomplishment in insight and tranquility, by taking up the issue of feeling tones. This takes the course of their discussion from high meditative attainments back to the common world of experience and its challenges. In line with the above-mentioned pattern, after the innocuous and easily answered query about the three types of feeling tones, the discussion quickly moves into deep waters, yielding clarifications about which feeling tones do not stimulate defilements or underlying tendencies.

The final part of their discussion proceeds through a series of terms that form counterparts to each other, until their exchange reaches the topic of Nirvana. When Visākha tries to push beyond this point, Dhammadinnā makes it clear that he has gone too far. In this way, she remains master of the situation even when it is not possible to reply to a question. Facing what would spell defeat in a normal debate setting, she self-confidently asserts that the question has moved beyond issues that can be discussed. This assertion, which must reflect her own firm establishment in the realization of the final goal, can be seen to form a fitting grand finale to her exposition.

The insightful explanations offered by Dhammadinnā in the present discourse have been a continuous source of inspiration in the history of Theravāda Buddhism, as can be seen from recurrent references to this exposition in the Pāli commentaries.[253] According to the commentary on the *Therīgāthā*, Dhammadinnā also served as an inspiring model for other women who had chosen to follow her example by going forth in a quest for awakening: One of those who had gone forth under Dhammadinnā and learned meditation from her became an arahant herself, after which this nun also became an outstanding teacher.[254] Another nun, unable to gain concentration for twenty-five years, was able to develop her practice and eventually attain the six supernormal knowledges after hearing a teaching delivered by Dhammadinnā.[255] In these various ways, Dhammadinnā indeed deserves to be reckoned foremost among those who "analyze the meaning and widely discourse on divisions and parts" of the teaching, as formulated in the *Ekottarikāgama* passage translated at the outset of the present chapter. She must have been indeed "foremost among those who give teachings," to borrow the formulation employed in the Pāli parallel.

Aspiring for Total Freedom

In addition to the above discourse, the *Therīgāthā* attributes a single verse to Dhammadinnā.[256] According to the commentary, she spoke this stanza when already established in stream-entry and aspiring to progress to full awakening.[257]

> "With desire for the final end aroused,
> Let her mind be pervaded by it.
> With her mind not bound to sensuality,
> She is reckoned one who moves upstream."

The verse in a way provides a poetic expression of the culmination point of the series of counterparts as the last topic in her exchange with Visākha: the final end of Nirvana. Arousing desire for this final end, and letting her mind be pervaded by it, was what led Dhammadinnā to the acme of spiritual perfection and thereby provided the foundation for her impressive ability to teach and instruct, thereby facilitating that others move similarly upstream.

Kajaṅgalā

A Difficult Question

THE OUTSTANDING TEACHING given by Dhammadinnā is not the sole instance showcasing a nun apt at delivering profound teachings, as the case of Khemā, taken up in a previous chapter, already demonstrates. The same can be seen again with a discourse extant only in Pāli that features the nun Kajaṅgalā as the speaker. After the standard introduction with information about the whereabouts of the Buddha, the Pāli discourse describes a group of lay followers approaching the nun Kajaṅgalā, paying respect to her, and then asking her the following question:[258]

> "Revered lady, the Blessed One said in the Great Questions: A question about one,[259] a brief statement of one, an analysis of one ... two ... three ... four ... five ... six ... seven ... eight ... nine ... a question about ten, a brief statement of ten, an analysis of ten. Revered lady, how should the meaning of this succinct statement by the Blessed One be viewed in detail?"

The pattern of a "question," a "brief statement," and an "analysis" applies equally for every number from one to ten. For the sake of ease of reading, in the above extract I have not fully treated the numbers from two to nine, as the resultant repetition can become a bit tiring. My presentation is in keeping with a standard procedure for abbreviation used in the discourses, where only the first and last item in a list will receive full treatment.[260]

The mention of the "Great Questions" to introduce this series refers to a discourse found in the same *Aṅguttaranikāya* collection right before the present one. This other Pāli discourse has parallels in a discourse extant in Chinese translation and in Gāndhārī fragments.[261] According to its introductory narration, Buddhist monastics had been challenged by outside practitioners. Such challenging of others appears to have been a common occurrence in the ancient Indian setting in order to initiate a debate.

When the monastics reported to the Buddha what had happened, he taught them a series of questions, presumably meant to silence those who try to pull them into a debate. These questions proceed from ones to tens. The whole set could be paraphrased as this: What liberating teaching involves the number one? And what liberating teachings involve the numbers two, three, four, five, six, seven, eight, nine, and ten? Each of these questions requires a brief statement by identifying a particular doctrinal item as the appropriate choice for the relevant number. This identification then should lead on to an analysis, which takes the form of relating this item to the final goal. Someone not knowing what progress to the final goal requires would not be able to give satisfactory answers to these questions.

The series of such questions seems to have two functions in the early discourses. One is to serve as an easily memorized list for those who wish to progress toward awakening. In an oral setting, such a numerical arrangement can serve as an aid for memory. This function stands in the background of a brief catechism of similar nature, which according to the commentarial explanation the Buddha gave to the novice Sopāka.[262] The other function, already mentioned, appears to be to offer a way out of getting bogged down in a debate with non-Buddhists. An actual implementation of this strategy can be seen in a discourse featuring a Buddhist householder facing the leader of the Jains.[263] The discourse reports that the lay follower had earlier made a statement that the head of the Jains at first misunderstood and approved. Once the householder clarified the intended meaning, the leader of the Jains reportedly reacted with verbal abuse. In reply, the lay follower noted that what the other said earlier did not match what he said later, followed by posing these ten questions. In this setting, employing this strategy reduced the leader of the Jains to silence and thus offered the householder the occasion to get up and leave.

The present case concerns the first function of this set of ten inquiries, as here the idea is obviously not to avoid a debate. Instead, the lay followers, who must have heard about this catechetical exposition, wish to be taught its doctrinal significance. In reply to this request, the nun Kajaṅgalā reportedly offered the following disclaimer before proceeding to expound on the topic:

> "Friends, I have not heard this in the presence of the Blessed One, not learned this in his presence, and I have also not heard this in the presence of meditating monastics, not learned this in their presence. Yet, listen and pay careful attention to what I will say, according to how it seems to me."

The injunction to pay careful attention to what is being said is a recurrent phrase used by those who are about to give a teaching, most often by the Buddha. It reflects the oral setting in which, due to a lack of written or other records, the teaching that is just being delivered will be irretrievably lost unless one pays careful attention.

The lay followers happily agree to Kajaṅgalā's suggestion that she will explain the matter as it seems to her, without being able to point to any authoritative source for her exposition. For Kajaṅgalā to expound this matter on her own is quite a challenging undertaking. It requires intimate and comprehensive acquaintance with the teachings in order to make a reasonable guess as to what particular teaching would best fit the numbers from one to ten under the overarching requirement of doctrines relevant to progress to full awakening.

Ones to Threes: Arousing Disenchantment and Dispassion

Kajaṅgalā's actual exposition begins as follows:

> "Now, it has been said by the Blessed One: 'A question about one, a brief statement of one, an analysis of one.' In relation to

> what has this been said? Friends, a monastic will make an end of *dukkha* in this very life on becoming fully disenchanted with one thing, fully dispassionate toward it, fully liberated from it, fully seeing its end, and fully penetrating its meaning. What is that one thing? All sentient beings subsist due to nutriment."

Kajaṅgalā's reply continues by repeating the indication that the final goal can be reached by becoming fully disenchanted, etc., with this one thing. This analysis precedes the question and again follows it, which reflects another feature of the oral setting, evident in the pervasive tendency to repeat passages so as to ensure their accurate storing in memory.

The Chinese parallel to the preceding Pāli discourse, which reports the Buddha's original delivery of the Great Questions, adds that sentient beings lacking nutriment will pass away, thereby making explicit what must be implicit in the Pāli version.[264] In this way, the teaching on "one" thing in all versions can be understood to throw into relief the dependence of sentient beings, including of course oneself, on a regular supply of food. Seen in a broader manner, this can be related to the predicament of the food chain, with all the killing and pain inevitably resulting from it, together with a reminder of mortality as an intrinsic dimension of having a physical body that needs to be kept alive through a regular food intake. A full appreciation of this predicament can indeed be expected to arouse dispassion and disenchantment and spur a practitioner onward on the path to freedom from rebirth.

Having dealt with the number one successfully, Kajaṅgalā turns to the next item, related to the number two, again first quoting the relevant statement by the Buddha and then offering her own explanation as follows:

> "Friends, a monastic will make an end of *dukkha* in this very life on becoming fully disenchanted with two things, fully dispassionate toward them, fully liberated from them, fully seeing their end, and fully penetrating their meaning. What are those two? Name and form."

The Chinese parallel to the preceding discourse in the *Aṅguttaranikāya* again furnishes additional information, as it defines "name" to stand for feeling tone, perception, intention,[265] contact, and attention, whereas "form" represents the four elements and their derivatives.[266] In this way, the mental functions assembled under "name" are those responsible for recognition and the formation of concepts, for quite literally giving something its name.[267] "Form" in turn represents the material dimension of experience.

The compound name-and-form occurs as the fourth link in the standard exposition of dependent arising, which takes the form of altogether twelve links. Some expositions of dependent arising show name-and-form to stand in a relationship of reciprocal conditioning with consciousness. Name-and-form depends on consciousness just as consciousness in turn depends on name-and-form. Together, these two links account for the continuity of existence during life and from one life to the next. Whereas consciousness stands for the receptive dimension of such continuity, for the knowing aspect of subjective experience, name-and-form is responsible for the way we make sense of the world. Disenchantment and dispassion toward name-and-form thereby goes right to the root of the construction of subjective experience.[268] Such dispassion can indeed be expected to have considerable awakening potential.

The next item in relation to which the cultivation of disenchantment and dispassion, etc., can lead to full awakening concerns the number three:

> "Friends, a monastic will make an end of *dukkha* in this very life on becoming fully disenchanted with three things, fully dispassionate toward them, fully liberated from them, fully seeing their end, and fully penetrating their meaning. What are those three? The three feeling tones."

The Chinese version again provides additional detail.[269] Based on the standard analysis into three feeling tones as pleasant, unpleasant, and neutral, the discourse relates pleasant feeling tones to a mind that is not scattered and unpleasant ones to a mental state of confusion and a lack of concentration. This offers a somewhat specific presentation. Although proceeding from a distracted to a collected mental condition is of considerable importance for the path to awakening, the insight potential of the three feeling tones is not confined to this particular dimension. Instead, penetrative insight into any occurrence of the three feeling tones, in whatever situation, carries a potential to awaken the mind. This relies in particular on a direct understanding of how feeling tones tend to trigger reactions of craving and clinging, thereby revealing a key aspect in the dependent arising of *dukkha*.

Fours to Eights: Cultivating the Mind

With the next set of questions, Kajaṅgalā's descriptions proceed from the need to cultivate disenchantment and dispassion toward the items mentioned, as was the case up to now, to topics that require being "well cultivated." This is noteworthy, as the preceding discourse in the same collection, the Great Questions, continues throughout with things that elicit a reaction of dispassion, etc. I will come back to this difference after having explored the remainder of the exposition.

A topic related to the number four, whose cultivation leads to liberation, takes the following form:

> "Friends, a monastic will make an end of *dukkha* in this very life on fully and well cultivating the mind in four things, fully seeing their end, and fully penetrating their meaning. What are those four? The four establishments of mindfulness."

Explicitly introduced as the direct path to Nirvana in the *Satipaṭṭhāna-sutta* and its parallels,[270] the four establishments of mindfulness are an excellent fit for a teaching that involves the number four and that leads toward making an end of *dukkha*.

The Chinese parallel to the preceding discourse instead mentions the four truths of *dukkha*, its arising, its cessation, and the path, followed by expounding each.[271] The four noble truths also feature in a brief catechism given to the novice Sopāka, already mentioned above, which similarly works through the numbers one to ten, each time providing a brief reference to a doctrinal topic that fits each category (though without establishing a relationship to either dispassion or cultivation). Its presentation corresponds to the items mentioned above under the categories of ones to threes, but for the number four it has the four noble truths.[272]

The *Aṅguttaranikāya* discourse that reports the Buddha's original delivery of the teaching under discussion continues throughout with the theme of dispassion, etc. For this reason, in relation to the number four this discourse has again something that can elicit attachment and clinging: the four kinds of nutriment.[273] These are edible food, contact, volition, and consciousness. Since they serve to sustain the continuity of existence, these four are reckoned to be "nutriments."[274] Note that the first of these corresponds to the item listed under "one," according to which sentient beings subsist due to nutriment.

Next in the exposition by Kajaṅgalā comes a doctrinal teaching that fits the number five and whose cultivation will enable reaching liberation:

> "Friends, a monastic will make an end of *dukkha* in this very life on fully and well cultivating the mind in five things, fully seeing their end, and fully penetrating their meaning. What are those five? The five faculties."

The Chinese version again obliges by explicitly listing the five faculties, which are confidence, energy, mindfulness, concentration, and wisdom, followed by expounding their individual significance:[275] Confidence takes the Buddha as its object. Energy is the effort to abandon what is unwholesome and cultivate what is wholesome. Mindfulness enables reciting without forgetfulness (an important requirement in an oral setting in order to preserve the teachings). Concentration corresponds to unification of the mind and the absence of distraction. Wisdom stands for insight into the four truths. A balanced cultivation of these five faculties is a key aspect for progress to awakening.

Since the *Aṅguttaranikāya* discourse that precedes the present one continues with the theme of dispassion, the doctrinal item that fits the case here are the five aggregates of clinging.[276] Dispassion toward them would indeed be a straightforward approach to reaching the final goal.

The number six calls up this aspect of the teachings for cultivation:[277]

> "Friends, a monastic will make an end of *dukkha* in this very life on fully and well cultivating the mind in six things, fully seeing their end, and fully penetrating their meaning. What are those six? The six elements of release."

The six elements of release comprise loving kindness or benevolence (*mettā*) as a release from ill will, compassion as a release from harming, sympathetic joy as a release from envy, equanimity as a release from passion and aversion,[278] signlessness as a release from signs, and overcoming conceit as a release from doubt. The point of the first part of this presentation is to show the potential of the four *brahmavihāra*s in leading to a substantial diminishing of defiled states like ill will, harming, etc. Although the *brahmavihāra*s do not lead on their own to full awakening,[279] they do weaken defilements and thereby can greatly facilitate such progress. In addition to these four types of release, the cultivation of signlessness presents a release from signs. In fact, its very cultivation involves not taking up signs, which here stand for those basic features of experience that the mind habitually takes up to recognize and then conceptualize. Finally, diminishing conceit leads to inner clarity and thereby naturally provides a release from doubt.

The Chinese version instead takes up the six elements conducive to communal harmony, which are loving kindness or benevolence by body, speech, and mind, sharing the gifts one has received with others, maintaining ethical conduct, and keeping to right view.[280] Without in any way intending to underrate the remarkable potential of these six for social harmony, a relationship to progress to the final goal is not as evident here as it is with the items previously listed in this discourse. Such a relation is certainly evident in the other *Aṅguttaranikāya* discourse, which recommends dispassion, etc., in relation to six internal sense spheres.[281] The awakening potential of such dispassion hardly requires comment.

A key teaching calling for cultivation comes up under the number seven:

> "Friends, a monastic will make an end of *dukkha* in this very life on fully and well cultivating the mind in seven things, fully seeing their end, and fully penetrating their meaning. What are those seven? The seven factors of awakening."

The cultivation of the seven awakening factors is perhaps the most important early Buddhist teaching for maturing the mind in its progress toward making an end of *dukkha*. The Chinese version and the other *Aṅguttaranikāya* discourse instead mention the seven stations of consciousness.[282] These comprise sentient beings who differ in body and perception, as is the case for human beings, and celestial beings that could differ in body but have the same perception, have the same body but different perceptions, or be alike in both respects. In addition to these four possibilities, the remaining three relate to the first three formless spheres of boundless space, boundless consciousness, and nothingness. Dispassion in regard to these seven stations of consciousness would imply a thorough disenchantment with a broad range of possible realms of existence. This would indeed be conducive to progress toward freedom from rebirth.

Another key teaching to be cultivated features under the number eight:

> "Friends, a monastic will make an end of *dukkha* in this very life on fully and well cultivating the mind in eight things, fully seeing their end, and fully penetrating their meaning. What are those eight? The eight [members of] the noble eightfold path."[283]

The awakening potential of the noble eightfold path hardly requires comment. The Chinese version and the other *Aṅguttaranikāya* discourse are again in agreement, as both refer to the eight worldly conditions.[284] These are loss and gain, disrepute and fame, blame and praise, and pain and pleasure. The eight worldly conditions stand representative for the ups and downs of life, in relation to which one should best remain unperturbed and equanimous. Cultivating such an attitude could indeed offer substantial support to progress toward awakening.

The Nines and the Tens

The next teaching, concerned with the number nine, shifts back to a type of topic that calls for disenchantment and dispassion:

> "Friends, a monastic will make an end of *dukkha* in this very life on becoming fully disenchanted with nine things, fully dispassionate toward them, fully liberated from them, fully seeing their end, and fully penetrating their meaning. What are those nine? The nine abodes of sentient beings."

All versions are in agreement on this item. These nine comprise the abodes of sentient beings that correspond to the seven stations of consciousness, mentioned above, and add to these the abode of unconscious beings and of neither-percipient-nor-nonpercipient beings. The present item is thus a more comprehensive restatement of the topic already taken up under the number seven in the Chinese version and the other *Aṅguttaranikāya* discourse. From a practical perspective, this does create some degree of redundancy in these two versions. If someone has already developed dispassion, etc., toward the set of seven, it would be hardly worth explicit mention that the same attitude should also be extended to these two additional realms. In contrast, since Kajaṅgalā presented the seven awakening factors (as something calling for cultivation) under the heading of the number seven, her present mention of the nine abodes of sentient beings does not create any redundancy. Each of the topics she has presented so far stands on its own as a significant perspective in addition to the others (in fact, by not mentioning the nutriments under the number four, she even avoids a partial overlap with the subsistence based on nutriment mentioned under the number one).

The final item in Kajaṅgalā's presentation is once again about something to be cultivated, this time involving the number ten:

> "Friends, a monastic will make an end of *dukkha* in this very life on fully and well cultivating the mind in ten things, fully seeing their end, and fully penetrating their meaning. What are those ten? The ten wholesome pathways of action."

The other *Aṅguttaranikāya* discourse broaches the same topic in a complementary way, as it commends dispassion, etc., in regard to the ten unwholesome pathways of action.[285] These comprise the three bodily actions of killing, stealing, and sexual misconduct. Another four pertain to the verbal domain, which are false speech, malicious speech, harsh speech, and gossiping. The final three concern the mind, namely being covetous, harboring ill will, and holding wrong view(s).[286] Dispassion toward these, just as cultivating their wholesome counterparts, will establish a firm foundation in morality. In combination with the presence of right view (aka dispassion toward wrong view), this will indeed lead forward on the path to freedom.

The Chinese version instead lists the ten recollections,[287] which are recollecting the Buddha, his teaching, the community of noble ones, one's own morality, one's own generosity, celestial beings, mindfulness of stilling, mindfulness of breathing, mindfulness of the body, and mindfulness of death. Several of these recollections can offer considerable support for progress to awakening.

The Pāli account of Kajaṅgalā's teaching continues by reporting that the lay disciples rejoiced in her teachings and then reported it to the Buddha, who approved of it wholeheartedly, stating that he would have expounded the matter in exactly the same way (similar to the case of Dhammadinnā, taken up in the previous chapter). His approval in the present case is particularly noteworthy, since Kajaṅgalā's presentation differs in several respects from the one given reportedly by the Buddha himself, the Great Questions, which the lay followers had wanted to be taught. Even though Kajaṅgalā had been asked to explain the Buddha's teaching on the matter, rather than being invited to give her own views, her lack of conformity to the actual teaching given by the Buddha receives full approval from the latter. As already noted by Elsa Legittimo (2012, 368):

> Her explanations indeed partly differ from those given by the Buddha. Nevertheless, when the lay followers, taking her advice, subsequently go to see the Buddha and repeat the nun's exposition, the Buddha is said to fully approve her teaching.

The implication of this approval must be that the appropriate responses to the series of ten queries are not set in stone. In fact, given the alternative function of employing this set when debating with non-Buddhists, it would be odd to try to reduce others to silence merely because they do not know the in-house associations these carry among Buddhist disciples. Instead, in such a setting the point would more reasonably be that in one way or another one needs to know what is required for awakening and then be able to combine such knowledge with a way of presenting matters in an easily memorized form, namely by way of a list from one to ten items.

The evidently flexible nature of this catechism sets a background for evaluating a remarkable difference between the Buddha's and Kajaṅgalā's presentations. Whereas the former consistently covers matters that call up dispassion (etc.), Kajaṅgalā shifts modes and thereby gives more room to the cultivation of positive states or qualities.[288] These amount to six items out of the whole set of ten. The approach taken in this way evokes an overall more positive or inspirational spirit that, at least to my mind, makes her presentation quite appealing. Moreover, it also enables her to avoid any redundancy, as already mentioned above.

In view of such evident advantages, it would even be possible to consider the teaching given by Kajaṅgalā to be an improvement compared to the precedent reportedly set by the Buddha himself, which was not known to her. In fact, it is precisely the circumstance that she did not know what the Buddha had said on the matter that prompted her delivery of this improved version in the first place. The present instance thereby testifies to the crucial importance of granting to Buddhist women the space to express the teachings in their own way, rather than restricting such expression to the male voice, even if that should be the one of the Buddha himself.

The balanced listing of items relevant to awakening, free of redundancy, that results from Kajaṅgalā expounding the matter in her own individual way can be summarized in the following manner:

One: dispassion toward nutriment.
Two: dispassion toward name-and-form.
Three: dispassion toward the three feeling tones.
Four: cultivation of the four establishments of mindfulness.
Five: cultivation of the five faculties.
Six: cultivation of the six elements of release.
Seven: cultivation of the seven awakening factors.
Eight: cultivation of the members of the noble eightfold path.
Nine: dispassion toward the nine abodes of beings.
Ten: cultivation of the ten wholesome pathways of action.

The main purpose of the numerical arrangement from one to ten must be to facilitate memorization, where one may even count on the fingers of the two hands alongside reciting the teaching. Nevertheless, and without intending to take a firm position that this must have been intended by Kajaṅgalā's exposition, the above listing could be read sequentially as a step-by-step delineation of progress on the path toward making an end of *dukkha*. Such progress would then have its starting point in an appreciation of the basic predicament of human (and animal) life due to being part of the food chain. Dispassion aroused in this way could then be broadened from what has been more a concern with the material side of existence ("form") to include the mental dimension as well ("name"). This can take the form of appreciating the degree to which the activities of the mind, especially when it is in a defiled condition, make their own and rather distinct contribution to *dukkha*.

With this broader compass of arousing dispassion in place, further cultivation of the same quality can then focus in particular on the three feeling tones. These correspond to the key link in the dependent arising of *dukkha* where craving can but does not have to manifest. Even arahants still experience these three feeling tones, yet without reacting to any of them with craving. Hence, it is right at the juncture of feeling tone that dispassion has a particularly eminent liberating potential. Cultivating such dispassion would moreover be a way of proceeding from a somewhat more reflective type of practice to an increasing emphasis on direct experience through the cultivation of mindfulness of feeling tones. Mindfulness is in fact a key factor in the interpretation of the list of ten presented here. Besides mindful recognition of each of the three feeling tones, mindfulness of their changing nature is an important asset in such practice, as growing insight into impermanence is precisely what arouses dispassion.

Now, recognition of the three feeling tones and their true nature is the task of the second establishment of mindfulness. Hence, from the foundation in dispassion laid in this way by the first three items from Kajaṅgalā's list, it is only natural to turn to a practice of all four establishments of mindfulness, placing the understanding gained in relation to feeling tones into a broader perspective. A cultivation of the four establishments of mindfulness is at the same time a cultivation of mindfulness as a faculty.[289] The other four faculties could in turn be visualized as the four sides or four corners of a field of meditation practice within which mindfulness evolves. Practice proceeds well and harmoniously when mindfulness is situated in the center of this field. If practice does not proceed well, then this can be visualized in terms of mindfulness not being in the center of this field, due to a lack of balance between the other faculties. This then calls for either balancing confidence with wisdom or else energy with concentration (in the sense of mental composure), by strengthening whichever quality is weak in order to restore balance and enable mindfulness to regain a position in the center of the field. Understood in this way, the teaching on the five faculties can be employed as a frame of reference for addressing imbalances that occur during the cultivation of mindfulness.

The quality of mindfulness has much in common with the four *brahmavihāras*, and in several ways these practices support and complement each other.[290] In the context of Kajaṅgalā's list, the four *brahmavihāras* feature together with the meditative cultivation of signlessness and the removal of conceit, thereby ensuring the presence of the insight component that is crucial for making any *brahmavihāra* practice become truly liberating in the Buddhist sense.

The same cultivation of mindfulness takes in turn a central place among the seven awakening factors, those sublime mental qualities that can quite literally awaken the mind. Here, mindfulness is always required, whereas the other six fall into two groups, one of which is more energetically stimulating (investigation, energy, joy) whereas the other tends more toward calming (tranquility, concentration, equipoise). Depending on the present condition of the mind, either the one or the other group may be more commendable to foster inner balance. Mindfulness monitors what is taking place and thereby provides the all-important feedback needed to know how to proceed.

After these four items more specifically related to meditation, the final set of three can be visualized as setting an overall context. The eightfold path offers the required foundation for mindfulness practice, which in the context of this path features under the heading of "right mindfulness." Central for the cultivation of the path is the guiding principle of right view. This combines with an undertaking of ethical conduct as a basic requirement for any mental cultivation to flourish.

The orientation provided by right view, in the form of the four noble truths, finds a practical expression in dispassion toward all types of possible existences (here expressed in terms of the nine abodes). Alongside the resultant overarching aspiration for freedom from *saṃsāra*, however, the attitude toward the world is one of kindness and compassion, in line with the earlier cultivation of the *brahmavihāra*s. Such a kind and compassionate attitude finds its practical expression in ever increasing degrees of perfection regarding the ten wholesome pathways of action. The earlier described four practices of mental cultivation, based on the triple foundation in dispassion, find their consummation in the unswerving maintenance of a type of conduct that never intentionally inflicts harm, be it on others or on oneself. Such conduct can become a brightly shining light of ethical perfection that inspires and encourages others in their search for a way out of *dukkha*.

Soṇā

> The foremost of those nuns who overcome outside practitioners and establish them in the right teaching is the nun called Soṇā.[291]

THE REFERENCE TO outside practitioners intends those who are "outside" of the Buddhist dispensation. An example is a recurrent reference to six well-known teachers who were contemporaries of the Buddha, already mentioned briefly earlier (see above p. 76). The tale to be taken up below indeed shows Soṇā overcoming them, although apparently not to the extent of actually establishing them in the right teaching. Soṇā also features in the corresponding listing in the *Aṅguttaranikāya*, which instead reckons her outstanding in the arousal of energy.[292] Although this is probably meant predominantly in the sense of dedication to the path of practice, a relationship to the *Ekottarikāgama* presentation could be established by noting that to debate with outsiders and successfully establish them in the right teaching can safely be expected to require a sustained dedication of energy.

The Six Teachers and the Buddha

The *Ekottarikāgama* report of how Soṇā singlehandedly defeated the six teachers begins with the following narration.[293]

> At one time the Blessed One was living by the side of the Monkey Pond.[294] The people of the country were supporting him with robes, food, bedding, and medicines in accordance with

their means. Each of them brought food for the Buddha and the community of monks, and they undertook the eight precepts without missing an opportunity to do so.

At that time six teachers had in the course of their wanderings come to stay in the city of Vesālī. That is, the six teachers were Pūraṇa Kassapa, Ajita [Kesakambalī], [Makkhali] Gosāla, Pakudha Kaccāyana, Sañjaya Belaṭṭhi[putta], and Nigaṇṭha [Nātaputta]. Then, the six teachers gathered in one place and said [to each other]: "This recluse Gotama is staying in the city of Vesālī, and he is supported by the people, but we are not being supported by the people. We could approach him and debate with him. Who [among us] would be victorious? Who [among us] would not be up to it?"

The description in the above *Ekottarikāgama* discourse, which is without a parallel in other discourse collections, revolves around the importance accorded in the ancient Indian setting to debate as a means of gaining public repute and hence receiving ample offerings from the people.

Pūraṇa Kassapa said: "All the recluses and brahmins who do not accept what he proclaims, they have in various ways cross-questioned him, [pointing out] what is contrary to the teaching of recluses and brahmins. Yet, this recluse Gotama did not accept what they say, and he cross-questioned them in many ways. In what way could we debate with him?"

Ajita [Kesakambalī] said: "There is no offering, there is no receiving [of results], there is no giver, there is neither this world nor a future world for living beings, and there is also no fruition of good and evil."

[Makkhali] Gosāla said: "[If] on the [right] side of the river Ganges someone kills people beyond measure, amassing them into a mountain of flesh, and to the left of the river Ganges someone does meritorious deeds, because of this there is still no fruition of good and evil."

Pakudha Kaccāyana said: "[If] to the left of the river Ganges someone properly engages in giving gifts and upholding morality, and at the appropriate time makes offerings so that there is no deficiency, there is also no fruition of this."

Sañjaya Belaṭṭhi[putta] said: "I make no statements, and I give no replies; I just enjoy keeping silent."

Nigaṇṭha [Nātaputta] said: "I make statements, and I also give replies. The recluse Gotama is a man, and I am also a man. What Gotama knows, we also know. The recluse Gotama has psychic powers; I also have psychic powers. If that recluse manifests one feat of psychic power, I will manifest two feats of psychic power.[295] [If] he manifests two feats of psychic power, I will manifest four feats of psychic power. [If] he manifests four, I will manifest eight. [If] he manifests eight, I will manifest sixteen. [If] he manifests sixteen, I will manifest thirty-two. I will continually make them increase until I have overcome him and completely had a trial of powers with him. Suppose he does not accept our teachings; he will be blamed. Having heard this, people will no longer support him, and we will in turn get their support."

The above presentation seems to be inspired by the Discourse on the Fruits of Recluseship (*Sāmaññaphalasutta*), in which a king reports to the Buddha his earlier visits to each of these six teachers.[296] Even though the king had asked each teacher to explain to him a visible fruit of their life of renunciation, these teachers are portrayed as just voicing their particular doctrines in reply, without really adjusting what they say to the actual inquiry. This of course failed to impress the king.

In the above passage Ajita Kesakambalī, Makkhali Gosāla, and Pakudha Kaccāyana act in the same manner, just professing their doctrine. The same may hold for Sañjaya Belaṭṭhiputta, as his doctrine was to avoid taking any position, although in the present context it could also be read to imply that he will not reply to the query by Pūraṇa Kassapa. The one who explicitly addresses the concerns voiced by Pūraṇa Kassapa is Nigaṇṭha Nātaputta, by affirming that he can defeat the Buddha in a contest of supernormal feats and thereby win the support of the populace. The claim to defeat the Buddha by a doubling of supernormal feats appears to take its inspiration from such a declaration made in another discourse by a different ascetic, who similarly felt ready to respond to any supernormal feat performed by the Buddha by doubling it.[297] In the present context, this claim sets the scene for Soṇā to intervene.

Soṇā's Challenge

> Then the nun [Soṇā] heard this being said: "The six teachers have come together in one place and have given rise to this discussion: 'We will be fully victorious over the recluse Gotama, who does not accept [our] teachings to the people.'" Then the nun Soṇā flew up into the sky and approached the six teachers,[298] speaking this poem:
>
> "My teacher has no equal,
> He is the most venerable one, whom none excels.
> I am that venerable one's disciple,
> Called the nun Soṇā.
>
> Establish your positions,
> And in turn debate them with me.
> I shall reply to all matters,
> Like a lion trapping a deer.
>
> Except for my venerable teacher,
> There is currently no Tathāgata.
> I am a nun who right now
> Can subdue outside practitioners completely."
>
> When the nun had said this, the six teachers were not even able to look at her face, let alone debate with her.

Soṇā's feat of levitation can be viewed in light of the similar feat attributed to Mahāpajāpatī Gotamī and her following of five hundred nuns, taken up in the first chapter (see above p. 15). The above feat differs as it does not involve the performance of the twin miracle and instead leads on to a challenge to debate doctrinal points. Both reflect an evolved notion of levitation, prevalent in later texts, as the feat is performed with the physical body rather than involving just a mental body.

The image of a lion trapping deer conveys Soṇā's self-confidence in challenging the six teachers. The term Tathāgata, as briefly mentioned earlier, can at times simply refer to fully awakened ones in general or else stand for the Buddha as the one who discovered the path to awakening on his own. The second sense seems to be the one relevant here, when Soṇā proclaims that only the Buddha is indeed such a Tathāgata and then follows this up with the challenge to a debate, confident that she is well able to subdue even all six teachers together.

In the present episode, the combination of the supernormal feat with such a challenge has its effect, as the six teachers are so embarrassed that they do not even dare to look at her face. In view of the traditional custom of expressing hierarchy through higher and lower seating, Soṇā's act of levitation has placed her at a level substantially higher than the six teachers. It follows that these would now have to levitate as well in order not to have to look up at her when making any argument. Presumably unable to perform such a feat and thereby unable even to start debating, the six teachers are publicly humiliated by a female disciple of the teacher whom they had wanted to best. With all due recognition to the underlying thrust of showcasing the superiority of the Buddha, from the perspective of the cultural setting the resultant scene is remarkable, as here a single woman is shown to be victorious over a group of male teachers.

The story continues by depicting the repercussions of this feat on the local populace, which turn out to be the exact opposite of what the six teachers reportedly had hoped for.

Soṇā's Victory

> Then the inhabitants of the city of Vesālī saw from afar that the nun was up in the air debating with the six teachers, yet the six

> teachers were unable to reply. Everyone praised and celebrated it, being delighted beyond measure, [saying]: "Today the six teachers have been defeated by her."
>
> Then the six teachers were highly upset. They went out of the city of Vesālī and left; they did not enter the city anymore. Then a group of many monastics heard that the nun Soṇā had debated with the six teachers and been victorious. Having heard this, they approached the Blessed One, paid respect with their heads at his feet, and fully reported to the Blessed One what had happened. The Blessed One said to the monastics: "The nun Soṇā has great psychic power, great might; she is wise and learned. For a long time, this thought has arisen in me: 'There is no one else who is able to debate with the six teachers, only the Tathāgata and this nun.'"
>
> At that time the Blessed One said to the monastics: "Have you seen another nun who is able to overcome outside practitioners like the nun Soṇā?" The monastics replied: "No, Blessed One." The Blessed One said: "Monastics, among my disciples, the foremost of nuns able to overcome outside practitioners is the nun called Soṇā." At that time the monastics, having heard what the Buddha said, were delighted and received it respectfully.

In the context of the reference to nobody else being able to debate with the six teachers, except for Soṇā and the Tathāgata, the latter term stands again specifically for the Buddha himself. In fact, among the early discourses there is no report of any monk defeating all of the six teachers together.[299] Although this type of presentation is part of a later tendency to narrative aggrandizement of the abilities and powers of the Buddha and consequently also of his disciples, nevertheless, the net result is to place Soṇā as foremost among all disciples, male or female, monastic or lay, for having defeated the six teachers. This puts a spotlight on a nun as the sole disciple capable of performing such a feat and thereby publicly defending the superiority of the Buddha's dispensation and ensuring the continuity of offerings from the local population. Soṇā achieves this by combining a display of her readiness to debate with a supernormal feat, whereby she successfully silences even the one out of the six teachers who, according to the preceding narrative, felt ready to defeat the Buddha in a competition of supernormal feats.

Liberation

In addition to the above description of her remarkable feat, verses attributed to Soṇā occur in the *Therīgāthā*:[300]

> "With this assemblage of material form
> I gave birth to ten sons.
> Then, being weak and aged,
> I approached a nun.
>
> She proclaimed to me the teachings:
> The aggregates, the sense spheres, and the elements.
> Having heard her teachings,
> I shaved off my hair and went forth."

The description in these two verses gives the impression that Soṇā went forth at an advanced age, after having worn herself out by giving birth to ten sons. If the same person should be intended, which is not certain, this would make her defeat of the six teachers even more remarkable. Soṇā's verses continue by describing her apprenticeship under the nun who had given her teachings:

> "Training under her,
> The divine eye was purified.
> I know my former births,
> Where I lived before.
>
> I cultivated signlessness,
> Being well composed and unified;

I was instantly freed,
Becoming quenched and free from clinging.

The five aggregates stand with their root cut off,
On being penetrated with understanding.
Shame on you, misery of old age![301]
There is now no more renewed existence."

The above verses show that, in spite of going forth at an advanced age, Soṇā was remarkably successful at putting the teachings into practice, as she acquired the three higher knowledges of recollection of past lives, the divine eye, and the destruction of the influxes. Her penetrative understanding of the five aggregates of clinging stands her in good stead when having to face the predicament of old age. To the extent to which such clinging is removed, to that extent one no longer suffers when the body becomes sick, old, and finally dies. Hence, from the vantage point of her lofty accomplishment, she can dismiss the miserable nature of old age in the firm knowledge that this is her last body.

Bhaddā Kaccānā

> The foremost of those nuns who have irreversibly attained liberation by confidence is the nun called [Bhaddā] Kaccānā.[302]

THE PĀLI LISTING of outstanding nuns highlights Bhaddā Kaccānā's eminence in having attained great supernormal knowledge (*mahābhiññā*).[303] If the two listings in the *Aṅguttaranikāya* and *Ekottarikāgama* intend the same person, then the qualities they highlight are quite different.[304] The extract translated above refers to reaching the final goal by relying prominently on the faculty of confidence or faith (*saddhā*), as distinct from achieving the same through wisdom. The reference in the Pāli list, however, concerns the six supernormal knowledges that, according to early Buddhist thought, can be reached through dedicated meditative practice. These already came up in an earlier chapter in relation to Uppalavaṇṇā (see above p. 42). The Pāli commentarial tradition considers Bhaddā Kaccānā's eminence in this respect to be particularly prominent in her ability to recall her own past lives.[305] This particular ability receives a highlight in the *Ekottarikāgama* discourse to be taken up below, which again reflects a somewhat more mature stage in the history of Buddhist thought, comparable in this respect to the Pāli commentaries rather than the Pāli discourses.

Also known under the names of Yasodharā and Rāhulamātā, Bhaddā Kaccānā was reportedly the chief wife of the Buddha-to-be and the mother of his son Rāhula. The circumstance that at times she is referred to by her role as "Rāhula's mother" does not imply that her personal importance and agency is being sidelined by emphasizing just her motherly role.[306] The same mode of referencing can also be seen, for example, in relation to the chief monk disciple of the Buddha, known as the "Son of Sārī," Sāriputta. He is thus called after his mother rather than by his personal name Upatissa. Such a mode of reference is probably best seen as simply a feature of the ancient Indian cultural setting. As noted by Bhikkhunī Dhammadinnā (2018, 301n53), taking a position on "the supposed negative implications of the use of the epithet Rahulamātā does not take into account the common family-based sociolinguistics of proper names in South-Asian societies," which therefore risks becoming "a value judgment on the alleged gender significance of certain terminology that is incorrectly based on linguistic-historical extrapolation."

A Meritorious Offering

The tale of Bhaddā Kaccānā's ability to recall her past lives occurs in a discourse reporting that King Pasenadi made offerings of robes, food, bedding, and medicine to the Buddha and the monastic community for a three-month period. At the completion of this offering, Pasenadi proclaims his satisfaction with the merit he has achieved in this way. Yet, the Buddha cautions him not to remain satisfied with the merit he has acquired, relating a story from one of his past lives by way of illustration.

At this juncture, the nun Bhaddā Kaccānā gets up from her seat and repeats the injunction just given by the Buddha to the king that he should seek to progress toward liberation, before relating her own past life experience as an additional illustration.[307]

> "I recollect that the Tathāgata Sikhin,[308] an arahant, fully awakened, had appeared in the world thirty-one eons [ago]. He was accomplished in knowledge and conduct, a well-gone one, a knower of the world, an unsurpassable person, a charioteer of the path of Dharma, a teacher of celestials and human beings, called a Buddha, a Blessed One. He was wandering in the Marīci region.[309]
>
> "At that time, when the time had come to beg for alms, that Buddha put on his robes, took his bowl, and entered the town of Marīci. At this time there was a messenger in the

> town, called Suddhakālaka. Then that messenger saw that the Tathāgata was carrying his bowl and had entered the town to beg for alms. Having seen him, he thought in turn: 'The Tathāgata has now entered the town; he must need food.'[310]
>
> "He entered his house and came out with food to give to the Tathāgata, generating this aspiration: 'Endowed with this merit, may I not fall into the three bad destinies. May this make me in a future life meet a venerable noble one like him. May it make me be taught the Dharma by that venerable, and may I then attain liberation.'"

The former Buddha Sikhin is the second of six former Buddhas recognized in early Buddhism.[311] The three bad destinies are being reborn in hell, as a ghost, or as an animal. These contrast with the two good destinies of being born as a human or a celestial. Considering birth as an animal in a negative light appears to reflect in particular the predicament of the food chain. According to Reiko Ohnuma (2017, 5), "to be an animal in a Buddhist cosmos is to live a miserable and pathetic existence, to suffer intensely, to lack the intelligence that makes spiritual progress possible, and to die in a state of abject terror."

The aspiration voiced by the messenger is meant to avoid such rebirth.[312] In the early discourses, being free from the prospect of rebirth in a bad destination features as a result of attaining stream-entry. The above tale reflects a mode of thought that became prominent with the gradual evolution of the bodhisattva ideal. Summarizing a complex development in a few words, the situation could be described as follows:

The type of thought presented in the early discourses in general does not yet reflect the idea that the Buddha intentionally prepared himself over a series of past lives to fulfill the role of a fully awakened teacher.[313] An important step taken in the direction of the emergence of that idea was the integration of various folk tales in the Buddhist narrative repertoire as *jātaka*s, based on choosing one particular character in such a story as corresponding to a past life of the Buddha. The resultant increasing interest in stories of past existences appears to have soon spread from taking the Buddha as their subject to doing the same with eminent disciples, resulting in various tales of their past-life exploits. Once the Buddha's former lives came to be seen as steps in an intentional career undertaken for the sake of accumulating the merits, mental qualities, and physical endowments required for Buddhahood, the same perspective naturally also came to inform past-life stories of disciples.

It is against the background of the development briefly sketched above that the present tale can best be understood, where a deed of merit leads to formulating an aspiration for future births and will eventually lead to encountering a Buddha who affords the occasion for the aspirant to reach full awakening at that future time. In line with a recurrent trope at the end of tales of the past, Bhaddā Kaccānā identifies the messenger in her story from the distant past to have been one of her own past lives:

> "Blessed One and King Pasenadi, may you both know this: Was the messenger Suddhakālaka at that time someone else? It should not be seen in this way. The reason is that the messenger Suddhakālaka at that time was me.
>
> "At that time, I fed the Tathāgata Sikhin and made this aspiration: 'May this make me in a future life meet a venerable noble one like this who teaches me the Dharma, and may I then attain liberation.' For thirty-one eons I did not fall into the three bad destinies. I was born among celestials and human beings, until at last I have now received this particular body. I met the Blessed One and gained the going forth to train in the path.[314] I have eradicated all the influxes and accomplished arahantship.
>
> "As the Blessed One said, so superbly and sublimely, in speaking to King Pasenadi: 'Let all the various activities performed by body, speech, and mind be completely for seeking liberation. Do not spend these meritorious deeds on life in *saṃsāra*.'"

With this proclamation, Bhaddā Kaccānā confirms the success of her aspiration made a long time ago, thereby highlighting the power of merit, followed by commending that the king make a similar aspiration in reliance on his merit. In this way, the king should not just rest satisfied with making merits as such but should also formulate the right aspiration for how he would want these merits to bear fruit and lead him eventually to liberation.

Regarding the reference to thirty-one eons, in the ancient imagination one such eon stands for a period longer than the time it would take to wear down a solid mountain several miles high by stroking it with a piece of cloth once every hundred years.[315] The imagery conveys quite palpably that an eon was seen as incredibly long.

According to Bhaddā Kaccānā's proclamation, a simple gift of food given thirty-one such eons ago ensured freedom from rebirth in bad destinations for all that time and then culminated in preparing the ground for her eventual attainment of full liberation. King Pasenadi had done more than that, as he had fed the Buddha and his community for three months and provided them with all of the monastic requisites. Hence, an aspiration formulated by him can reasonably be expected to yield abundant fruit.

The type of thought in the background to such tales involves to some extent a shift of perspective from the early teachings, where the overarching concern is to reach stages of awakening in this very life rather than postponing such progress to the distant future. At the same time, Bhaddā Kaccānā's repetition of the statement made earlier by the Buddha places into context the prospect of safe transmigration in *saṃsāra*, the cycle of birth and death, free from the suffering of the bad destinations. This context is an orientation toward liberation. Although such an orientation could in principle have motivated the messenger to seize the opportunity to progress to liberation under the guidance of the former Buddha Sikhin right away, this need not be seen as the only possible option. The present story expresses another option, where the certainty of the fruition of merits ensures the successful outcome of an orientation toward liberation, even after a very long time.

Looking After the Needs of Others

With this backdrop from the distant past in place, Bhaddā Kaccānā continues by describing how her former attitude of combining generosity with devotion to a Buddha still informs her present mode of behavior:

> "If I see monks, nuns, male lay followers, and female lay followers, with their hearts delighting in the Tathāgata, the thought in turn arises in me: 'Do not all these distinguished beings still need to have a mind of loving regard and reverence toward the Tathāgata?'
>
> "If I see the four assemblies,[316] I approach them and say: 'Virtuous ones, what things do you require: Robes and bowls? Sitting cloths? Needle cases? Bathing vessels? Any other sundry requisites of recluses? I will supply them all.' Being permitted to do so, I in turn seek for them by begging anywhere. If I get them, that is a great fortune. If I do not get them, then I will go to Uttarakuru, [Apara]goyāna, and Pubbavideha, seeking an offering. The reason is that through all this the four assemblies will gain the path to Nirvana."

Uttarakuru, Aparagoyāna, and Pubbavideha are three of the four great continents that in ancient Indian cosmology make up a world system. India itself corresponds to the fourth continent of Jambudīpa. The idea is thus that Bhaddā Kaccānā is so keen to look after the needs of others, who are still striving to reach what she has already accomplished, that she will go anywhere to get what is needed, even beyond India.

Bhaddā Kaccānā's disposition to take care of the needs of others could be considered a trait in line with her gift to the past Buddha, motivated by the realization that "he must need food." Similarly, her present willingness leads her to do whatever she can to take care of the needs of members of the four assemblies. The reference to all four assemblies is of interest here, as these cover male and female, monastics and laity. In the present context, the reference to these four assemblies being on the path to Nirvana shows that her concerns are particularly with those who have dedicated themselves to progress to awakening. That is, the passage does not imply that Bhaddā Kaccānā, herself being a nun, tries to take care of the needs of any lay person living the household life. Instead, the point would rather be that, in addition to supporting her monastic peers, she was also willing to do the same for lay practitioners wholeheartedly dedicated to the path, perhaps even living at a monastery together with monastics, or else having adopted a lifestyle of renunciation that made them reliant on others for the basic "requisites of recluses."

Bhaddā Kaccānā's teaching to the king, based on relating her own past experiences as well as her present generosity, meets with the Buddha's explicit approval:

> At that time the Blessed One, having examined the mind of the nun [Bhaddā] Kaccānā, said in turn to the monastics: "Have you seen such liberation of the mind by faith as in the nun [Bhaddā] Kaccānā?" The monastics replied: "We have not seen it, Blessed One." The Blessed One said: "Among my disciples, the nun who is foremost in attaining liberation by faith is reckoned to be the nun [Bhaddā] Kaccānā."

The final pronouncement by the Buddha corresponds to the listing of eminent nuns, given at the outset of this chapter.

The *Ekottarikāgama* discourse studied in this chapter provides a helpful perspective on the *Apadāna* of Yasodharā. This reports her accompanying a listing of her meritorious past deeds with a recurrent injunction: "Great King, listen to me."[317] The significance of this reference is not clear in the *Apadāna* itself.[318] From the viewpoint of the above tale, however, this could be interpreted to be her addressing King Pasenadi.

Be that as it may, it is remarkable that the *Ekottarikāgama* discourse shows Bhaddā Kaccānā getting up in front of the local king and giving expression to her own view on a matter that had been broached by the Buddha, relating the story of her former life to illustrate the teaching King Pasenadi had just received. The narrative conveys the impression that Bhaddā Kaccānā was not at all apprehensive that expressing her own opinion and even going so far as to detail her personal past life could be perceived as inappropriate, perhaps even as a form of disrespect toward the Buddha, her former husband and present teacher. In fact, the Buddha reacts by praising her as a foremost disciple. In this way, on a rather official occasion, namely the conclusion of a three-month period of offerings, the

Buddha endorses the action of a nun disciple who gets up on her own initiative to give a talk, without having been invited to do so, in front of the local king. This offers a clear-cut endorsement of female agency and self-confidence by none other than the founder of the tradition himself.

Bhaddā Kāpilānī

> The foremost of those nuns who recollect their own past lives for innumerable eons is the nun called Bhaddā Kāpilānī.[319]

In the case of Bhaddā Kāpilānī, the Pāli listing of eminent nuns is in full agreement with the above quote from the *Ekottarikāgama* that she was foremost in recollection of past lives.[320] Such ability, which relies on mastery of the four absorptions, is not a necessary component of the early Buddhist path to awakening.[321] Hence to recollect one's past lives is already in itself a remarkable feat, even in the case of an arahant. For Bhaddā Kāpilānī to be foremost in this respect then conveys that she was able to expand such recollection into the distant past to a greater extent than others. Her ability in this respect comes to the fore in a discourse in the *Ekottarikāgama*, translated below. Similar to the discourses from the same collection surveyed in the two previous chapters, this discourse also reflects a stage in the development of Buddhist thought that is somewhat move evolved than what is usually found in the early discourses.

A Telling Smile

After the standard introductory indication regarding the whereabouts of the Buddha, the *Ekottarikāgama* discourse featuring Bhaddā Kāpilānī's abilities in the recollection of past lives proceeds as follows:[322]

> At that time in Sāvatthī there was a nun called Bhaddā, who was dwelling together with five hundred nuns, of whom she

> was the leader. Then, being in a secluded place, the nun Bhaddā was reflecting by herself. Seated cross-legged and with mindfulness collected in front, she was recollecting events from her innumerable past lives, whereupon she smiled.
>
> A nun saw from afar that the nun Bhaddā was smiling. Having seen this, she in turn approached the [other] nuns [and said]: "The nun Bhaddā is now alone beneath a tree and she is smiling. What will be the reason?"

The motif of a smile leading on to a story from the past occurs in another discourse, where it is the Buddha himself who displays such a smile.[323] Here, too, the smile being witnessed by others, in this case his attendant Ānanda, motivates an inquiry after the reason for the smile. The point behind such episodes is the notion that arahants and Buddhas do not smile without a reason, and such reason can safely be assumed to have a deeper significance. Hence, inquiring from a Buddha or an arahant after the reason for displaying a smile can be expected to result in the delivery of an edifying instruction. In the present case, this is indeed what happens, thereby showing Bhaddā Kāpilānī to act in the same way as the Buddha himself by displaying her knowledge of past lives and employing that to convey a teaching.

> Then the five hundred nuns together approached the nun Bhaddā and paid respect with their heads at her feet. Then the five hundred nuns said to Bhaddā: "What causes you to smile, as you sit alone beneath a tree?"
>
> Then the nun Bhaddā said to the five hundred nuns: "Just now beneath this tree I was recollecting events from my innumerable past lives, seeing again my life experiences of former times, dying here and being reborn there. I was contemplating it all."
>
> Then the five hundred nuns further said: "We only wish that you would tell us of those former events."
>
> Then the nun Bhaddā said to the five hundred nuns: "In the distant past, ninety-one eons ago, a Buddha called Tathāgata

> Vipassin appeared in the world. He was an arahant, fully awakened, accomplished in knowledge and conduct, a well-gone one, a knower of the world, an unsurpassable person, a charioteer of the path of Dharma, a teacher of celestials and human beings, called a Buddha, a Blessed One, who had manifested in the world.

With this introductory narration in place, the stage is set for storytelling about the distant past. The reference to the Buddha Vipassin, believed to have lived ninety-one eons ago, shows that Bhaddā Kāpilānī's account sets in at a time in the past further removed than Bhaddā Kaccānā's recollections, which had their starting point thirty-one eons ago, at the time of the Buddha Sikhin.

Aspiring for a Female Rebirth

> "At that time the region called Bandhumatī was flourishing with a population beyond counting. At that time the Tathāgata was wandering in that country, leading a community of one hundred and sixty-eight thousand monastics. Surrounded by them on all sides, he was teaching them the Dharma. Then the Buddha's name was renowned in the four directions thus: 'The Buddha Vipassin possesses all of the marks [of a Buddha]; he is a good field of merit for everyone.'
>
> "At that time in that region there was a youth called Brahmadeva, who was of beautiful appearance, rarely found in the world. Then that youth was walking in the streets and alleys holding a bejeweled parasol in his hand. A female householder, who was beautiful as well, was then also walking along that road. All the people were looking at her.
>
> "Then the youth thought in turn: 'Now I too am beautiful, and I am holding a bejeweled parasol in my hand. [Yet,] none of the people look at me. All of these people together are looking at this woman. I should now devise a means to make people look at me.'

> "Then that youth went out of that town and approached the Buddha Vipassin. Holding the bejeweled parasol [over the Buddha] with his hands,[324] he worshipped him for seven days and seven nights, and made this aspiration: 'Granted that the Buddha Vipassin has such psychic power, such supernormal strength, and is a supreme field of merit in the world and in the heavens, being endowed with this merit, may it make me in a future life have a female body, such that on seeing it there will be no one who will not be thrilled with joy.'
>
> "At that time, having worshipped that Buddha for seven days and seven nights, the youth lived out his lifespan and was after that in turn reborn in the Heaven of the Thirty-Three with a female body of utmost beauty, foremost among female celestials, surpassing other female celestials in the five types of excellence. What are the five? That is, they are divine lifespan, divine complexion, divine happiness, divine might, and divine dominion."

A particularly noteworthy feature of the above episode is the aspiration by a male to be reborn as a female. The youth could instead have aspired to be reborn as a male of such beauty as to outshine any female beauty. That the aspiration instead explicitly stipulates the acquisition of a female body shows that the mere wish to get the attention of others was sufficient to overrule any other concerns, which therefore could not have been very substantial. This implies that in this tale female rebirth as such is not considered in a strongly negative light, even though this was the traditional perspective in the ancient Indian setting.

The additional indication that with her heavenly rebirth Bhaddā Kāpilānī came to be endowed with divine lifespan and divine complexion, superior to all other celestials, mirrors descriptions of the condition of the Buddha-to-be when he was reborn in the Tusita heaven.[325] Bhaddā Kāpilānī's account of past lives, to be explored below, will come back repeatedly to celestial rebirths endowed with these divine qualities, thereby showing the power of her meritorious deed in service of the former Buddha Vipassin, which led to her endowment with a superior status comparable, at least in this respect, to the status of the Buddha Gotama in his penultimate life in the Tusita realm.

A Celestial Beauty

"Then, having seen her, the celestials of the Thirty-Three said to one another: 'This female celestial is superb; no one is her equal.' Some celestials among them said: 'This female celestial and I should become husband and wife.'[326] Competing with each other, they quarreled. Then the great king of the celestials said: 'Do not quarrel with each other. Whoever among you is able to proclaim the most excellent poem can in turn take this female celestial for his wife.'[327]

"At that time, one celestial spoke this poem:

'Whether I get up or whether I sit down again,
Being awake or falling asleep, there is no joy for me.
When I am asleep for a while,
Only right after that am I without desire [for you].'

"At that time, another celestial spoke this poem:

'You are right now the cause of my delight.
Being asleep [he] does not miss you,
[But] I am now aroused by thoughts of desire,
Like the beating of a battle drum.'

"At that time, another celestial spoke this poem:

'Even if the battle drum is beaten again,
Yet there comes a time when it becomes still.
[But] my desire [for you] is a quickly spreading disease,
Like flowing water that never stops.'

"At that time, another celestial spoke this poem:

'Even water that carries away great logs,
Does in time become still.
[But] I constantly think [of you] with desire,
Unblinking, like a slain elephant.'

"At that time, the most respected celestial among all the celestials spoke this poem:

'You [others] are still at ease,
[As] each of you is able to speak a poem.
Now I do not know about myself:
Am I dead or alive?'

"At that time all the celestials said to that celestial: 'Well done, celestial. The poem you have spoken is the most clear and excellent one. Today this female celestial should wait on the king of celestials.' Then the female celestial entered the palace of the king of celestials.

"Sisters,[328] you should not have any doubt about this, the reason being [that you think]: 'The youth who at that time worshipped the Buddha by [holding] a bejeweled parasol above him, was he someone else?' Do not see it in this way. The youth at that time was me."

The emphasis in the above tale on Bhaddā Kāpilānī's attractiveness and on all the celestials wanting her in marriage needs to be read keeping in mind the ancient Indian narrative setting, where for a woman not to be physically attractive and not to be wanted in marriage was seen as a serious misfortune. In fact, the attention she receives from the celestials in the Heaven of the Thirty-Three is a direct outcome of her aspiration for a female body of such beauty that "on seeing it there will be no one who will not be thrilled with joy."

The poetic competition among her suitors then shows a gradual buildup of such joy, where each competitor outdoes the others by proclaiming how much he has fallen in love with her. The first one already expresses this in a stark manner, by stating that he is only able to find respite from his joyless condition of not being united with her when having been asleep for a while. The next one turns this on its head by saying that the other at least does not miss her when asleep, whereas he is as tense as a battle drum. This evokes an image from ancient Indian warfare, where a drum served as an important means of communication, able to make itself heard over the cacophony of an ongoing battle. Yet, the next suitor outdoes his predecessor by noting that a battle drum at times is still, whereas his desire is as continuous as flowing water. Even this image is in turn bested by the next celestial, who notes that even strongly flowing water will eventually become still, perhaps intending when a river enters the ocean. In order to prevent others from surpassing him, this celestial illustrates his desire with the unblinking eyes of a dead elephant. Yet, the king of celestials outdoes even this description by stating that his own condition is such that he is no longer even able to speak a poem. The entertaining competition ends and Bhaddā Kāpilānī, in her former birth as a celestial, becomes the wife of the king, the ruler over the Heaven of the Thirty-Three. Having spent a long time as the foremost beauty in heaven, her story continues with an episode situated at the time of the former Buddha Sikhin.

Offerings to Past Buddhas

> "In the past, thirty-one eons ago, the Tathāgata Sikhin appeared in the world. He was wandering in the Marīci region, accompanied by a great community of monastics, one hundred and sixty thousand persons. At that time that female celestial, after her lifespan had in turn come to its end, was reborn among human beings, with a female body of utmost beauty, rarely found in the world.
>
> "Then the Tathāgata Sikhin, when the time had come to beg for alms, put on his robes, took his bowl, and entered the town

> of Marīci. Then that female celestial had again become the wife of a householder. With excellent food and drink, she waited on the Tathāgata Sikhin, and she also made this aspiration:[329] 'Endowed with the merit of this deed, wherever I am reborn, may I not fall into the three bad destinies, and may I be of such beautiful appearance as is unusual among human beings.'
>
> "At that time that woman, after her lifespan had in turn come to its end, was reborn in the Heaven of the Thirty-Three. She again came to have a female body of the utmost beauty, possessing the five types of excellence and surpassing all the other celestials. Was the female celestial at that time someone else? Do not see it in this way. The reason is that the woman was me.
>
> "In that eon the Tathāgata Vessabhū appeared in the world. At that time the female celestial, having lived out her lifespan, had after death come to be reborn among human beings, taking a female body of beautiful appearance, rarely found in the world. She had again become the wife of a householder. At that time the householder's wife, having offered excellent robes of superb cloth to the Tathāgata, made again this aspiration: 'May this make me have a female body in a future life.' Then, after death, that woman was reborn in the Heaven of the Thirty-Three, with a beautiful appearance surpassing that of the other female celestials.
>
> "Was that woman at that time someone else? Do not see it in this way. The reason is that the woman at that time was me."

The above episodes move the narrative thread to the time of the Buddha Sikhin, who also afforded Bhaddā Kaccānā's past life as a messenger an opportunity to acquire merits. Bhaddā Kāpilānī's account of her past lives then proceeds from the Buddha Sikhin to the ensuing Buddha Vessabhū.

Note that her last aspiration no longer mentions being beautiful and just wishes for a female body. Her rebirth in the Heaven of the Thirty-Three still involves an exceptionally beautiful body, presumably a residue from her earlier aspirations when donating to the Buddhas Vipassin and Sikhin. But with her next human life the pattern of being beautiful breaks, and she becomes a female servant of ugly appearance. From the viewpoint of the early Buddhist notion of karma and its fruit, this need not be considered a surprising turn of events. During the timeless faring on in the round of rebirths, all kinds of different karmic forces have been accumulated, awaiting an opportunity to ripen. Hence, the lack of an explicit aspiration for beauty would have left the door open for some other karma from a different past time to gain an opportunity to exert its influence (after an interim stay in the Heaven of the Thirty-Three).

Offerings to a Paccekabuddha

> "Then that woman lived out her lifespan and after death came to be reborn among human beings in the great town of Vārāṇasī. She was a female servant of the wife of the householder Candābha and her appearance was ugly, displeasing to the sight of people. Since Vessabhū had departed from the world, no further Buddha had appeared.[330] [But] a Paccekabuddha was wandering around at that time.[331]
>
> "Then the wife of the householder Candābha said to her female servant: 'Go around outside and look for a recluse who is of such beautiful appearance that he will inspire me.[332] Lead him to the house. I wish to worship him.'
>
> "At that time that female servant went out of the house and looked outside for a recluse. She came across the Paccekabuddha, who was wandering in the town begging [for alms]. However, he was of ugly and repulsive appearance. Then that female servant gave the message to the Paccekabuddha: 'The lady of the house wants to meet you, wishing you would condescend to come to the house.' She then entered and said to her mistress: 'A recluse has come. You can come and meet him.' When the householder's wife had seen the recluse, her mind was displeased. She said to her female servant: 'Send him away again. I will not give to him. The reason is because of his ugly appearance.'

"At that time that female servant said to the housewife: 'If the housewife does not make an offering to the recluse, then I will now take my food allowance for today and use it all to make an offering to him.' Then that housewife brought out the food allowance, one measure of finely broken rice.[333] Then that female servant took it and in turn offered it to the recluse. When the Paccekabuddha had received this food, he flew up into the air and performed the eighteen transformations. Then the householder's female servant made the aspiration again: 'Endowed with this merit, wherever I am reborn, may I not fall into the three bad destinies, and may it make me in a future life have a female body of the utmost beauty.'

"Then that Paccekabuddha, holding in his hand the bowl with the food in it, flew around the town three times. The householder Candābha was leading a gathering of five hundred merchants in the community hall. Then the townspeople, men and women, adults and children, saw the Paccekabuddha holding in his hand the bowl with the food and flying through the air. Having seen it, they said to one another: 'Whose merit is this? Who has met this Paccekabuddha and offered him food?'[334]

"Then the householder's female servant said to the housewife: 'I wish you would come outside to look at the power of the recluse.[335] He is flying through the air and performing the eighteen transformations. His powers are immeasurable.' Then the householder's wife said to her female servant: 'If you give to me all the merit you gained from offering food to the recluse today, I shall give you two days' food right away.' Her female servant replied: 'I cannot agree to transfer the merit.'[336] The housewife said: 'I will give you four days' food right away ... up to ... ten day's food right away.' Her female servant replied: 'I cannot agree to transfer the merit.' The housewife said: 'I will now give you a hundred gold coins.' Her female servant replied: 'I do not need that either.'[337] The housewife said further: 'I will now give you two hundred ... up to ... a thousand gold coins.' Her female servant replied: 'I do not need that either.'

"The housewife said: 'I will set you free, making you no longer be a servant.' Her female servant replied:[338] 'I do not seek to be an independent person either.' The housewife said further: 'You will become the housewife and I will become the servant.'[339] Her female servant replied: 'I do not seek to become the housewife either.'

"The housewife said: 'I will now take hold of you and beat you, mutilate you by cutting off your ears and nose, cutting off your hands and feet; I will cut off your head.' Her female servant replied: 'All such pain I can bear with, but I will not transfer the merit from the offering. My body is subject to the lady of the house; the goodness of my mind is a different matter.' At that time, the householder's wife beat her female servant.

"Then each of the five hundred merchants said: 'This saintly person has come today to beg for food. He will certainly have been given an offering at my home.' Then the householder Candābha dismissed all of the people, returned to his house, and went inside. He saw that his wife had taken hold of the female servant and was beating her. He asked: 'Why is this female servant being beaten?' Then the female servant informed him fully of the events. Then the householder Candābha was delighted and thrilled [that the Paccekabuddha had received food at his house], unable to contain himself. He had the housewife become a female servant and made the female servant be in the position of the housewife.

"At that time the king who ruled the town of Vārāṇasī was called Brahmadatta. Then the great king heard that the Paccekabuddha had been given food [at the house] of the householder Candābha. He was extremely pleased that an arahant had been received and a timely offering had been made to him. King Brahmadatta dispatched a man to summon the householder Candābha. He said to him: 'Is it true that food was given to the saintly arahant at your [house]?' The householder replied to the king: 'It is true that the arahant was received, and food was offered to him.' Then, having investigated it, King

> Brahmadatta gave him a reward and also promoted him to a higher position.
>
> "Then the [former] female servant of the householder lived out her lifespan and after death was reborn in the Heaven of the Thirty-Three. She was of beautiful appearance, rarely found in the world, and she surpassed all the other celestials in the five types of excellence.
>
> "Sisters, [was the female servant at that time someone else?] Do not see it in this way. The householder's female servant at that time was me."

As mentioned above, the circumstance of being reborn ugly and in a servile position could be understood as the unintended consequence of not formulating the aspiration for becoming beautiful when making offerings to the Buddha Vessabhū, which presumably left room for some unwholesome deed(s) from the past to ripen. In contrast, her next aspiration, reported above, makes sure to stipulate beauty alongside the wish to be reborn as a female.

At the same time, however, the very fact of being ugly appears to have been to her advantage. Unlike Buddhas, who teach and thereby inevitably become widely known for their qualities, Paccekabuddhas awaken on their own but do not teach and do not have a following of disciples. This in turn makes it more difficult to recognize them. The reaction of everyone else on seeing the Paccekabuddha perform a series of miracles shows the high esteem that would have been afforded him, had his true nature been already recognized before he performed the miracles.[340]

In this respect, Bhaddā Kāpilānī in her former life as an ugly servant was at an advantage, since she would have known from her own experience in that life what it means to be despised by others for being ugly. Presumably for this reason she would have been able to see the Paccekabuddha in a way quite different from her mistress. Instead of foregrounding his ugly physical appearance, she apparently saw him first of all as a recluse begging for food. Since as a Paccekabuddha he would naturally have been endowed with a calm and collected bearing, it could well be that she gave more importance to that than to his physical appearance, even though this is not explicitly expressed in the narration translated above. Perhaps from her perspective he was indeed inspiring, the quality stipulated by the housewife, due to the beauty of his demeanor. In fact, she must have been deeply inspired by him, otherwise she would hardly have been willing to forgo her own food for the day in order to be able to make an offering to him. In a way, her lack of concern for the stipulation to bring someone who fulfills the housewife's expectation of physical beauty in turn set the scene for the ensuing events. In particular her willingness to offer her own food to the Paccekabuddha eventually led to a complete reversal of her earlier subservient situation.

The Pāli tradition also knows of a former life of Bhaddā Kāpilānī in Vārāṇasī when, at a time when no Buddha had arisen, she made an offering to a Paccekabuddha.[341] According to this narrative, she was not a servant but a housewife herself. Moreover, at first, she filled the bowl of the Paccekabuddha with mud. However, she quickly repented her foolish deed, cleaned his bowl, and then made a proper offering to him.[342]

Bhaddā Kāpilānī's account of past life experiences in the *Ekottarikāgama* proceeds from her encounter with the Paccekabuddha and a subsequent period in heaven to her meeting a Buddha again.

More Offerings and the Wish to Remain a Woman

> "In this auspicious eon a Buddha appeared in the world called the Tathāgata Kakusandha. Then that female celestial lived out her lifespan and after death was reborn among human beings. At that time, she became the wife of the brahmin Yajñadatta. Then this woman, having fed the Tathāgata, again made an aspiration, wishing to have a female body [in a future life]. After death she was reborn in the Heaven of the Thirty-Three. She was of beautiful appearance, supreme among all female celestials. After dying there, she was reborn among human beings again.
>
> "At that time the Buddha Konāgamana had appeared in the world. Then that female celestial became a householder woman. Having worshipped the Buddha Konāgamana with

golden flowers, she again [made the aspiration]: 'Endowed with this merit, wherever I am reborn, may I not fall into the three bad destinies, and may it make the body I take hereafter be a female body.'

"Then this woman lived out her lifespan and after death was reborn in the Heaven of the Thirty-Three. She was very beautiful, supreme among the assembly of female celestials, and she possessed the five types of excellence, such that [the other celestials] could not match her. Was the householder woman who at that time worshipped the Buddha Konāgamana someone else? Do not see it in this way. The householder woman at that time was me.

"Then that female celestial lived out her lifespan and came to be reborn among human beings. Being again the wife of a householder, she was of very special appearance, rarely found in the world.[343] At that time the Tathāgata Kassapa had appeared in the world. Then the householder's wife worshipped the Buddha Kassapa for seven days and seven nights and made [this] aspiration: 'May this make me obtain a female body in the future.'

"Then the householder's wife lived out her lifespan and after death was reborn in the Heaven of the Thirty-Three. She possessed the five types of excellence, surpassing other female celestials. Was the householder's wife who at that time worshipped the Buddha Kassapa someone else? Do not see it in this way. The householder's wife at that time was me.

"In this auspicious eon the Buddha Sakyamuni appeared in the world.[344] Then that female celestial, after having passed away, was reborn in the town of Rājagaha. She became the wife of the brahmin Kapila.[345] She was of beautiful appearance, surpassing the appearance of all [other] women. The brahmin Kapila's wife resembled a polished golden image,[346] as a result of which other women were [in comparison] as if blackened by ink. Her mind had no desire for the five sensual pleasures. Was this wife someone else? Sisters, do not see it in this way. The brahmin's wife at that time is me.

"Sisters, you should know, because of the merits of former events I became the wife of Pippali-Māṇava,[347] that is, of Mahākassapa. The venerable Mahākassapa first went forth himself; on a later day I went forth on my part.[348] Just now I smiled to myself because I was recollecting my lives in former days with a female body. Because it had been hidden to me, I did not know that I had worshipped six Tathāgatas, seeking to get a female body. This is the reason why I smiled, because of my experiences in former days."

According to the above account, Bhaddā Kāpilānī repeatedly made an aspiration to be reborn as a female, until eventually she became an arahant nun. This series of aspirations starts off from the wish to get the attention of others, when a beautiful male youth finds that, even though he is carrying a bejeweled parasol, he cannot compete with a beautiful female's ability to attract public attention. This suggests that the first aspiration reflects the idea that by changing from male to female, she will certainly be able to outdo anyone else in attractiveness. This is indeed what happens. Once reborn in heaven, Bhaddā Kāpilānī's former existence is of such dazzling female beauty that the male celestials in the realm of the Thirty-Three, which was renowned in ancient Indian imagery for the already outstanding beauty of its women, all fall completely in love with her and stage a poetry contest to determine who will be allowed to become her partner.

The theme of beauty comes up again in the aspiration made at the time of the former Buddha Sikhin, but the next aspiration is just for becoming a woman. Presumably due to the complexity of karmic retribution, where at times deeds from the far distant past can come to fruition unless other, more recent deeds obstruct such fruition, the lack of wishing for beauty results in her rebirth as an ugly person. Yet, as already mentioned above, this appears to have been to her advantage, as it enabled her to remain unprejudiced by the ugly appearance of the Paccekabuddha and facilitates her becoming so inspired by him that she is even willing to forgo her day's ration of food in order to make an offering to him. In view of her own experience of being despised for her ugly appearance, it is perhaps natural that once more she aspires to being a woman of utmost beauty. Nevertheless, this is the last time for her to do so. In fact, the merits accumulated by then apparently suffice to ensure that she will be beautiful, to the extent that in her last life she resembles an image made of gold.[349] Perhaps precisely her seeing through physical ugliness to discern inner beauty when meeting the Paccekabuddha should be understood to have served as a contributive factor here. Be that as it may, according to the above account, her aspirations when making offerings to the former Buddhas Kakusandha, Konāgamana, and Kassapa are only concerned with having a female body in the future, in one instance combined with the wish to avoid rebirth in the lower realms.

The Pāli tradition's account of Bhaddā Kāpilānī's former lives does not present her wish to be reborn as a female in a comparably explicit manner, although the same is implicit in the report that, at the time of yet another past Buddha, she had witnessed a nun being declared foremost in recollection of past lives and then aspired to the same honor in the future.[350] This implies that on that occasion she was aspiring for a rebirth as a woman.

A Foremost Nun

The *Ekottarikāgama* account of Bhaddā Kāpilānī's report of her former lives, during which she repeatedly wished for a female body, concludes with the Buddha expressing his approval:

> At that time a group of many monastics, who had heard that the nun Bhaddā had recollected events from her own innumerable past lives,[351] approached the Blessed One. They paid respect with their heads at his feet, sat down to one side, and told the Tathāgata all that had happened. Then the Blessed One said to the monastics: "Have you seen any [other] nun

among my disciples who recollects events from innumerable lives like her?" The monastics said to the Buddha: "We have not, Blessed One."

The Buddha said to the monastics: "Among my disciples, the foremost disciple in recollecting events from innumerable lives is the nun Kapilānī."

The discourse concludes with the standard description of the delighted reaction of the listeners to what the Buddha has said. In the present case, this delighted reaction would refer to the Buddha's extolling of Bhaddā Kāpilānī's outstanding abilities at recollecting past lives. At the same time, it also serves as a form of endorsement, making it clear that her memories of her past lives should be trusted. In this way, the Buddha commends and the monks receive with delight a tale of repeated aspirations to be born as a female rather than a male, which in view of the ancient Indian setting is certainly a remarkable aspiration.

A Liberated Couple

The *Therīgāthā* has preserved a set of verses by Bhaddā Kāpilānī.[352]

"The heir of the Buddha, his 'son,'
Kassapa, who is well composed,
Knows his former births,
And sees heaven and hell.

And having gained the destruction of birth,
He is a sage, perfected in the supernormal knowledges.
Through these three higher knowledges
He is a [true] brahmin with triple knowledge."

Bhaddā Kāpilānī's first two verses eulogize her former husband Mahākassapa. She continues by clarifying that she had reached the same superb degree of accomplishment:

"In the same way Bhaddā Kāpilānī,
With the triple knowledge, has overcome death.
She bears her last body,
Having conquered Māra and his retinue.

Having seen the peril in the world,
We both went forth.
With influxes eradicated, tamed,
We have become cool and quenched."

After her many lives spent as a celestial or human wife, Bhaddā Kāpilānī's last marriage forms the converging point and ultimate completion of her many lives of aspiring to be a beautiful woman, which in the ancient Indian setting comes intrinsically interwoven with becoming married. In this case, however, both husband and wife decide to shun sensuality and go forth in quest of supreme freedom.

Mallikā

WITH THE PRESENT chapter my exploration proceeds from outstanding nuns, surveyed up to now, to the accomplishments and abilities of exceptional lay women.

> The foremost of those female lay disciples who have reverence for the Tathāgata is the female disciple Queen Mallikā.[353]

Although the Pāli listing of outstanding female lay disciples does not mention Mallikā, her firm confidence in the Buddha is quite evident in the episode to be taken up below.

Mallikā's Teachings on the Drawbacks of Worldly Affection

The discourse that features Mallikā's firm confidence in the Buddha is extant in Pāli and in several parallels in Chinese.[354] The narrative that precedes the part to be taken up below describes a householder informing the Buddha of his thorough affliction by grief at the death of his only son. When the Buddha points out that sorrow and grief arise from those whom one holds dear, the householder becomes upset and leaves in disapproval. The story of their exchange reaches the court of King Pasenadi. When Queen Mallikā expresses her acceptance of what the Buddha reportedly had said, the king takes her facile agreement to be a sign of her blind faith in her teacher. His reaction conveys the impression that the present episode should be located at a time when the king, unlike Mallikā, had not yet become a follower of the Buddha.

According to the discourse parallels, the king sends a messenger to the Buddha to find out if the latter had really made such a statement, a natural procedure in an oral setting where there is a constant need to verify hearsay. This is even more needed in the present case, as the Buddha's pronouncement runs counter to a widespread popular belief and for this reason was as puzzling to the king as it had been to the Buddha's earlier visitor.

The Buddha confirms that he had indeed made this statement and then relates to the messenger several stories showcasing deep sorrow and grief caused by the death of a family member. A difference between the parallels occurs at this juncture, as in the Pāli and one Chinese discourse version this messenger relates all the Buddha had said to Mallikā, whereas according to another two Chinese discourse versions he only confirms, in the presence of the king, that the Buddha had indeed made the statement that sorrow and grief arise from those whom one holds dear.

As a result of this difference, the explanation given by Mallikā to the king, translated below, is either inspired by having heard the messenger's report of what the Buddha had explained or else accomplishes the same without her having been informed about the Buddha's explanation. In addition to the four discourse parallels, another version extant in an *Udānavarga* collection does not report any messenger being sent,[355] so that here, too, Mallikā's exposition is entirely the result of her own insight. Be that as it may, the exchange that ensues between Mallikā and Pasenadi takes the following form in the *Madhyamāgama* version:[356]

> Having heard [the messenger's report], King Pasenadi of Kosala said to Queen Mallikā: "The recluse Gotama has truly made this statement: 'If affection arises, then grief, lamentation, despair, sadness, and distress will in turn arise.'"
>
> Queen Mallikā said: "Great King, I [would now] ask the great king a question; [please] answer according to your understanding. What do you think, does the king have affection for General Viḍūḍabha?" He replied: "I truly have affection [for him]." Queen Mallikā asked again: "If an alteration

> [were to happen to] General Viḍūḍabha, how would that be for the king?" He replied: "Mallikā, if an alteration [were to happen to] General Viḍūḍabha, it would certainly arouse in me grief, lamentation, despair, sadness, and distress." Mallikā said: "Because of this matter, one can understand that, when affection arises, then grief, lamentation, despair, sadness, and distress will in turn arise."

The example provided by Mallikā concerns the king's son. The reference to an "alteration" intends something untoward that would seriously affect the health and even life of General Viḍūḍabha, which due to the affection the king has for his son will result in Pasenadi experiencing grief. By bringing the discussion directly to bear on the king's personal sphere of experience, Mallikā is able to make him realize that the Buddha's statement, which at first sight seemed just baffling to him, contains a kernel of truth.

She then continues to pursue the same line of inquiry with other examples:

> Mallikā asked again: "Does the king have affection for the senior minister Sirivaḍḍha ... affection for his elephant Ekapuṇḍarīka ... affection for his daughter Vajīrī ... affection for Vāsabhā ... affection for the countries of Kāsi and Kosala?" He replied: "I truly have affection [for them]." Mallikā asked again: "If an alteration [were to happen to] the countries of Kāsi and Kosala, how would that be for the king?" He replied: "Mallikā, my [ability to] enjoy myself on being endowed with the five types of sensual pleasures depends on these two countries. If an alteration [were to happen to] the countries of Kāsi and Kosala, I would even be without a livelihood. How could that not arouse [in me] grief, lamentation, despair, sadness, and distress?" Mallikā said: "Because of this matter, one can understand that, when affection arises, then grief, lamentation, despair, sadness, and distress will in turn arise."

After having taken up the king's son, an example that combines family affection with the political concern of a king to have a successor, Mallikā turns to other examples related to both fields, covering his minister and elephant as well as his daughter and another of his wives. Next, she homes in on the whole realm ruled by Pasenadi, the countries of Kāsi and Kosala. As a last step, she takes up her own case:

> Mallikā asked the king: "What do you think, do you have affection for me?" He replied: "I truly have affection for you." Queen Mallikā asked again: "If one day an alteration [were to happen to] me, how would that be for the king?" He replied: "Mallikā, if one day an alteration [were to happen to] you, it would certainly arouse in me grief, lamentation, despair, sadness, and distress." Mallikā said: "Because of this matter, one can understand that, when affection arises, then grief, lamentation, despair, sadness, and distress will in turn arise."
>
> King Pasenadi of Kosala said: "Mallikā, because of this matter, from today onward the recluse Gotama is my teacher and I am his disciple. Mallikā, now I myself take refuge in the Buddha, the Dharma, and the monastic community. I only wish that the Blessed One accepts me as a lay follower starting from today, having myself taken lifelong refuge, until life ends.

The above presentation implies that Mallikā's dexterous exemplification of the Buddha's dictum on affection and its sorrowful repercussions converted the king to the Buddhist fold. Given the dependency of the Buddhist mendicant community on material support and political protection, the conversion of the local king is a matter of highest importance. Whether Mallikā accomplished this after having heard the Buddha's explanation of his statement, as reported in some of the discourse versions, or whether she did the same entirely of her own accord, as is the case in other versions (including the one translated above), her ability to adjust the matter to the king's personal sphere of experience was certainly highly skillful.

More Affection Results in More Grief

The basic message that affection leads to sorrow recurs in a different form in a discourse in the *Udāna* that has the eminent female lay disciple Visākhā as the main protagonist. Since the early discourses do not report a full teaching given by Visākhā, which I could have examined in a separate chapter dedicated to her, I would like to take up the relevant episode briefly here before returning to Queen Mallikā.

The relevant introductory narration reports that Visākhā, whom the listing of outstanding disciples in the *Aṅguttaranikāya* considers foremost in making offerings,[357] had come to visit the Buddha. She had wet clothes and hair, due to having just participated in the funeral of her beloved grandson.[358] On informing the Buddha of this, the following exchange reportedly ensued:

> [The Buddha asked:] "Visākhā, would you like to have as many sons and grandsons as there are inhabitants in Sāvatthī?"
>
> [Visākhā replied:] "Blessed one, I would like to have as many sons and grandsons as there are inhabitants in Sāvatthī."
>
> [The Buddha asked:] "Visākhā, but how many inhabitants die daily in Sāvatthī?"
>
> [Visākhā replied:] "Venerable sir, ten inhabitants die daily in Sāvatthī, or nine, eight, seven, six, five, four, three, two, or one inhabitant dies daily in Sāvatthī. Venerable sir, Sāvatthī is never without inhabitants who die."
>
> [The Buddha said:] "What do you think, Visākhā, would you ever be with dry clothes and dry hair?"
>
> [Visākhā replied:] "No, venerable sir. Enough, venerable sir, with me having so many sons and grandsons."

The basic message of this exchange is the same as the teaching given by Mallikā to King Pasenadi: affection for others will sooner or later involve the experience of sorrow. Hence, there is a need to accord recognition to the impermanent nature of whatever one has affection for, in order to become less lost in the pleasurable and rewarding dimensions of affectionate relationships and be better prepared to face sorrow whenever it occurs. The teachings given in this way can help with becoming more aware of potential drawbacks of affection, rather than just trying to intensify and prolong one's loving and being loved in all possible ways. Such increased awareness will enable cultivating a kind of warmth of the heart and care for others that remains balanced and unperturbed when an alteration occurs and something untoward happens. I will return to this topic in the next chapter.

Another parallelism with the case of Mallikā concerns the conversion of others, as according to the commentarial tradition Visākhā had succeeded in converting her father-in-law, Migāra, to Buddhism. In recognition of this, from then on Migāra formally considered her to be like a mother to him,[359] rather than a daughter-in-law, a shift in position which in the ancient Indian setting implies a rather substantial increase in respect and authority. Visākhā came to be known as Migāramātā, the "mother of Migāra." As noted by Pascale Engelmajer (2020, 93), this case exemplifies that the relevant texts "do not limit their understanding of the status of mother to the biological functions of gestation and breastfeeding," as in the present context the notion of being a mother clearly carries spiritual connotations.

Mallikā Reveals the Primacy of Affection for Oneself

Mallikā's wisdom, so plainly evident in the discussion translated in the first part of the present chapter, comes to the fore in yet another exchange with her husband. This is found in a discourse in the *Udāna* as well as a discourse in the *Saṃyuttanikāya*. The relevant part proceeds as follows:[360]

> At that time King Pasenadi of Kosala had gone together with Queen Mallikā to the upper terrace of the palace. Then King Pasenadi of Kosala said to Queen Mallikā: "Mallikā, is there anyone dearer to you than yourself?"

The commentary reports that the king had asked this question expecting her to reply that she loved him more than herself.[361] Mallikā had been elevated by the king from being just the daughter of a family of garland makers to becoming his chief wife and thereby queen of the country; hence he expected her to express her gratitude. Yet, this expectation was not fulfilled:

> [She replied:] "Great King, there is nobody dearer to me than myself. Great King, is there anyone dearer to you than yourself?" [He replied:] "Mallikā, for me, too, there is nobody dearer to me than myself."

Presumably touched by Mallikā's sincerity, the king had to admit that he also loved himself most. The discourse continues with the king reporting the conversation to the Buddha. By way of expressing his approval, the Buddha uttered a poem confirming the insight expressed by Mallikā. Taking the affection one naturally has for oneself as a starting point, the Buddha's reply then endows the same with an altruistic dimension by recommending that one should not harm others, in the understanding that they also have such affection for themselves. The Buddha's approval of Mallikā's wisdom, also evident in the episode that led to Pasenadi's conversion, confirms the impression of her skillful ability to convey the truth of a particular matter to the king.[362]

The present episode could be set in contrast to Māra's reference, in his challenge to Somā discussed above (see p. 96), to women's "two-fingers' wit." The basic idea behind such a reference appears to be a dismissal of the possibility that a woman could be wise, alleging that all she can do is kitchen chores. In addition to the dismissal of such foolish ideas by Somā and the evident wisdom and high accomplishment of other outstanding nuns, surveyed in previous chapters, in the present case a woman who has decided not to ordain amply proves her wisdom and the sharpness of her intellect. Moreover, she does that precisely in relation to what common opinion believes to be women's main concern: dear and loved ones. In the first episode taken up above, Mallikā shows her ability to make sense of the initially puzzling statement by the Buddha that affection is a cause of grief, dexterously explaining the matter to her husband. In the second episode, she sees through the sentiments of love and gratitude she has for her husband to such an extent as to be able to discern that love for herself is still stronger. This combines with her honesty in admitting to this state of affairs, which in turn makes her husband admit that the same actually holds for himself as well. Clearly, Queen Mallikā was quite a remarkable woman.

Nakulamātā

ALTHOUGH THE *EKOTTARIKĀGAMA* listing of outstanding female lay disciples does not mention Nakulamātā, she does feature in the Pāli counterpart as foremost in trustworthiness.[363] This type of quality is indeed evident in a teaching she delivers to her husband, given when the latter was seriously ill. Although a full version of this teaching, to be translated below, has only been preserved in Pāli, a remnant of a version of this discourse appears to be extant in two lines in a Gāndhārī fragment.[364] If the identification should be correct, which due to the small amount of text preserved remains somewhat uncertain, it would testify to the existence of this discourse in another reciter lineage.

TEACHINGS TO AN AILING HUSBAND

The introductory narration to the instruction given by Nakulamātā, translated below,[365] reports that her husband Nakulapita was seriously ill, seemingly on the verge of passing away. This motivated Nakulamātā to deliver the following teaching to him:

> "Householder, do not die full of concern! To die full of concern is distressful, householder, and to die full of concern has been censured by the Blessed One. Now, householder, suppose it should occur to you: 'After my demise, the housewife Nakulamātā will not be able to look after the children and maintain the household.' Yet, householder, you should not see it like this. Householder, I am skilled in weaving cotton and preparing wool. After you are gone, I am able to look after the

> children and maintain the household. Therefore, householder, do not die full of concern! To die full of concern is distressful, householder, and to die full of concern has been censured by the Blessed One."

According to the Pāli commentary, Nakulamātā and her husband had been a couple for many past lives, during which they were also in a family relationship with the Buddha in several of his previous existences.[366] In their present lives, as recorded in another discourse, they had such profound affection for each other that each of them could declare in front of the Buddha never to have transgressed against the other in thought, much less in deed.[367] The same discourse reports their aspiration to continue to be united in future lives.

Such a longstanding relationship appears to stand in the background of the present teaching given by Nakulamātā, where she first of all encourages her husband to let go of any worries about what might happen when he is no longer there to ensure the family's income.

The present case can in a way serve as an illustration of the teachings on affection for others that emerged from the episodes involving Mallikā and Visākhā, taken up in the previous chapter. The point at issue is not to censure any affection whatsoever. Nakulamātā had deep and longstanding affection for her husband. Nevertheless, when faced with the prospect of his death, she was able to remain balanced and to face the situation in an exemplary manner. Rather than acting out personal distress and bereavement, her response took the form of the affectionate wish to help her partner meet his death with a mind at ease and in peace. Instead of revolting against what is happening or becoming overwhelmed by it, her calm reaction expressed her deep love by way of supporting her partner in confronting the inevitable with composure.

Having settled any possible concern regarding her ability to maintain the household, Nakulamātā turns to another potential source of worry:

> "Now, householder, suppose it should occur to you: 'After my demise, the housewife Nakulamātā will take another husband.'[368] Yet, householder, you should not see it like this.

> Householder, you know and I know that for sixteen years we have lived the household life in celibacy. Therefore, householder, do not die full of concern! To die full of concern is distressful, householder, and to die full of concern has been censured by the Blessed One."

The above part takes up the anxiety her husband might feel that she will take another husband. Given the longstanding affection the two have for each other, this suggestion is probably best read as expressing the concern, quite reasonable in the ancient setting, that in case she should find it difficult to maintain the household in the way she has just described, to find another husband may appear as an easier solution to ensure a regular income. Nakulamātā dispels such worries by reminding him of the long time they had lived together in celibacy, an apparently not altogether uncommon form of conduct among lay disciples of the Buddha in those times. Perhaps the idea here is not just to affirm her fidelity to him and her lack of sensual desire, but also to convey that a new husband would hardly be willing to marry an aged widow who is committed to celibacy, hence a concern regarding such an option is not particularly realistic.

Nakulamātā's Inspiring Qualities

After having settled her husband's two interrelated concerns, Nakulamātā turns to her own qualities:

> "Now, householder, suppose it should occur to you: 'After my demise, the housewife Nakulamātā will not wish [to go] to see the Blessed One and not wish [to go] to see the community of monastics.' Yet, householder, you should not see it like this. After you are gone, householder, I will even more wish [to go] to see the Blessed One and even more wish [to go] to see the community of monastics. Therefore, householder, do not die full of concern! To die full of concern is distressful, householder, and to die full of concern has been censured by the Blessed One."

In this way, after having clarified that she will keep the household going without any need for another husband, Nakulamātā describes her own qualities as a way of providing her husband with inspiration to let go of any concerns he may have. Should he pass away, her spiritual interests, expressed by wishing to visit the Buddha and his monastic disciples, will increase rather than abate.

She continues with a set of three qualities related to her accomplishment in morality, concentration, and wisdom:

> "Now, householder, suppose it should occur to you: '... the housewife Nakulamātā does not fulfill morality.'[369] Yet, householder, you should not see it like this. Householder, I am one of the Buddha's female lay disciples who, wearing white, fulfill morality. Now, whoever has doubts or reservations about this, having approached the Blessed One, the arahant, the fully awakened one, who [at present] lives among the Bhaggas at Mount Suṃsumāra, in the deer park at Besakalā Grove, should ask that Blessed One. Therefore, householder, do not die full of concern! To die full of concern is distressful, householder, and to die full of concern has been censured by the Blessed One.
>
> "Now, householder, suppose it should occur to you: 'The housewife Nakulamātā is not one who gains inner tranquility of the mind.' Yet, householder, you should not see it like this. Householder, I am one of the Buddha's female lay disciples who, wearing white, have gained inner tranquility of the mind. Now, whoever has doubts or reservations about this, having approached the Blessed One, the arahant, the fully awakened one, who [at present] lives among the Bhaggas at Mount Suṃsumāra, in the deer park at Besakalā Grove, should ask that Blessed One. Therefore, householder, do not die full of concern! To die full of concern is distressful, householder, and to die full of concern has been censured by the Blessed One.
>
> "Now, householder, suppose it should occur to you: 'The housewife Nakulamātā is not one who dwells having gained a foothold in this teaching and discipline, gained a firm stance,

> gained assurance, having crossed over doubt, being free of uncertainty, having gained self-confidence, being independent of another in the dispensation of the teacher.' Yet, householder, you should not see it like this. Householder, I am one of the Buddha's female lay disciples who, wearing white, dwell having gained a foothold in this teaching and discipline,[370] gained a firm stance, gained assurance, having crossed over doubt, being free of uncertainty, having gained self-confidence, being independent of another in the dispensation of the teacher. Now, whoever has doubts or reservations about this, having approached the Blessed One, the arahant, the fully awakened one, who [at present] lives among the Bhaggas at Mount Suṃsumāra, in the deer park at Besakalā Grove, should ask that Blessed One. Therefore, householder, do not die full of concern! To die full of concern is distressful, householder, and to die full of concern has been censured by the Blessed One."

In this way, she is able to assert publicly that she is in full possession of morality, concentration, and the inner confidence gained from having reached the transcendence of doubt with the attainment of stream-entry.

Regarding these three qualities, given the close association between the two and their common interest in the Buddha's teaching, it does not seem likely that the point of the above presentation is that she only now reveals these to him. Instead, from the viewpoint of the narrative setting it can safely be assumed that he must have known about these all along. At the very least her moral conduct could hardly have gone unnoticed by him, especially when living together in celibacy for sixteen years. But even the gaining of inner tranquility of the mind is something that one could hardly hide in a close relationship, and the same may well hold for the inner clarity about the Buddha's teachings that results from the successful attainment of stream-entry. Besides quite probably showing up in her behavior, there is also no reason why the two should not have been discussing their meditative experiences and understandings with each other.

From this perspective, then, it seems quite probable that this part of her presentation is also directed at whoever else was present on that occasion.

In fact, the last three cases come with an open invitation to anyone who has doubts about her accomplishments to go and check with the Buddha himself, to the extent of informing them of the precise location where the Buddha can be encountered right now. My full translation of all three instances, rather than abbreviating, is meant to draw attention to this repetitive element and the sense of emphasis it conveys. Particularly in an oral setting, repetition is an important means to make sure a particular point has been fully taken in by the audience.

The repetitive invitation given in this way is obviously not addressed to her husband, who to all appearances is on his deathbed and thus would hardly be able to go and meet the Buddha to get confirmation of her claims. Instead, her statements must be intending others who, not knowing her as well as her husband does, may be in doubt about her accomplishments.

This is not to take the position that her proclamations were not *also* directed at her husband. In fact, according to the commentarial explanation,[371] her asseverations functioned as a declaration of truth, which in the ancient Indian setting was believed to be invested with a supernormal potential to bring about a fervent wish of the speaker of such a truthful statement.[372] From this perspective, then, her public announcement of her accomplishments would have been meant to help her husband regain his health. This is indeed what happened, as the discourse continues by reporting that, having heard this teaching by Nakulamātā, her husband recovered from the disease. On a later occasion, he visited the Buddha and recounted what had happened. In reply, the Buddha congratulated him for his good fortune in having received such an instruction from his compassionate wife.

The Buddha's praise endorses the appropriateness of the teaching given by Nakulamātā. Besides thereby providing a public confirmation of her qualities, the endorsement also implies that this episode can be taken as a model for how one may try to comfort one's partner if the latter is seriously ill and perhaps even on the brink of passing away.[373] Needless to say, such comforting needs to be adapted to the contemporary living situation, which differs in several respects from ancient India. But the basic pattern of addressing any possible concerns head-on, rather than avoiding them, and doing such with an attitude of compassion and self-confidence similar to Nakulamātā, by replacing worries with inspiration related to the Dharma, can indeed be just the type of medicine required in such a situation.

On this understanding, then, the teaching given by Nakulamātā provides a model to be emulated not only through the calm and composed manner with which she faces the possible death of her beloved partner, but also for the contents of her actual teaching, aimed at helping another to gain freedom from worries and achieve calmness of the mind.

Nandamātā

The foremost of those female lay disciples who dwell guarding their actions is the female lay disciple Nandamātā.[374]

ACCORDING TO THE Pāli parallel, Uttarā Nandamātā was rather outstanding among female lay disciples for her meditation.[375] Both qualities eulogized in this way, the ability to guard oneself as well as proficiency in meditation, come up in the course of the discourse to be taken up below.

Before turning to that discourse, however, it needs to be mentioned that there is some uncertainty about the identity of its protagonist. The Pāli listing of eminent disciples refers to Uttara Nandamātā, whereas the protagonist in the Pāli discourse to be taken up below refers to Veḷukaṇṭakī Nandamātā. This is not necessarily problematic, as it could just be that the same person is referred to in different ways, the second version qualifying her by the name of her place of residence. Some scholars have followed the lead provided by Caroline Rhys Davids in assuming that the two are probably identical, although there has also been dissent with her opinion.[376] This disagreement relates to a problem already taken up in an earlier chapter (see above p. 64), in that proper names do not fare particularly well in oral transmission, something that happens for male protagonists just as much as for females. Without being able to solve the uncertainty, my suggestion is to follow for the time being the lead provided by Caroline Rhys Davids, given that the indications in both listings of eminent disciples fit the tale below quite well.

Meeting the Heavenly King Vessavaṇa

A discourse in the *Aṅguttaranikāya*, of which no parallel is known, reports that on one occasion Nandamātā was by herself reciting the Chapter on the Beyond (*Pārāyanavagga*), a collection containing profound poems, many of which concern progress to the final goal. A celestial king, overhearing and rejoicing in her recitation, informed her that a group of monks headed by Sāriputta and Mahāmoggallāna were on their way to the location where she was living. Knowing about this beforehand, Nandamātā was able to prepare food in advance and offer it to them as soon as they arrived. Surprised at this unexpected turn of events, at the end of the meal Sāriputta wanted to find out how she had come to know ahead of time about their arrival:[377]

> [Sāriputta asked:] "But, Nandamātā, who told you about the arrival of the community of monks?"
>
> [Nandamātā replied:] "Venerable sir, having gotten up in the last part of the night and having recited the Chapter on the Beyond, I became silent. Then, venerable sir, having seen that I had finished, the Great King Vessavaṇa rejoiced: 'Very well, sister, very well, sister!' [I asked:] 'Now, who is this being of auspicious countenance?' [He said:] 'Sister, I am your brother, the Great King Vessavaṇa.' [I said:] 'Very well, one of auspicious countenance, then let the exposition of the teaching I just recited be for you my gift to a guest.'"
>
> [He said:] "Very well, sister, and let this also be a gift to a guest for me: The community of monks headed by Sāriputta and Mahāmoggallāna will come to Veḷukaṇṭaka without having had a meal in the morning. Having served that community of monks, dedicate the offering to me and that will also be a gift to a guest for me, [saying]: 'Venerable sirs, let any merit and abundance of merit from this offering be for the happiness of the Great King Vessavaṇa.'"[378]
>
> [Sāriputta said:] "It is marvelous, Nandamātā, it is amazing, Nandamātā, that you should have a direct conversation with

> the Great King Vessavaṇa, who is a celestial of such great power and such great might."

Vessavaṇa is one of the four Great Heavenly Kings in ancient Indian cosmology. The Pāli commentary explains that he was a stream-enterer, hence he introduced himself to Nandamātā, who was a nonreturner, as her "brother."[379] Similar to the case of Visākhā Migāramātā, mentioned earlier (see above p. 188), here, too, a term reflecting family relationship instead serves to express a spiritual sense. His being a stream-enterer would also explain his appreciation for the Chapter on the Beyond. Sāriputta's expression of amazement at her having a personal conversation with a celestial being of such power and might stimulates Nandamātā to reveal more of her outstanding qualities. Before turning to these, the setting of this exchange calls for a comment.

Nandamātā, as will become clear from her proclamations below, was not only a lay woman but even a widow, which in her cultural setting usually implied being relegated to a rather low hierarchical standing. Stephanie Jamison (2006, 205) reports that, from the viewpoint of ancient Indian law and society, a "widow was one whose role in life was over by definition, and given that women were considered untrustworthy ... it made sense to place as many restrictions as possible on a widow's way of life." In addition, Nandamātā had also lost her only son, which made her situation still worse. Yet, after having been visited by the Great Heavenly King Vessavaṇa and treated by him as his sister, which already implies a remarkable reversal of ancient Indian hierarchical ideas, at the present juncture she is in dialogue with the Buddha's foremost monk disciple Sāriputta.[380] In fact, she is not just speaking to him but self-confidently disclosing her own exceptional qualities, to each of which Sāriputta responds with an expression of his admiration.

The remainder of the discourse does not explicitly indicate that the other monks were still present during this exchange between Nandamātā and Sāriputta, although this seems a very probable scenario. They would all have been curious to know how come that, when they had set out on their journey in the expectation of not getting a meal, on arrival they found that everything was ready for them. This would make it natural for

Sāriputta to inquire about the matter right after the meal was over and thus in front of everyone. Moreover, it is a standard procedure that the donor(s) will be given a talk on the Dharma at the conclusion of a meal, which Sāriputta does *after* the present exchange. This makes it safe to conclude that the whole group of monks was still present.

From this viewpoint, then, after having devotedly served the community of monks with food, Nandamātā gets a chance of complementing this with a display of her extraordinary accomplishments. The appreciation she receives in this way from two leading male figures in the heavens and the Buddha's dispensation respectively, together with her evident self-confidence, must have turned Nandamātā into a source of inspiration for everyone present in the audience. In fact, Sāriputta's repeated acknowledgment of the marvelous nature of her qualities may well be on purpose to encourage her to continue further, in the knowledge that it will leave a deep impression on his monastic companions to come to know about the extraordinary nature of the woman who has just offered them food.

Nandamātā's Superb Balance of Mind

> [Nandamātā said:] "Venerable sir, this is not the only marvelous and amazing quality in me. There is indeed another marvelous and amazing quality in me. Here, venerable sir, I had an only son called Nanda, dear and precious to me. On account of some matter, the rulers took him by force and killed him. Yet, venerable sir, when my child was being arrested or had been arrested, was being imprisoned or had been imprisoned, was being killed or had been killed,[381] I did not know of any alteration in my mind.
>
> [Sāriputta said:] "It is marvelous, Nandamātā, it is amazing, Nandamātā, that you should keep pure even the arousal of your mind."

The experience Nandamātā relates here reflects a basic uncertainty for the inhabitants of one of the petty kingdoms in the ancient Indian setting, where the power of the local ruler(s) was such that they could simply abduct and kill someone, even if the latter was innocent of whatever the ruler(s) was suspecting. The outrageous nature of such injustice is further strengthened by the circumstance that the present case concerns Nandamātā's only son. In addition to the love she naturally felt for him, giving birth to a son was invested with considerable importance in the ancient Indian setting, all the more so if he was the only son. This was precisely why Kisāgotamī had experienced such excessive grief when her only son died, as discussed earlier (see above p. 49).

Understood in this way, the episode reported by Nandamātā combines several strands that make it indeed marvelous and amazing that she should have been able to witness the killing of her only son directly, as is implicit in her description, without giving rise even to an unwholesome state of mind. This story thereby stands out as an inspiring illustration for the degree of mastery of the mind and profound equanimity that a dedicated lay disciple can in principle achieve.

Nandamātā continues with yet another of her qualities, also related to her family:

> [Nandamātā said:] "Venerable sir, this is not the only marvelous and amazing quality in me. There is indeed another marvelous and amazing quality in me. Here, venerable sir, my husband passed away and was reborn in a certain realm of sprites. He appeared to me in his previous form. Yet, venerable sir, I did not know of any alteration in my mind because of that."
>
> [Sāriputta said:] "It is marvelous, Nandamātā, it is amazing, Nandamātā, that you should keep pure even the arousal of your mind."

This quality continues to throw into relief Nandamātā's profound equanimity and mastery of the mind, as she remained unperturbed even when her dead husband suddenly appeared out of nothing, looking just as he did when still alive. It is rather challenging to remain completely balanced with such an unexpected appearance of one's dead spouse.

Worthy of note at this point is also the fact that, even though her husband had evidently died and her son had been killed, she remained living a lay life and did not go forth. Although there would have been reasons for this choice, it is nevertheless noteworthy that, even at the time of the Buddha, not all accomplished disciples are on record for adopting the monastic path.

Her next two marvelous qualities relate to her ethical perfection:

> [Nandamātā said:] "Venerable sir, this is not the only marvelous and amazing quality in me. There is indeed another marvelous and amazing quality in me. Venerable sir, since as a young girl I was given to my young husband in marriage, I do not know of any transgression against him even in mind, much less by deed."
>
> [Sāriputta said:] "It is marvelous, Nandamātā, it is amazing, Nandamātā, that you should keep pure even the arousal of your mind."
>
> [Nandamātā said:] "Venerable sir, this is not the only marvelous and amazing quality in me. There is indeed another marvelous and amazing quality in me. Venerable sir, since I declared myself to be a lay follower, I do not know of any intentional breach of a training precept."
>
> [Sāriputta said:] "It is marvelous, Nandamātā, it is amazing, Nandamātā."

With these two achievements in the realm of moral conduct in place, Nandamātā has done more than ample justice to the quality eulogized in the *Ekottarikāgama* listing of outstanding female lay disciples, which considers her foremost in guarding her actions. Her ability in this respect is already evident in relation to the killing of her only son. The present two instances of her impeccable moral conduct, even in the mental realm, confirm her outstanding ability in this respect.

At the same time, the source of this ability is to be found in the extraordinary condition of her mind, which makes it hardly surprising that the continuity of her exposition to Sāriputta turns to accomplishments related to mental cultivation. This thereby relates to the quality highlighted in the *Aṅguttaranikāya* listing of outstanding female lay disciples, namely her being foremost in matters of meditation.

Nandamātā's Meditative Accomplishment

[Nandamātā said:] "Venerable sir, this is not the only marvelous and amazing quality in me. There is indeed another marvelous and amazing quality in me. For as much as I wish, venerable sir, being secluded from sensual desires and secluded from unwholesome states, with application and sustaining, with joy and happiness born of seclusion, I dwell having attained the first absorption. With the stilling of application and sustaining, with inner confidence and unification of the mind, being without application and without sustaining, with joy and happiness born of concentration, I dwell having attained the second absorption. And with the fading away of joy I dwell equipoised, mindful, and clearly knowing, and experiencing happiness through the body, being one whom noble ones designate as 'one who dwells happily with equipoise and mindfulness,' I dwell having attained the third absorption. With the abandoning of happiness and the abandoning of pain, and with the previous disappearance of joy and sadness, without pain and without happiness, and with purity of mindfulness and equipoise, I dwell having attained the fourth absorption."

[Sāriputta said:] "It is marvelous, Nandamātā, it is amazing, Nandamātā."

[Nandamātā said:] "Venerable sir, this is not the only marvelous and amazing quality in me. There is indeed another marvelous and amazing quality in me. Venerable sir, of the five lower fetters that have been declared by the Blessed One I see not a single one that has not been abandoned in me."

[Sāriputta said:] "It is marvelous, Nandamātā, it is amazing, Nandamātā."

With these final two qualities, Nandamātā clarifies that she has mastery of the four absorptions and is a nonreturner, making her indeed an outstanding lay meditator. These lofty achievements stand in the background of her superb balance of the mind when facing the killing of her only son or the sudden appearance of her dead husband. All of these are expressions of her highly accomplished mind as a result of dedicated meditation practice. In the light of her attainments, it becomes quite natural to picture her getting up in the early morning and reciting the Chapter on the Beyond, as reported in the introductory narration to the present discourse.

With this exceptional display of Nandamātā's abilities, my survey of teachings given by lay women comes to an end (the subject of the next and final chapter is also a lay woman, but her role is not to deliver her own teachings). The reason for that is mainly that the early discourses do not report many teachings given by lay disciples in general, as the standard setting is rather that the Buddha or one of his senior monastic disciples will give a teaching. When viewed from this perspective, it is already remarkable that three different lay women are on record for actually giving teachings, namely Queen Mallikā, Nakulamātā, and Nandamātā. The present case is even more remarkable, as Nandamātā delivers her exposition to Sāriputta, who in the early discourses features as the monk disciple who is second only to the Buddha himself.

A lay man by the name of Citta is also on record for giving teachings to some Buddhist monks.[382] Since he was also a nonreturner and had mastery of the four absorptions, he could be considered the male counterpart to Nandamātā in this respect. Nevertheless, none of his eloquent expositions is addressed to Sāriputta himself, nor is he on record for facing with complete equanimity such challenging experiences as Nandamātā encountered. In view of her extraordinary nature, it is not surprising that Nandamātā should have been chosen as one of the two role models for lay women, a choice to which I turn in the next chapter.

Khujjuttarā

> The foremost of those female lay disciples who are supreme in wisdom is the female lay disciple Khujjuttarā.[383]

The Pāli parallel reckons Khujjuttarā outstanding in being learned.[384] In the oral setting of ancient India, such learnedness refers literally to "having heard much," as that was the sole mode of delivery of teachings. This quality implies not only the fact of having heard much but also of retaining it in memory, without which the hearing will not be of long-term use.

Role Models for Female Lay Disciples

Khujjuttarā and Nandamātā, studied in the previous chapter, serve as role models for lay women. The two are thereby the counterparts to the nuns Khemā and Uppalavaṇṇā, who serve as role models for nuns, discussed in an earlier chapter (see above p. 35).[385] Needless to say, these two female lay disciples also have male counterparts, as the householders Citta and Hatthaka Āḷavaka serve as role models for other male lay disciples.

Comparable to the mental propensities of the two outstanding nuns Khemā and Uppalavaṇṇā, it seems that Khujjuttarā serves to exemplify wisdom (or the related quality of learnedness), whereas Nandamātā stands representative of meditative mastery of the mind. The relevant indication in a Chinese discourse, which has several Pāli parallels, proceeds as follows:[386]

> A trustworthy female lay disciple should instruct her daughter: "Now that you are living as a householder, you should be like the female lay disciples Khujjuttarā and Nandamātā. The reason is that this is the measure, this is the standard,[387] being disciples of the Blessed One who have experienced realization, namely Khujjuttarā and Nandamātā.

The teaching by Nandamātā, examined in the previous chapter, surveys a whole range of her marvelous and amazing qualities that can easily serve as an inspiration for taking her as one's role model. Key qualities would be the ability to remain equanimous with the ups and downs of life and a firm commitment to maintain ethical conduct, allowing such commitment to cover in its purview even what happens in the mind. Proceeding beyond these two pillars in daily life, dedication to meditation practice would be another inspiring quality to emulate, as such practice led Nandamātā to the heights of her mental accomplishment. This could be combined with the acknowledgment that, although in principle the monastic life is the best fit for someone wishing to live a life dedicated to meditation,[388] Nandamātā's case shows that remarkable progress is possible while remaining a lay practitioner. Needless to say, actualizing this potential would nevertheless require structuring one's life as a householder in such a way that it resembles as closely as reasonably possible the normative lifestyle of monastics, with an emphasis on renunciation and seclusion over sensual indulgence and socialization.

In comparison with the inspiration that can be gained from making Nandamātā one's role model, the equivalent function of Khujjuttarā would revolve around her having memorized a whole collection of Pāli discourses now extant as the *Itivuttaka*. According to the relevant story from the Pāli commentarial tradition, she had been a servant of Queen Sāmāvatī and was regularly sent into town to buy flowers for her lady.[389] On one such occasion of going to buy flowers, she had to wait as the Buddha had come and was giving a teaching. Overhearing his teaching, she became a stream-enterer. On her return to the royal harem, she gave a teaching to the queen and her following, establishing them in stream-entry as well. From then onward, she would regularly go to listen to the

Buddha's teachings, whenever he was in the area, and then return to repeat them in the royal harem. The collection of teachings that she had memorized eventually became the *Itivuttaka*. Characteristic of this collection are unusual opening and closing formulas, which differ from those employed in other discourses.[390] These presumably reflect the unusual circumstances of how this collection came into existence.

Her role in this respect makes her a female counterpart to the Buddha's attendant Ānanda, who according to tradition had memorized the discourses now found in the other collections. An explicit reference to this correspondence occurs in the discussion between Nāgasena and the King Milinda, already taken up in a previous chapter in relation to the chariot simile (see above p. 92). The Pāli and Chinese versions agree that Nāgasena explicitly mentioned Ānanda and Khujjuttarā when discussing the topic of memory.[391] Khujjuttarā as a counterpart to Ānanda can thus be taken to be a central implication of her function as a role model. This would in turn point to an encouragement of training in mindfulness as a central quality for having a good memory, combined with developing a good acquaintance with the Buddha's teachings.

The same already came up implicitly in the previous chapter in the description of Nandamātā's early morning recitation, showing that she had memorized the Chapter on the Beyond. This description helps to clarify that to develop a good acquaintance with the teaching is not confined to book learning. For example, inspiring passages can be read out aloud (even if that involves just a translation), as a way of letting their oral nature come more alive, and perhaps even be memorized. Recitation done from memory can in turn become part of one's meditation practice, as it can be skillfully employed when the mind is distracted in order to give it something to do and allow it to settle down, which can then become an entry door into the more silent dimensions of meditation. In fact, from a traditional perspective the cultivation of mindfulness embraces all the three types of activities that engender wisdom: hearing (= learning), reflecting, and meditating.[392] It can be quite helpful to step out of a rigid division between theory and practice, sometimes found in Western thought, and instead adopt an open attitude that enables flexibly adjusting to the requirements of the present moment. If the mind is distracted, perhaps some recitation and/or recollection of the teachings is adequate. Once the mind settles, however, this can be let go of in order to allow the deeper domains of meditative experience to unfold.

An additional dimension of inspiration could be derived from the circumstance that, without Khujjuttarā's role as a messenger of the Buddha's teachings to the royal harem, the discourses preserved in the *Itivuttaka* would no longer be extant (the Buddha's attendant Ānanda was presumably not present during the delivery of this series of teachings). As noted by Karen Lang (2019, 36), Khujjuttarā "was recognized for her important role in transmitting the Buddha's teaching." This in a way reflects the requirements of ensuring the preservation of the teachings, which in the ancient Indian oral setting was memorization. It is thanks to generation after generation of reciters memorizing and rehearsing these teachings that they have come down to us. Reflecting on this naturally arouses a sense of gratitude, which could lead over to attempting to make one's own contribution, however possible within the range of one's means, to support the continuity of the teachings for the benefit of future generations.

The importance of the role taken by Khujjuttarā in this respect can be illustrated with two excerpts from the *Itivuttaka* that present information otherwise not found among the Pāli discourses. Even though, strictly speaking, these are teachings given by the Buddha and not by Khujjuttarā, her crucial role in ensuring their preservation merits inclusion of these two extracts as the concluding point of the present study, which otherwise has focused on teachings actually delivered by women.

Three Faculties Related to Penetrative Knowledge

The discourse to be taken up first concerns three faculties that are related to progress toward awakening. These three are also listed in other Pāli discourses and their parallels, which for the most part do not provide any further explanations, except for a *Saṃyuktāgama* discourse that follows the listing with verses.[393] Such verses are also found in the Pāli version of the *Itivuttaka*, to which the Chinese parallel adds explanations. After the standard introduction to a discourse, the relevant Chinese version proceeds as follows:[394]

> "You should know that there are three types of faculties whose nature is very profound and whose clear understanding is very profound, whose nature is difficult to see and whose clear understanding is difficult to see. What are the three? The first is the faculty of coming to know what has not yet been known; the second is the faculty of knowing; and the third is the faculty of being endowed with knowledge.
>
> "What is called the faculty of coming to know what has not yet been known? That is, noble disciples in my teaching produce joyful desire, diligently endeavor, collect the mind, and take hold of the mind for the sake of vision and for the sake of knowledge in regard to the noble truth about all [kinds of] *dukkha*, which has not yet been seen and known. They produce joyful desire, diligently endeavor, collect the mind, and take hold of the mind for the sake of vision and for the sake of knowledge in regard to the noble truth about the arising of *dukkha* ... in regard to the noble truth about the cessation of *dukkha* ... in regard to the noble truth about progressing on the true path to the cessation of *dukkha*, which has not yet been seen and known.[395] This is called the faculty of coming to know what has not yet been known.
>
> "What is called the faculty of knowing? That is, noble disciples in my teaching understand it as it really is: 'This is the noble truth of *dukkha*,' 'this is the noble truth of the arising of *dukkha*,' 'this is the noble truth of the cessation of *dukkha*,' 'this is the noble truth of progressing on the true path to the cessation of *dukkha*.' This is called the faculty of knowing.
>
> "What is called the faculty of being endowed with knowledge? That is, noble disciples in my teaching who have eradicated all the influxes and truly gained being influx-free, being well liberated in the mind and being well liberated by wisdom, are able to rightly understand: 'Birth has been eradicated for

me, the holy life has been established, what was to be done has been done, there will be no experiencing of further becoming.' This is called the faculty of being endowed with knowledge.

In this way, these are called the three types of faculties whose nature is very profound and whose clear understanding is very profound, whose nature is difficult to see and whose clear understanding is difficult to see."

These three faculties in a way provide a map for progress from being unawakened to becoming an arahant, expressed in terms of the four noble truths, which, according to the traditional account, formed the main topic of the first sermon given by the Buddha after his awakening.[396] Such progress relies on joyful desire in the sense of sincerely aspiring to liberation, on diligently applying oneself to the practice, and on collecting and composing the mind. Based on these qualities, one cultivates the faculty of coming to know what has not yet been known. In other words, one directs those qualities toward the growth of insight. The faculty of knowing in turn relates to the attainment of stream-entry, whereby the insight described with the help of the scheme of four truths comes to be directly known and seen. Further progress then eventually leads to becoming an arahant, at which point what needed to be done has been done and transcendence from the cycle of rebirth has been achieved, corresponding to the faculty of being endowed with knowledge.

The Chinese parallel to the *Itivuttaka* continues with a set of verses by the Buddha that convey the nature of the three faculties in the following manner:

"In my right teaching,
A noble disciple in training
Properly cultivates the right and true path;
This is called the first faculty.

Rightly knowing the noble truth of *dukkha*,
The arising of *dukkha* and the cessation of *dukkha*,

Progressing on the path to the cessation of *dukkha*;
This is called the second faculty.

It should be known that the third faculty
Is the complete and perpetual eradication of the influxes,
The realization of being truly influx-free,
Being well liberated in mind and by wisdom.

It is the knowledge that birth has been eradicated for me,
As well as that the holy life has been established,
That what was to be done has all been done,
And that there will be no experiencing of further becoming.

Body and mind are constantly at peace,
All the [sense-]faculties are well restrained.
Bearing one's last body,
Māra and his retinue have been defeated."

The verses in the Pāli parallel proceed differently; their concern is not to delineate the implications of each of the three faculties. Instead, they provide indications about the trainee and the arahant. Regarding the trainee, the indication is that knowledge of cessation occurs first and will then immediately be followed by penetrative knowledge.[397] The next verse then highlights that an arahant's liberation is unshakable. The final verse in the Pāli version is similar to the last of the verses translated above, specifying that the peaceful one is endowed with (restraint of) the faculties, bears the last body, and has defeated Māra and his retinue.

The Two Nirvana Elements

Another *Itivuttaka* passage, which has no counterpart among the remainder of the Pāli discourses, describes two elements of Nirvana.[398] The corresponding description in its Chinese parallel proceeds as follows (leaving out the standard introduction):

"You should know that the Nirvana element is, in brief, of two types. What are the two? The first is the Nirvana element with a residue; the second is the Nirvana element without a residue.

"What is called the Nirvana element with a residue? That is, monastics who have become arahants, have eradicated all the influxes, have established the holy life, have done what was to be done, have shed the heavy burden, have realized their own aim, have eradicated the fetter of becoming, have rightly understood, are well liberated in mind, and have gained penetrative knowledge of the conditions of former karma.

"Yet, their [sense] faculties continue to remain. Even though their [sense] faculties are capable and contacts of various types manifest with attractive and repulsive perceptual objects, still they are able to be dispassionate, do not cling to anything, and their minds are not beset by craving and aversion, because they have forever cut off completely the bondage of craving, aversion, and so on ...

"Even though there is the mind and there are attractive and repulsive mental objects, still they are without lustful desire and also without irritation. Why is that? It is because they have forever and completely cut off the bondage of craving, aversion, and so on.

"As long as there is the body, they continue to remain in the world, having not yet [entered] final Nirvana, being constantly looked up to, revered, respected, and supported by celestials and humans. This is called the Nirvana element with a residue.

"What is called the Nirvana element without a residue? That is, monastics who have become arahants, have eradicated all the influxes, have established the holy life, have done what was to be done, have shed the heavy burden, have realized their own aim, have eradicated the fetter of becoming, have rightly understood, are well liberated in mind, and have gained penetrative knowledge. In the present, because there are no more impulsions and no more longings, which have all forever been

> extinguished, all that is being felt comes to be finally at peace, ultimately becomes cool, disappears, and no longer manifests.
>
> "Only purity is still there in the absence of what is of the substance of conceptual proliferation. Purity like this in the absence of what is of the substance of conceptual proliferation cannot be reckoned as 'it exists,' cannot be reckoned as 'it does not exist,' cannot be reckoned as 'that exists as well as does not exist,' and cannot be reckoned as 'that neither exists nor does not exist.' It can only be called what cannot be designated, the ultimate, Nirvana. This is called the Nirvana element without a residue."

The Pāli parallel is considerably shorter for both types of Nirvana. Regarding the Nirvana element without residue, the Pāli discourse just notes, after describing an arahant with the same terms used earlier for the Nirvana element with residue, that for such a one all felt experience, not being delighted in, will become cool right here.[399]

The additional description in the paragraph translated above is intriguing. Usually in the early discourses a reference to all feeling tones becoming cool intends the passing away of an arahant. If that is the sense intended above, which seems highly probable given the context of a discussion of the Nirvana element without residue, then the reference to purity would be describing the condition of an arahant after death. To the best of my knowledge, such a description is not found anywhere else among the early discourses.

The above description of purity would be considerably less surprising if it were to intend the mental condition of an arahant still alive. The absence of conceptual proliferation is indeed a characteristic condition of an arahant. The same holds for the impossibility of adequately reflecting the nature of an arahant in terms of the fourfold mode of reasoning. As Khemā aptly illustrated (see above p. 29), once an arahant (referred to alternatively as a Tathāgata) is free from identifying with any of the five aggregates of clinging, there is no more room left for identifying the arahant with the five aggregates of clinging. For this reason, the fourfold mode of reasoning in terms of existence and nonexistence no longer applies. This prevents making predictions of an arahant after death and also holds for an arahant still alive. Once clinging has been removed for good, the arahant becomes, to use her words, "deep, immeasurable, and difficult to fathom, just like the great ocean."

Yet, an interpretation of the tetralemma in the above passage as referring to the arahant while still alive would not work in view of the next sentence, according to which the condition just described is called "the ultimate, Nirvana." This phrase would more naturally fit the condition of the arahant after death. This is in fact the whole point of distinguishing between two Nirvana elements. In other words, the reference to purity could hardly intend the same as what the first part of the discourse describes to be the Nirvana element with a residue. In sum, the description of purity in the absence of conceptual proliferation does indeed appear to refer to the after-death condition of an arahant.

In this way, the above passage provides a unique perspective, as far as the early discourses are concerned, on a topic that has been debated from ancient to modern times: What exactly happens when an arahant passes away? Whatever may be the final word on this topic, after confirming to the audience that these are the two Nirvana elements, the Chinese version continues with the Buddha concluding his exposition with a verse:

> "Liberation of the mind with the eradication of the influxes,
> Bearing one's last body,
> This is called the Nirvana [element] with a residue;
> All formations still continue.
>
> The complete cessation of all that is felt,
> The peaceful, forever cool,
> This is called the Nirvana [element] without a residue,
> Where all the many conceptual proliferations stop.
>
> These are the two Nirvana elements,
> Supreme and unparalleled.

That is, the present and the future one,
Peaceful and forever at ease."

The above verses, in themselves unproblematic, further support an interpretation of the purity described in the prose as referring to the after-death state of an arahant. The corresponding two verses in the Pāli version proceed differently, although touching on similar topics. The first verse lists the two Nirvana elements, with the specific indication that in the one without residue all forms of becoming (*bhava*) cease completely. The second verse indicates that those who have fully understood this are free from becoming. Having attained the essence of the teachings, they have left behind all forms of becoming. The repeated emphasis on the ending of all forms of becoming is in line with the general position taken in the early discourses.

Alongside the various and at times intriguing differences between the presentation translated above from the Chinese and its Pāli parallel, from the viewpoint of the present study it is particularly noteworthy that the preservation of an exposition on the two Nirvana elements appears to be entirely due to the role reportedly played by Khujjuttarā. Without her memorizing the exposition and passing it on to others, this intriguing teaching would no longer be extant. In this way, the case of Khujjuttarā complements the survey in the preceding pages, which throws into relief the amazing and impressive contributions made by ancient Indian female disciples of the Buddha.

Epilogue

The present epilogue summarizes the remarkable and inspiring qualities of the spiritual daughters of the Buddha,[400] surveyed in the preceding pages, and at the same time places these within a wider context. The frame of reference for doing so is the listing of outstanding disciples in the *Ekottarikāgama*, extracts from which came up in the introductory section of most of the chapters of my study. The survey in what follows also includes outstanding nuns mentioned in the *Ekottarikāgama* list that have not yet come up in the preceding chapters. In such cases, I refrain from providing their names, as the reconstruction of names from the Chinese original is at times highly uncertain. Although I would in principle have preferred to provide names, in some cases I would have had to invent Indic names that may never have existed. For this reason, after some deliberation, I decided it would be preferable to focus on their respective qualities, as this is after all the main purpose of the present epilogue.[401]

For fully appreciating the implications of this listing of eminent disciples in the *Ekottarikāgama*, as well as in its Pāli parallel, it needs to be kept in mind that each of the nuns and female lay disciples eulogized in this way should not be considered a unique case, where a single woman has a particular quality or ability. Rather, a woman can only be declared foremost in some respect if at the same time there were other women who had similar qualities or engaged in comparable conduct. Viewed from this perspective, then, the listing of outstanding women is a survey of qualities and modes of behavior that were held to be to some degree common among a number of early Buddhist nuns and female lay disciples.

Outstanding Nuns

According to the *Ekottarikāgama* list, Mahāpajāpatī Gotamī was foremost in seniority and in being respected by the king of the country. Her being foremost in this respect implies that other senior nuns were also respected by local rulers. Even though such respect is not explicitly mentioned in the Pāli parallel, the appropriateness of the idea as such could be deduced from the Pāli discourse reporting the visit paid by King Pasenadi to the nun Khemā, who features as the only religious teacher in the whole area really worth a visit.

Returning to the case of Mahāpajāpatī Gotamī, the very existence of other senior nuns, including Khemā, is directly related to Mahāpajāpatī Gotamī's petitioning the Buddha to start an order of nuns at what appears to have been an early period in his teaching activities. The narrative of Mahāpajāpatī Gotamī's spectacular passing away involves her setting an example for others to follow, in line with her leadership role throughout.

The topic of respect comes up again with another nun, also included in the *Ekottarikāgama* listing of eminent disciples but not yet covered in the preceding pages of my study, presented as foremost among nuns in being respected and liked by the people. This in a way complements Mahāpajāpatī Gotamī's role of being respected by the king. The two eminencies in combination convey that, even though apparently not popular among some of those who were responsible for the shaping of the narrative that reports the founding of their order, the nuns had been able to earn the respect of the local rulers and the population in general.

The already-mentioned Khemā was foremost among the nuns for wisdom, which of course implies that other nuns were also wise. Her dexterous teaching to King Pasenadi on the nature of the Tathāgata, illustrated with the examples of the impossibility of counting the sand grains in the Ganges or the water in the ocean, confirms her outstanding wisdom. This has its complement in her complete disinterest in sensuality, highlighted in her verses. Early Buddhist thought considered such aloofness from sensual attractions to be indeed a matter of wisdom and insight.

The *Ekottarikāgama* list mentions another two outstanding nuns that could be related to the topics just broached. One of these was foremost in contemplating impurity and analyzing dependent arising. The first of these qualities directly relates to aloofness from sensuality; the second highlights the basic principle that stands in the background of Khemā's exposition on the nature of a Tathāgata. Another eminent nun was foremost in being widely learned and also in being kind. The combination with kindness is noteworthy, as this directs attention to the type of attitude and disposition that rounds off learnedness.

Together with Khemā, Uppalavaṇṇā can serve as a role model for other nuns. Her forte lies in excellence in psychic powers. Uppalavaṇṇā's powerful personality becomes evident in the composed and self-confident way she handles a sexual threat, in reply to which she is able to proclaim that even a hundred thousand rogues would not be able to frighten her.

The ability to gain psychic powers relies on concentrative mastery. In this respect, Uppalavaṇṇā was certainly not alone, as the *Ekottarikāgama* list mentions another two nuns outstanding in entering concentration on the elements of water and fire, respectively. Two more nuns were foremost in entering concentration with a mind that is not scattered and in having a mind that is always calm. Yet another two nuns gained the rank of being foremost in sitting at the root of a tree with an unmoving mind or else in having calm senses and a unified mind. Clearly, a range of nuns stood out for excellence in various dimensions of the cultivation of concentration.

Kisāgotamī ranks as foremost among nuns undertaking ascetic practices. The *Ekottarikāgama* list mentions several nuns outstanding in related practices, namely in sitting on a grass mat without a cloth on top, in always being out in the open without caring for a cover, in delighting in abandoned cemeteries, in wandering everywhere and begging among a range of people, and in begging for alms without choosing between rich and poor. Once again, for each of these nuns to be foremost implies that other nuns were also dedicated to such types of conduct. It follows that the early Buddhist nuns were quite distinguished in matters of asceticism. This has its basis in cultivating wishlessness, a quality in relation to which yet another nun ranks foremost.

Stern conduct is also a quality of Paṭācārā, who had gone through a series of calamities that made her become insane. Having recovered her mental balance and reached complete mental health through awakening, she became outstanding among nuns in upholding the disciplinary rules without infraction. Such keen concern in matters of moral conduct can be seen also with several other nuns, who according to the *Ekottarikāgama* list were foremost in being restrained during all activities, in never being separate from the three robes, in wearing the robes in an orderly manner, in not being ashamed of wearing rough robes, and in wearing rag robes and begging in order. The ability to undertake such conduct can be related to the mental quality of cherishing patience in the heart, for which yet another nun features as foremost. Keeping in mind that each of the nuns just mentioned represents a whole group of nuns acting in like manner, which holds similarly for the nuns mentioned above together with Kisāgotamī, throws into relief the degree to which moral conduct and renunciation were held in high esteem among a range of the ordained daughters of the Buddha.

Vijayā, who rebuffed Māra by proclaiming her preference for meditation over musical entertainment, ranks foremost in the four analytical knowledges. Her verses report how a teaching, received from Khemā, helped her to emerge from restlessness and gain such deep realization that she sat motionless for seven days. Other nuns in the *Ekottarikāgama* list are considered outstanding for quickly accomplishing the fruits of the path, for attaining final realization, and for delighting in the attainment of the path.

Upacālā stood out for delighting in empty places and in not being among people. In her encounter with Māra, Upacālā made it quite clear that the same preference for solitude applies to the possibility of being in heavenly company. The *Ekottarikāgama* list mentions another two nuns outstanding for related qualities, namely for always being in secluded places, instead of among people, and for sitting alone in a single place without moving at all.

Somā's affirmation of the ability of women to reach the highest is to my mind one of the most inspiring episodes covered in the preceding pages. Of what relevance could the distinction between male and female be to one who has mastery of the mind? Her clarification in this respect may well be related to her outstanding quality in having compassion for living beings who have not yet awakened. The *Ekottarikāgama* list features other nuns foremost in related qualities, namely in delivering people, in teaching and transforming people, in widely teaching the development of the path, and in dwelling much in *mettā* and empathy. Once again, keeping in mind that each of these needs to be visualized at the head of a group of nuns endowed with the same qualities, the early Buddhist nuns clearly made a substantial contribution to the compassionate task of spreading the liberating teachings.

The same holds for Dhammadinnā, of course, who was outstanding in analyzing and widely discoursing on the Buddha's teachings. Her eminence in teaching becomes quite apparent in her discussion with her former (or would-be) husband, covering a range of subtle and intricate points that have made her exposition a lasting inspiration for generation after generation of Buddhist practitioners and scholars. The *Ekottarikāgama* list mentions related qualities in relation to two eminent nuns, who were foremost in widely explaining the meaning of profound teachings and in never tiring of contemplating the Dharma.

Soṇā's excellence in overcoming non-Buddhist practitioners finds ample illustration in her feat of levitation, challenging the leaders of other traditions to face her in debate. Another two nuns feature in the *Ekottarikāgama* list for eminence in discussing in various ways without hesitation and in composing stanzas in praise of the Buddha.

The Buddha's former wife, Bhaddā Kaccānā, was according to the *Ekottarikāgama* account foremost in being liberated by confidence, whereas the Pāli counterpart presents her as outstanding for great supernormal knowledge. Her ability to recall past lives came to the fore in the teaching she delivered in front of the Buddha, addressed to the local king on the power of merits. In line with the topic of her teaching, the same episode shows her doing her very best to provide other practitioners with the things they need. Another nun in the *Ekottarikāgama* listing was foremost in this respect, namely in supporting people, giving them what is lacking. Bhaddā Kaccānā's self-confident manner of delivering her teaching could be related to yet another nun, mentioned in the same

Ekottarikāgama listing for being foremost in having a courageous mind, without attachment.

Chief in recollecting past lives is Bhaddā Kāpilānī, who in the episode translated above was able to relate a series of past lives informed by the wish to be reborn with a female body. Another nun in the *Ekottarikāgama* list was exceptional in the closely related possession of the divine eye. Another two outstanding nuns could be added here as exemplifying concentrative mastery, required for recollection of past lives and the divine eye. The two nuns in question stood out for excellence in delighting in signlessness and in keeping to emptiness.

Remarkable Nuns

The above survey of various nuns explicitly declared in the *Ekottarikāgama* list as foremost in various qualities does not yet exhaust the material surveyed in the previous chapter, as some remarkable nuns are not included in this listing. One of these is Cālā, who eloquently expressed her total disinterest in birth. Sīsupacālā and Vīrā in turn stood out for delighting in nothing apart from the Buddha's teachings and in deconstructing substantialist notions attributed to a sentient being. The same deconstruction takes a particularly powerful form in Selā's (or Vajirā's) delivery of the chariot simile, with which she made a substantial contribution to Buddhist thought that has been of continuous interest up to present times.

Going completely beyond the attractions of sensuality comes up again with the nun Āḷavikā in her encounter with Māra. This is one in a series of instances where Māra acts as a tempter and at times even as a sexual aggressor, each time being quickly recognized and rebuffed by the nuns he attempts to disturb. Another nun not included in listings of foremost nuns is Kajaṅgalā, whose dexterous exposition of ten replies to ten questions shows her impressive grasp of the teachings. This comes combined with an ability to present these topics in a way that gives pride of place to positive qualities and thereby avoids any possible redundancy. This makes Kajaṅgalā's teaching truly worth memorization and reflection.

Outstanding Female Lay Disciples

Besides nuns, the *Ekottarikāgama* listing of outstanding women also covers a range of female lay disciples.[402] Queen Mallikā who, in two episodes surveyed above, stood out for her inner clarity in explaining matters to her husband, should be reckoned foremost among female lay disciples in having reverence for the Buddha. The same listing mentions several other queens as outstanding for honoring the true Dharma, for having reverence for the noble community, for admiring noble sages of the past and the future, and for being good at teaching others.[403] The last mentioned was presumably superior even to Queen Mallikā herself. A quality related to her eminence is attaining liberation by confidence, for which another female lay disciple features as foremost in the *Ekottarikāgama* listing (whereby this woman becomes a lay counterpart to the nun Bhaddā Kaccānā).

Nakulamātā does not feature in the *Ekottarikāgama* list and is only found in its Pāli counterpart, a status she shares with Visākhā and several other lay women. Even when the two lists share a particular name, such as is the case for Nandamātā, they do not necessarily agree on her qualities. Whereas the *Ekottarikāgama* reckons her outstanding in guarding her actions, the Pāli version sees her as foremost in meditation. The discourse revealing her marvelous and amazing qualities confirms both indications. The topic of guarding one's actions can be related to several qualities of other outstanding female lay disciples, who were foremost in being capable at upholding morality, in constantly dwelling in patience, in being courageous and energetic, and also in never being intimidated. Another quality in which another woman disciple excelled, and which to some extent can also be connected to Nandamātā, is being foremost as a munificent donor.

The eminence accorded to Nandamātā in the Pāli version, which fits her equally well, could be linked to other lay women outstanding for qualities related to meditation practice. These cover being of composed appearance, having all the faculties at peace, constantly delighting in sitting in meditation, constantly dwelling in concentration on *mettā*, dwelling in compassion and empathy, having a mental attitude of sympathetic joy, as well as dwelling in concentration on emptiness, on signlessness, and on desirelessness. This long list implies that meditation was a rather prominent concern among lay women at the Buddha's time, evidently resulting in considerable mastery of the mind among them.

Khujjuttarā features as supreme in wisdom among female lay disciples. Her eminence in this respect can be connected to a range of qualities for which other women were outstanding. These comprise clearly understanding with the faculty of wisdom, being capable in teaching the Dharma, expounding the meaning of the discourses well, and being able to compose verses. Others were foremost in having a clear voice, being able to debate in various ways, and vanquishing outsiders. Still other lay women were chief in being learned and having extensive knowledge, and in gaining realization. The above goes to show that, even though going forth to become a nun was the normative avenue for spiritual progress in the ancient setting, those women who, for one reason or another, chose to remain householders still excelled in a range of abilities and practices held in high esteem in the early Buddhist community.

With the above survey of the staggering range of extraordinary qualities and achievements completed, there is still one more thing to be said. In view of the potential intersectional combination of the pervasive discrimination against women in ancient and modern times with the persistency of the racist belief that lacking whiteness of skin implies some sort of inferiority, it could be noted that all the protagonists of the amazing accomplishments and impressive feats surveyed in this book were what we would nowadays call "women of color."

Abbreviations

Abhidh-k	*Abhidharmakośabhāṣya*
AN	*Aṅguttaranikāya*
Ap	*Apadāna*
CBETA	Chinese Buddhist Electronic Text Association
D	Derge edition
DĀ	*Dīrghāgama* (T 1)
Dhp	*Dhammapada*
Dhp-a	*Dhammapada-aṭṭhakathā*
DN	*Dīghanikāya*
EĀ	*Ekottarikāgama* (T 125)
EĀ²	partial *Ekottarikāgama* (T 150A)
It	*Itivuttaka*
Khp	*Khuddakapāṭha*
Kv	*Kathāvatthu*
MĀ	*Madhyamāgama* (T 26)
Mil	*Milindapañha*
MN	*Majjhimanikāya*
Mp	*Manorathapūraṇī*
P	Peking edition
Pj	*Paramatthajotikā*
Ps	*Papañcasūdanī*
PTS	Pali Text Society
SĀ	*Saṃyuktāgama* (T 99)
SĀ²	partial *Saṃyuktāgama* (T 100)
SHT	Sanskrithandschriften aus den Turfanfunden
Si	Sichuan edition

SN	*Saṃyuttanikāya*
Sn	*Suttanipāta*
Spk	*Sāratthappakāsinī*
T	Taishō edition (CBETA)
Th	*Theragāthā*
Th-a	*Theragāthā-aṭṭhakathā*
Thī	*Therīgāthā*
Thī-a	*Therīgāthā-aṭṭhakathā* (1998 ed.)
Ud	*Udāna*
Ud-a	*Paramatthadīpanī*
Up	*Abhidharmakośopāyikāṭīkā*
Uv	*Udānavarga*
Vin	*Vinaya*
Vism	*Visuddhimagga*

Notes

1 Needless to say, these textual sources cannot yield definite information about what actually happened in ancient India. For this reason, what I report is what the reciters of these texts believed to have happened, without intending to present what I survey as undisputable historical facts.
2 See in more detail the survey on Buddhist androcentrism in Anālayo 2021g, 5–39.
3 EĀ 5.1 at T 2.125.558c20.
4 AN 1.14.5 at AN I 25,18: *rattaññūnaṃ*.
5 AN 1.14.1 at AN I 23,15; see also below note 131.
6 DN 2 at DN I 47,18.
7 DN 18 at DN II 202,2.
8 Contrary to the assumption by Garling 2021, 158, this holds even for accounts of this event reporting that Mahāpajāpatī Gotamī's followers also received ordination by accepting the eight stipulations, reportedly promulgated by the Buddha, as is the case for T 22.1428.923c2 and T 24.1463.803b20. In the former version, Mahāpajāpatī Gotamī accepts these eight stipulations (and therewith ordination) on behalf of the rest, making her naturally the most senior among them. The same can safely be assumed to apply to the latter version as well, which is overall rather short and for this reason does not explicitly delineate the role played by Mahāpajāpatī Gotamī at this juncture.
9 See Anālayo 2016a (on the Tibetan versions see also Dhammadinnā 2016); for a reply to criticism see Anālayo 2019f: 51–67 and below note 23.
10 MĀ 116 at T 1.26.605a11 and T 1.60.856a8.
11 AN 8.51 at AN IV 274,6.
12 AN 8.51 at AN IV 276,10.
13 For a critical reply to the suggestion by Dutt 1957, 145, Schumann 1982/1999, 217, Harvey 1990, 218, Samuels 1999, 238, Bluck 2002, 10, and Somaratne 2009, 153 that the early discourses show evidence to the existence of arahants who continue to live on as lay disciples see Anālayo 2010c, 8n19. Thomas 1933/2004, 26 sums up the situation in the following manner: "It has been a matter of discussion whether a layman can win arahatship. The question is not properly put, for the real question is whether he can exercise the necessary training while living in a house. If he can and does, then he becomes an arahat, but he at the same time ceases to be a laymen" in orientation, since, if "such a one does cast off all the fetters, he has freed himself from everything that binds him to a life of pleasure," being for this reason unable to continue living the life of a householder.
14 AN 8.51 at AN IV 274,30.

15 MĀ 180 at T 1.26.721c24 and T 1.84.903b28; for a comparative study that takes into account a range of parallels see Anālayo 2011b, 810–19. A monograph publication based on the relevant Gāndhārī fragment version is at present under preparation by Ingo Strauch.

16 MN 148 at MN III 253,2.

17 See Anālayo 2008a, 108–10.

18 Contrary to the assumption by Garling 2021, 114, combinations of the tale of Mahāpajāpatī Gotamī's gift of a robe with episodes related to Maitreya are distinctly late and the result of considerable textual evolution. In fact, the very idea that there will be a future Buddha by this name can already be identified as a later development; see Anālayo 2010a, 95–113 and 2014d.

19 MĀ 116 at T 1.26.606c14 and T 60 at T 1.60.857b10.

20 The translation is based on adopting a variant.

21 Here and below, I follow the precedent set by Bodhi 2012, 1804n1742: "Rather than use an obscure Pāli or Latin term, I freely render the name of the flower as 'lilies.'" The reference in the original could according to Dhammika 2015/2018, 34 perhaps be to *Hiptage madablota* or according to Cone 2001, 66 perhaps to *Ougeinia oojeinensis*.

22 AN 8.51 at AN IV 278,5.

23 For a comparative study of this episode see Anālayo 2016a, 91–116. Although most parallel versions illustrate the function of the eight rules with the example of a dyke or dam, T 22.1428.923b19 speaks of 橋梁 and T 24.1463.803b15 of 橋船, on which von Hinüber 2019, 94 comments that the first character in each couplet can render "Skt. *saṃkrama* or *setu*, both of which do not mean 'bridge' but 'causeway' or 'dam.'" This assertion is unexpected, as Monier-Williams 1899/1999, 1127 and 1246 lists "bridge" as one of the possible meanings for each of the two Sanskrit terms. For the first rendering as 橋梁, Hirakawa 1997, 670 gives *tīrtha*, in addition to *saṃkrama* and *setu*, which can mean a "ford." The additional reference to 船 in the second rendering is to a "boat," whose function to convey across water is similar to a bridge and not to a dam. In fact, both versions explicitly indicate that the purpose of the contrivance under discussion is to enable one "to cross over," 渡. Whatever the Indic original may have been, the idea the Chinese translations convey does not seem to be that the eight rules function to restrain water but much rather that they serve as something that enables crossing over water, such as a bridge. The illustrations provided in these two versions thereby convey positive connotations, in line with what other canonical occurrences of the dyke simile suggest to be relevant even in the case of the similes employed in the parallel versions; see Anālayo 2016a, 92–93 and 2019f: 58–59. In sum, closer inspection makes it to my mind reasonable to propose that the similes illustrating the promulgation of the eight rules could have been intended to call up positive associations.

24 Thī 157 to Thī 162.

25 It is noteworthy that the sequence of listing follows the order of the medical scheme of diagnosis that appears to have inspired the formulation of the four truths; see Anālayo 2011c. In this way, the 'cure' of the path stands in third position and cessation in the fourth, whereas the order adopted for the standard presentation of the four noble truths has cessation as the third and the eightfold path as its fourth. On the coherence of the resultant pattern see also Anālayo 2021g, 128–30.

26 On the motif of a mother's love see also Dhammadinnā 2019.

27 This is the interpretation offered for this verse in Thī-a 137,19, with reference to a statement reportedly made by the Buddha to the monk Vakkali, SN 22.87 at SN III 120,28; for a comparative study of this discourse see Anālayo 2011e.

28 See in more detail Anālayo 2016c.

29 The translated portion begins in EĀ 52.1 at T 2.125.821b26; already translated in Anālayo 2015d. The tale has parallels in Ap 17 at Ap 529,22, Thī-a 138,1, T 2.144.867a24, T 2.145.869b14, T 4.201.333a23, and in the Mūlasarvāstivāda *Vinaya*, T 24.1451.248b13 and D 6 *tha* 111a6 or P 1035 *de* 106b6. For a comparative study based on T 201 see Lévi 1908, 160–74 (for reservations regarding his conclusions see Oldenberg 1912, 207n3, Winternitz 1920/1968, 129, and Bechert 1958, 20); for a study of the Mūlasarvāstivāda *Vinaya* versions see Dhammadinnā 2015.

30 See Anālayo 2011b, 417.

31 Ap 17.2 at Ap 535,27 and Thī-a 138,16. T 2.144.867a26 and T 2.145.869b16 also mention that all members of her following of five hundred were arahants, without a reference to the following of the Buddha.

32 Ap 17.3 at Ap 529,28, to which Thī-a 138,21 adds Mahākassapa. In T 2.144.867b2 she also mentions Śāriputra and Mahāmaudgalyāyana, who appear to be implicit in her statement in T 2.145.869c12 (their names are given at 869b19).

33 Waldschmidt 1951, 382,10 (40.48), T 1.5.172b1, T 1.6.187c29, and T 1.7.204b23.

34 Ud 8.9 at Ud 92,29 and its parallels SĀ 1076 at T 2.99.280b27 and SĀ[2] 15 at T 2.100.378b1; for a more detailed study see Anālayo 2012b.

35 EĀ 26.9 at T 2.125.640a12.

36 The translation "reciting" is based on adopting an emendation that has been suggested in the CBETA edition.

37 The usual number of circumambulations in the early discourses is three.

38 The translation is based on adopting a variant reading that adds "at this time."

39 The reconstruction of some of the names of the nuns is only conjectural.

40 On this custom see, for example, Altekar 1956, 115–42, Nandy 1980, Datta 1988, Sharma, Ray, Hejib, and Young 1988/2001, Leslie 1991, Hawley 1994, Courtright 1995, van den Bosch 1995, Weinberger-Thomas 1996, Garzilli 1997, Mani 1998, Adhya 2006, and Brick 2010.

41 This has been assumed by Wilson 2011, 134–35: "Gotami frets about the death of male kinsmen ... because she may end up as a socially stigmatized woman if she does not relinquish her life before the death of her close kinsmen ... Gotami wishes to avoid the fate of the surplus woman, the woman without male guardianship."

42 The translation is based on adopting a variant.

43 Skilling 1997, 315 explains that "the Mūlasarvāstivādins, Sarvāstivādins, Lokottaravādins, Mahīśāsakas, Aśvaghoṣa, and Asaṅga along with the *Ratnaguṇasaṃcaya*, *Ekottarikāgama*, *P'u yao ching*, and *Book of Zambasta*, agree against the Theravādins that an auditor as well as a Buddha could perform the *yamakaprātihārya*."

44 Ap 17.85+88 at Ap 536,7 and Thī-a 146,3.

45 Ap 17.79 at Ap 535,24 and Thī-a 145,13.

46 The indication that she "returned to" enter the sphere of nothingness and the second absorption is based on adopting a variant, whereas in other instances this indication is found in the original.

47 For a comparative study see Anālayo 2014a.

48 Ap 17.146 at Ap 540,10 and Thī-a 151,4; this difference, compared to the report of the Buddha's practice on the eve of his decease, has already been noted by Pruitt 1998/1999, 197n1. The same absence of the attainment of cessation holds for the account in the Mūlasarvāstivāda *Vinaya* T 24.1451.248c19 and D 6 *tha* 112b3 or P 1035 *de* 108a1 (where this description applies to her and the five hundred nuns), which also differ insofar as the actual passing away takes place from the first absorption; see the discussion in Dhammadinnā 2015, 43–45. T 2.144.868a10 and 868a17 and T 2.145.869c25 do not precede her attainment of final Nirvana (or that of the five hundred nuns) with a meditative tour through the absorptions and the formless spheres.

49 Walters 1994, 375 argues that "Gotamī is the Buddha for women," even going so far as to speak of "the Buddhī, Gotamī" (p. 376) and to refer to "Her Buddhahood" (p. 378); reaffirming again in Walters 1995, 117 that "Gotamī is represented as the Buddha for women." Influenced by Walters, Crosby 2014, 251 in turn reasons that "Mahāpajāpatī Gotamī functions as a female Buddha or 'quasi-Buddha' in the *Apadāna*."

50 Walters 1994, 375n52 supports his suggestion by proposing that "the earthquakes caused by Gotamī define her as a Buddha de facto." Although a listing of eight causes for earthquakes in DN 16 at DN II 108,28 indicates one such cause to be when a Tathāgata mindfully gives up the life formation, it needs to be kept in mind that the listing of eight causes for an earthquake did not limit the evolution of the earthquake motif in Buddhist texts to these eight occasions only. Moreover, the listing of eight could in turn be the result of an elaboration of a list of three; see Przyluski 1918, 424, Waldschmidt 1944, 107, Frauwallner 1956, 157–59, Bareau 1979, 79, and Anālayo 2013a, 19 (for a detailed study of earthquakes see Ciurtin 2009 and 2012). In line with the impression that there is no definite and closed list of such events, earthquakes tend to occur in later texts without such occasions corresponding to one or the other of the list of eight instances. In fact, in Ap 17.6 at Ap 530,5 and Thī-a 138,26 the earthquake marks the decision of Mahāpajāpatī *and* of her following of five hundred nuns to enter final Nirvana, which obviously does not imply that they should all be considered Buddhas. As already noted by Faure 2003, 183, "Walter's claim that Gotamī Mahāprajāpatī [sic] is a female buddha seems exaggerated."

51 In relation to a prediction given at an earlier point in the same section on Mahāpajāpatī Gotamī in Thī-a 135,31 that she and Māyā will give birth to a *cakkavattin*. Garling 2021, 35 reasons that, since only Māyā actually gave birth to a child that could have become a *cakkavattin* (but instead became a Buddha), a way of interpreting the prediction that goes beyond "rigid conventional views" is that "Mahapajapati *herself* was a *chakravartin*, destined to become the 'wheel-turning' mother of Buddhism" (p. 36). A more convincing interpretation of the same prediction is the suggestion, given a few years earlier by the same author, Garling 2016, 62, that "each sister was predicted to become the mother of a universal king. Who knew this would someday mean sharing the same great son?" On the narrative function of the motif of the *cakkavattin*, which would indeed not fit the case of Mahāpajāpatī Gotamī, see Anālayo 2011d and 2014d.

52 Ap 17.173 at Ap 542,13 and Thī-a 153,14.

53 T 51.2087.908b28.

54 EĀ 5.1 at T 2.125.558c22.

55 AN 1.14.5 at AN I 25,19.

56 Speyer 1909/1970: 50,9; already noted by Skilling 2001, 143.

57 The translated portion begins in SN 44.1 at SN IV 375,3.
58 See in more detail Anālayo 2022d, 47–50.
59 See in more detail Anālayo 2022b.
60 MN 63 at MN I 426,9, MĀ 221 at T 1.26.804a25, and T 1.94.917b18; see also Anālayo 2018b, 40–42.
61 SN 22.86 at SN III 116,20. The parallel SĀ 106 at T 2.99.32c16, however, does not report him making such a statement. A Sanskrit fragment in de La Vallée Poussin 1913, 579 (Kha ii 3 R2) has preserved a phrase showing that its presentation was similar to SN 22.86 in this respect, making it fairly probable that the reading in SĀ 106 is the result of an error.
62 SN 22.85 at SN III 109,20 and its parallel SĀ 104 at T 2.99.30c17.
63 The simile of the sand in the Ganges occurs in SN 15.8 at SN II 184,4 to illustrate the difficulty of counting the eons that have passed by. The simile of the water in the great ocean occurs in SN 55.41 at SN V 400,8, AN 4.51 at AN II 55,19, AN 5.45 at AN III 52,16, and AN 6.37 at AN III 336,30 to illustrate the difficulty of measuring merit. In each instance, the speaker is the Buddha himself.
64 Commenting on Khemā's exposition, Harvey 1983, 36 reasons that this shows a Tathāgata "is free *from being reckoned*, known or fathomed *by means* of material shape [etc.], and not freed *by* reckoning *it* or freed *from* reckoning *it*."
65 Karunadasa 1994, 8 points out that "there is no identifiable self-entity called Tathāgata, either to be perpetuated or annihilated after 'death.'"
66 MN 72 at MN I 487,31; see also Anālayo 2011b, 393.
67 Thī 139 to Thī 144.
68 Spk I 191,24; see Bodhi 2000, 427n343.
69 See Anālayo 2014b, 116–19.
70 SN 5.3 at SN I 131,11.
71 SĀ 1204 at T 2.99.328a6 and SĀ² 220 at T 2.100.455b17.
72 Thī-a 122,19.
73 MN 22 at MN I 130,28 and SN 5.1 at SN I 128,25; see also Anālayo 2011b, 148n17.
74 Ud 1.10 at Ud 9,5; the commentary Ud-a 98,10 relates the whole verse to Nirvana. A similarly worded parallel occurs in Uv 26.26–27, Bernhard 1965, 330.
75 EĀ 5.1 at T 2.125.558c23, with a parallel in AN 1.14.5 at AN I 25,20.
76 EĀ 9.2 at T 2.125.562b19, with parallels in SN 17.24 at SN II 236,16, AN 2.12.2 at AN I 88,16, and AN 4.176 at AN II 164,7. The *Mahāvastu*, Senart 1882, 251,21, lists Kṣemā and Utpalavarṇā as the two chief nuns.
77 The text actually speaks of shaving off their hair *and beard*. Since this must be a copyist's mistake influenced by the more frequently occurring corresponding phrase for males, the reference to the beard has not been translated.
78 The Chinese character employed here, which literally means "limit," appears to be a rendering of *pramāṇa*.
79 SĀ 1201 at T 2.99.326c13 (discourses SĀ 1198 to SĀ 1207 have already been translated in Anālayo 2014b), with parallels in SN 5.5 at SN I 131,18 and SĀ² 217 at T 2.100.454b11 (a translation and study of discourses SĀ² 214 to SĀ² 223 can be found in Bingenheimer 2011, 151–81).
80 Vin III 35,6.
81 SN 5.5 at SN I 132,11.

82 SĀ² 217 at T 2.100.454b29.
83 MN 50 at MN I 332,4 and its parallels MĀ 131 at T 1.26.620b11, T 1.66.864b7, and T 1.67.867a7 report that Māra entered the belly of Mahāmoggallāna/Mahāmaudgalyāyana. According to T 1.5.165a12, on another occasion Māra entered Ānanda's belly.
84 SĀ² 217 at T 2.100.454c5.
85 SN 45.167 at SN V 57,8.
86 The verses translated here are Thī 227 to Thī 235.
87 According to Thī-a 189,4, the relevant verses reflect a rather complex narrative whose thread results in both mother and daughter being married to the same man. A considerably more complex story in the Mūlasarvāstivāda *Vinaya* combines various types of repeated incest and in this case is related to Utpalavarṇā herself; see Silk 2008/2009, 137–63.
88 The first two verses, however, do not employ the third person singular.
89 See in more detail Anālayo 2017d, 96–114.
90 The Pāli editions differ here, so that an alternative to "such-like" would be "glorious" as a way of qualifying the Buddha in his role as a protector.
91 Thī-a 190,15.
92 Dhp-a III 211,21; see also Mp I 356,13.
93 This tale can be found, for example, in SĀ 604 at T 2.99.169c25 (this text does not belong to the original discourse collection and only became part of it due to a mix-up of folios from different Chinese translations), EĀ 36.5 at T 2.125.707c4 (and in its commentary T 25.1507.37c29), and in the Chinese counterpart to the *Aṭṭhakavagga*, T 4.198.185c9; see also the *Divyāvadāna*, Cowell and Neil 1886: 401,24, and for further references Lamotte 1949/1981, 634n1. Although not all of these versions explicitly mention a chariot, the same can be assumed to be implicit, as such a chariot would have been the most appropriate means of travel for a wheel-turning king.
94 Strong 2010, 974 comments that "she magically takes on the form of a cakravartin king, complete with the 32 marks of the great man. In this way she goes 'up' to greet the Blessed One. This is all the more remarkable since, as is well known, becoming a cakravartin king is precisely one of the things that women, at least in the *Lotus Sūtra*, are said to be incapable of doing." On the lateness of this stipulation on what is impossible for women see Anālayo 2009a.
95 T 25.1509.137a13; the title of this work, only extant in Chinese, is often reconstructed as the *Mahāprajñāpāramitāśāstra*, although *Mahāprajñāpāramitopadeśa* would probably be more accurate.
96 Thī-a 190,30. Dhammadinnā 2021: 90n43 notes, regarding such references in the *Therīgāthā* in general to a nun being just by herself, that a "poetic hagiography in verse with the spotlight on specific features and symbols of the ascetic live need not be taken literally, for example ruling out that another nun would be meditating not far from the *therī* in question yet allowing her enough seclusion, or [ruling out] that the featured nun would be accompanied by a follower on her tours."
97 SN 5.5 at SN I 131,29: *na c' atthi te dutiyā vaṇṇadhātu*, "and there is none second to you in the sphere of beauty."
98 SĀ² 217 at T 2.100.454b22.
99 The commentary quoted above in note 96 in fact relates her unrivalled beauty to her being alone in a place without people.
100 See in more detail Anālayo 2020/2022.

101 EĀ 5.1 at T 2.125.558c24.
102 Anālayo 2015b, 14n20.
103 For discussions of such variations see, for example, Bapat 1937, Dantinne 1991, 24–30, Ganguly 1989, 21–23, Nanayakkara 1989, 584, Ray 1994, 293–98, and Wilson 2004, 33.
104 Vism 59,16.
105 AN 1.14.5 at AN I 25,30.
106 SĀ 1200 at T 2.99.326b22, with parallels in SN 5.3 at SN I 130,4 and SĀ² 216 at T 2.100.454a22.
107 Thī-a 169,10; for a similar story see T 4.212.618b12.
108 Thī 213 to Thī 215 and Thī 222 to Thī 223.
109 A reference to "in all" (as a rendering of *pi* when this is related to a numeral) is not found in the PTS edition.
110 Thī-a 172,5.
111 Thī-a 106,14.
112 EĀ 5.1 at T 2.125.559a3, with its counterpart in AN 1.14.5 at AN I 25,21.
113 The Pāli editions differ, with the alternative that she said this with her mind "well" released.
114 DN 26 at DN II 93,14 (for a comparative study of the parallels see Waldschmidt 1944, 70–72) and SN 55.8 at SN V 357,11, with parallels in SĀ 852 at T 2.99.217b8 and Up 9035 at D 4094 *nyu* 94a2 and P 5595 *thu* 142b1.
115 EĀ 5.1 at T 2.125.559a6.
116 Some Pāli discourses without parallel reflect the high regard in which the four *paṭisambhidā*s were held: AN 5.86 at AN III 113,12 notes that other monastics will highly esteem a monastic who possesses five qualities, four of which are the *paṭisambhidā*s. AN 5.95 at AN III 120,1 specifies that a monastic endowed with five qualities will quickly attain to the highest, the five again including the four *paṭisambhidā*s. AN 4.173 at AN II 160,21 reports Sāriputta's attainment of the four *paṭisambhidā*s within a fortnight of being ordained.
117 AN 1.14.3 at AN I 24,29 and EĀ 4.3 at T 2.125.557b24.
118 SĀ 1204 at T 2.99.327c22, with parallels in SN 5.4 at SN I 130,30 and SĀ² 220 at T 2.100.455b7.
119 SĀ² 220 at T 2.100.455b13.
120 Thī 169 to Thī 174.
121 Thī 37 and Thī 42.
122 Thī-a 42,22.
123 AN 6.55 at AN III 374,10 (= Vin I 182,5), MĀ 123 at T 1.26.612a2, SĀ 254 at T 2.99.62b24, EĀ 23.3 at T 2.125.612a24, T 22.1428.844b9, T 22.1421.146a24, and Gnoli 1978, 142,9; see also Waldschmidt 1968.
124 Thī-a 157,23.
125 See in more detail Anālayo 2013c, 201–5.
126 SĀ 1205 at T 2.99.328a21, parallel to SN 5.6 at SN I 132,21 and SĀ² 221 at T 2.100.455c2; see also Enomoto 1994, 43.
127 The translation is based on adopting a variant.
128 See in more detail Anālayo 2018b and 2019d.
129 The text supplemented in square brackets appears to have been lost.
130 On specific conditionality as against interdependence or interconnectedness see Anālayo 2021b.

131 For a comparative study of what according to tradition was the Buddha's first sermon see Anālayo 2012a and 2013a .
132 SN 5.6 at SN I 132,23.
133 Thī-a 159,21.
134 Thī 189 to Thī 195.
135 Thī-a 162,4.
136 SN 5.6 at SN I 132,27.
137 SN 5.6 at SN I 133,1.
138 EĀ 5.3 at T 2.125.559b2.
139 AN 8.30 at AN IV 229,1 and its parallels MĀ 74 at T 1.26.540c24, T 1.46.835c17, and EĀ 42.6 at T 2.125.754a21.
140 MN 122 at MN III 110,16 and its parallel MĀ 191 at T 1.26.738a20 and a Tibetan parallel, Skilling 1994, 194,13.
141 SĀ 1206 at T 2.99.328b22, parallel to SN 5.7 at SN I 133,9 and SĀ[2] 222 at T 2.100.455c29.
142 See in more detail Gethin 1997.
143 For a discussion of the range of meanings of the term *saṅkhāra* see Anālayo 2006c.
144 SN 5.7 at SN I 133,17.
145 SĀ[2] 222 at T II 456a12.
146 Thī-a 165,21, commenting on the corresponding verse Thī 200. For a Tibetan parallel to the relevant verses in SĀ 1206 see Chung 2008, 229.
147 DN 33 at DN III 217,19 and its parallels in Sanskrit fragments, Stache-Rosen 1968, 79, DĀ 9 at T 1.1.50a23, and T 1.12.228b11.
148 Thī 196 to Thī 203.
149 My understanding of *asecanaka* is indebted to the discussion in Bailey 1958, 530–31 and Rotman 2009, 235n46, which in the present case of being combined with *ojava* gives me the impression that the relevant line intends to convey that, in a spiritual sense, Nirvana (= the state of peace) is profoundly nourishing in such a way that one will never get enough of it, one will never get tired or be sated of such nourishment.
150 Thī-a 164,7.
151 SN 5.7 at SN I 133,14.
152 The explicit reference "to me" is not found in all Pāli editions.
153 SN 5.7 at SN I 133,21.
154 SĀ 1207 at T 2.99.328c25, parallel to SN 5.8 at SN I 133,27 and SĀ[2] 223 at T 2.100.456a27; see also SHT VI 1399, Bechert and Wille 1989, 118, and SHT X 4236, Wille 2008, 331.
155 SN 5.8 at SN I 133,29.
156 SĀ[2] 223 at T 2.100.456b3.
157 DN 2 at DN I 52,21, DĀ 27 at T 1.1.108a27, T 1.22.271b25, EĀ 43.7 at T 2.125.763b4, and a discourse quotation in the *Saṅghabhedavastu*, Gnoli 1978, 220,22.
158 The parallel versions mentioned in the previous note differ considerably regarding which doctrine should be attributed to what teacher; see Bapat 1948, 109–12, Basham 1951, 21–24, Vogel 1970, Meisig 1987, 124–69, and MacQueen 1988, 148–68.
159 T 23.1440.536a22, already noted by Deeg 2005, 310n1512.
160 See Anālayo 2009b, 183–85.
161 See Anālayo 2006a and 2020f, 21–25.

162 Thī 182 to Thī 188.
163 Thī-a 160,29.
164 On the range of meaning of the corresponding Pāli term *dhamma* see the detailed study by Geiger and Geiger 1920.
165 SN 5.8 at SN I 134,2.
166 SĀ 1203 at T 2.99.327b24, parallel to SN 5.9 at SN I 134,11 and SĀ² 219 at T 2.100.455a12.
167 SN 5.9 at SN I 134,13 and Spk I 193,21.
168 See in more detail Bingenheimer 2011, 156–59, who concludes that the identifications in the Chinese versions are probably more reliable than their Pāli counterparts.
169 For a survey of several examples see Anālayo 2007b.
170 SN 5.9 at SN I 134,27. SĀ² 219 at T 2.100.455a23 mentions just the earth, which Bingenheimer 2011, 173n46 considers to be due to a loss of text.
171 AN 3.76 at AN I 223,21 (noted by Ñāṇananda 2003, 75 as the key to understanding SN 5.9); see also EĀ² 42 at T 2.150A.881c11.
172 SĀ 1328 at T 2.99.365b21, parallel to SN 10.11 at SN I 213,18 and SĀ² 326 at T 2.100.483b10. In the Pāli tradition there is some uncertainty regarding her name, in fact Bodhi 2000, 314 follows the alternative reading Dhīrā. As noted by Bingenheimer 2011, 153, the Chinese parallels support the reading Vīrā (see also below note 176).
173 SĀ 1327 at T 2.99.365b1 and SĀ² 327 at T 2.100.483c3. Bingenheimer 2020, 807 reasons that, since in both collections the "two discourses correspond closely in structure and content to each other," it can be assumed that "they formed early on through reduplication." Yet, closer inspection shows several minor variations between SĀ 1327 and SĀ 1328 as well as between SĀ² 326 and SĀ² 327, which makes the assumption of a reduplication considerably less probable.
174 SN 10.9 at SN I 212,27 (= Thī 54–55), SN 10.10 at SN I 213,6, and SN 10.11 at SN I 213,18.
175 This is the *Vinaya* of the Mahāsāṅghika-Lokottaravādins, Roth 1970, 112,18, which reports verses by a celestial in praise of Śuklā (although in the reverse order, as the first stanza praises the gift of a robe to her and the second and third stanza then eulogize her qualities).
176 Thī 7; a similar pun in relation to Sukkā can be found at Thī 56, preceded by two verses reporting the verses of the sprite in the episode discussed above. In the case of Thī 7, some editions read *dhīrā*, "firm," instead of *vīrā*, "heroic," and then refer to the speaker as "another Dhīrā." This is the name of the nun speaking the preceding verse Thī 6. It seems safe to assume that a transmission error has occurred, influenced by this preceding verse, leading to a replacing of *vīrā* in Thī 7with *dhīrā* both in the verse and in the name of the speaker (see also above note 172). As this results in two single verses by a nun of the same name, an attempt to make sense of this situation could then have led to the addition of *aññatarā*, "another," to the second reference to Dhīrā.
177 SĀ 1202 at T 2.99.327a25, parallel to SN 5.10 at SN I 135,4 and SĀ² 218 at T 2.100.454c18; see also Enomoto 1994, 42 and Up 9014 at D 4094 *nyu* 82a1 or P 5595 *thu* 128a2 (for a detailed study of the latter see Dhammadinnā 2020).
178 This has already been noted by Vetter 2000, 157.
179 Mil 28,5, which in line with the identification in SN 5.10 speaks of the nun Vajirā (through curiously qualified as having delivered this simile in the presence of the

Buddha); see also Kv 66,13. The Chinese parallel, T 32.1670B.706b12, does not mention her name (strictly speaking this is one of two extant Chinese parallels, both of which appear to stem from a single original; see Takakusu 1896, Demiéville 1924, and Guang Xing 2009).

180 See in more detail Anālayo 2013b, 17–23.

181 See, e.g., von Hinüber 1996/1997, 83 and for a detailed comparative study Minh Chau 1964.

182 Mil 28,4: *paramatthato pan' ettha puggalo nūpalabbhati.* This relates to a position taken by Nāgasena at the outset, when being asked his name, Mil 25,12: *na h' ettha puggalo upalabbhatī ti.* These statements are not found in the Chinese version; see in more detail Anālayo 2021f.

183 Vism 593,16: *na satto na puggalo atthī ti* and 593,32: *paramatthato ekekasmiṃ aṅge upaparikkhiyamāne ratho nāma n' atthi.*

184 T 48.2005.294a7: "Master Yue'an asked a monastic: 'Xi Zhong made chariots [with wheels that had] one hundred spokes. However, take [the wheels] at its two ends and put them apart from the axle. Explain: how is this state of affairs?' Wumen comments: 'If you gain understanding right away, your [wisdom] eye is similar to a comet; your [mind's] movement as fast as lightening.' He said in verse: 'The place where the wheel rotates confuses even an adept about the four directions, above and below, north, south, east, and west.'"

Master Yue'an is an eminent Chan master of the eleventh to twelfth century. Xi Zhong is the legendary inventor of chariots in ancient China. Wumen is the compiler of the *Gateless Barrier* (無門關), in which he usually presents a particular case, followed by offering a comment in prose and in verse to bring out the meaning of the case he has quoted. His comment on what is the eighth case in his collection implies that an instant understanding of the problem posed by Master Yue'an would be highly exceptional, comparable to a comet or to lightening.

185 Thī 57 to Thī 59.

186 EĀ 5.4 at T 2.125.559b11.

187 SĀ 1199 at T 2.99.326a21, parallel to SN 5.2 at SN I 129,11 and SĀ² 215 at T 2.100.454a1.

188 SN 5.2 at SN I 129,15. Rajapakse 1995, 13n14 comments that "it is interesting to note that the doubts in question are raised by Māra ... who thus assumes the role of a 'male chauvinist' in this setting." Abeynayake 2003, 3 adds that this challenge probably reflects "the condemnation that the society had towards women during this period."

189 SĀ² 215 at T II 454a2.

190 Thī-a 65,7.

191 Spk I 189,19; see Bodhi 2000, 425n336.

192 See, for example, the *Mahāvastu*, Marciniak 2019, 503,16 and 504,6 (= Senart 1897, 391,19 and 392,13).

193 In addition to the publications mentioned elsewhere in the present chapter, examples are Dhirasekara 1967, 157, Church 1975, 57, Gokhale 1976, 104, Lang 1986, 77, Bancroft 1987, 82, Kusumā 1987/2010, 26, Falk 1989, 161, Sponberg 1992, 9, Dewaraja 1999, 67, Harvey 2000/2005, 359, Dhammavihari 2002/2011, 6, Faure 2003, 120, Bentor 2008, 126–27, Anālayo 2009a, 137 (also 2010d, 74), and Choubey 2009, 6–7.

194 See in more detail Anālayo 2014b, 116–19 and 138–39.

195 SĀ 964 at T 2.99.246c14 (the original abbreviates the description of full awakening,

which has been supplemented from T 2.99.53c21) and 246c22, parallel to MN 73 at MN I 490,24, SĀ^2 198 at T 2.100.446b13, and T 24.1482.963b17; the assumption by Garling 2021, 172 that the wanderer was at this point already a disciple of the Buddha is not correct.

196 See in more detail Anālayo 2017a.

197 Thī 60 to Thī 62.

198 SĀ 1198 at T 2.99.325c22, parallel to SN 5.1 at SN I 128,9 and SĀ^2 214 at T 2.100.453c3.

199 The translation "torture" is based on adopting a variant reading.

200 SN 5.1 at SN I 128,26.

201 SN 4.25 at SN I 124,24 and its parallels SHT V 1441 R, Sander and Waldschmidt 1985, 257, SĀ 1092 at T 2.99.286c29, and SĀ^2 31 at T 2.100.383c1; see also the *Lalitavistara*, Lefmann 1902, 378,14, and the *Mahāvastu*, Marciniak 2019, 361,17 (= Senart 1897, 282,4).

202 For a comparative study of the dictum according to which only men can occupy certain positions, one of them being Māra, see Anālayo 2009a.

203 SN 4.21 at SN I 117,23 and its parallel SĀ 1099 at T 2.99.289a15.

204 In addition to the case mentioned in the previous note, see SN 4.16 at SN I 112,17 and SĀ 1102 at T 2.99.290a17; SN 4.17 at SN I 113,16 and SĀ 1103 at T 2.99.290b2; and SN 4.22 at SN I 119,18 and SĀ 1100 at T 2.99.289b28. In each of these episodes, the monk(s) fail to recognize Māra. Not all monks, however, are unable to recognize Māra. In MN 50 at MN I 332,11 and its parallels MĀ 131 at T 1.26.620b17, T 1.66.864b14, and T 1.67.867a11 a monk (who was an arahant) immediately recognizes Māra. Another case is EĀ 16.1 at T 1.125 578c22, where a monk, on being addressed by Māra, recognizes him.

205 EĀ 5.2 at T 2.125.559a13.

206 AN 1.14.5 at AN I 25,22.

207 Up 1005 at Si 3323 *ju* 14,21, which corresponds to D 4094 *ju* 6b4 or P 5595 *tu* 7b2, already translated in Anālayo 2011a (see also 2019a), with parallels in MN 44 at MN I 299,5 and MĀ 210 at T 1.26.788a17. Up 1005 relates to the discourse quotation in the *Abhidharmakośabhāṣya* that cessation has no counterpart, *asabhāgo nirodha*, Abhidh-k 1.6, Pradhan 1967, 4,7; see also the *Abhidharmakośavyākhyā*, Wogihara 1932, 16,27.

208 Ps II 355,29; see also Mp I 361,6, Thī-a 15,26, and Dhp-a IV 229,1.

209 See Finnegan 2009, 157–60 and 202–8 as well as Clarke 2014, 48–50 and Yao 2015.

210 Up 1005 at Si 3323 *ju* 14,19 refers to him as "venerable [Vi]sākha," *tshe dang ldan pa sa ga*, though the next sentence introduces him as a lay follower, *dge bsnyen sa ga*, an expression used throughout the remainder of the discourse. The qualification "lay follower," *dge bsnyen*, makes it clear that "venerable," *tshe dang ldan pa*, in the present context cannot have the meaning of marking him off as a monastic. In fact, a similar usage to address laity features in the monastic code of rules in the Mahāsāṅghika *Vinaya*, Tatia 1975, 14,11, the Mūlasarvāstivāda *Vinaya*, Banerjee 1977, 26,10, the Sarvāstivāda *Vinaya*, von Simson 2000, 186,14, and the Theravāda *Vinaya*, Pruitt and Norman 2001, 32,8. The Tibetan version of the Mūlasarvāstivāda code of rules, Vidyabhusana 1915, 67,2, indeed uses *tshe dang ldan pa*. In such contexts, the translation "venerable" would not fit and instead another form of address like "honorable" is required.

211 Up 1005 at Si 3323 *ju* 15,10 here speaks of the "view of [a reified sense of] identity," *'jig tshogs la lta ba*, even though the inquiry was just about "[a reified sense of] identity," *'jig thogs*, and afterward the discussion continues speaking just of the same. My translation is based on emending the present reference to read just *'jig thogs*, assuming that a transmission error occurred, influenced by the circumstance that later on the subject of *'jig tshogs la lta ba* will be broached.
212 Here and below, my translation is based on emending *srid pa* to *sred pa*, following Vetter 2000, 122.
213 See Anālayo 2008b, 405–6.
214 On this type of presentation see also Wayman 1979.
215 On stream-entry see, e.g., Anālayo 2021d.
216 MN 44 at MN I 299,27.
217 The discussion proceeds from inquiring after the nonexistence of the "view of [a reified sense of] identity" in MĀ 210 at T 1.26.788b4 to inquiring about the cessation of "[a reified sense of] identity" at T 1.26.788b12. This stands a bit out of context and may be a remnant of an earlier examination of the arising and cessation of [a reified sense of] identity.
218 MĀ 210 at T 1.26.788a17: 法樂.
219 Anālayo 2007b, 32–34.
220 MN 44 at MN I 300,31 and MĀ 210 at T 1.26.788b25.
221 See in more detail Anālayo 2020/2022.
222 MN 44 at MN I 301,8; see the discussion in Anālayo 2011b, 280–81.
223 For a more detailed discussion see Anālayo 2016b.
224 An example for such a confusion is the position taken by Thompson 2020, 78 that "nirvana, in being the unconditioned, can't be the result of any cause ... this implies that nirvana can't be the result of following the Buddhist path." For a critical reply see Anālayo 2022e.
225 On the early Buddhist perspective on mental construction and the role of bare awareness as a meditative tool for a potential deconstruction see Anālayo 2019c and 2023.
226 MĀ 210 at T I 788c16.
227 The first two factors mentioned here correspond to *vitakka* and *vicāra* in Pāli, on the significance of which see Anālayo 2017c, 123–28.
228 MĀ 210 at T I 788c19.
229 MN 43 at MN I 294,28.
230 See in more detail Anālayo 2017c, 109–50, 2019e, 2020b, and 2022c, 178–97.
231 MĀ 210 at T 1.26.788c24 and MN 44 at MN I 301,13.
232 On the latter see in more detail Anālayo 2022c, 198–207.
233 Anālayo 2019e.
234 MĀ 210 at T 1.26.788c26.
235 The translation is based on deleting a repetition of "formations" in the question.
236 MN 44 at MN I 301,17 and MĀ 210 at T 1.26.789a1 respectively.
237 MN 43 at MN I 296,11.
238 MN 44 at MN I 301,21.
239 See Bodhi 1998, 57–63.
240 In a comment on Visākha's inquiry about how the attainment of cessation takes place, Mahāsi 1981/2006, 118 notes that this "question was asked to find out whether

Dhammadinnā had ever achieved attainment of cessation ... and whether she was able to accomplish it completely with success."

241 MN 50 at MN I 333,19 and its parallels MĀ 131 at T 1.26.620c22, T 1.66.864c19, T 1.67.867a28, and Up 2049 at D 4094 *ju* 75b7 or P 5595 *tu* 85b4. On the attainment of cessation see also Griffiths 1986/1991.

242 On this topic see also Schmithausen 1987/2007, 19–20 and Pieris 2003.

243 MĀ 211 at T 1.26.792a9, which differs insofar as, according to its account, the bodily formation ceases first and arises last; see also Anālayo 2007a, 51–52.

244 MN 44 at MN I 302,26 and MĀ 210 at T 1.26.789b10.

245 MN 44 at MN I 302,22; see also Choong 1999, 62–63.

246 The term used in Up 1005 at Si 3323 *ju* 22,1 is *rgyas par 'gyur*.

247 See also Anālayo 2017e.

248 For a more detailed exploration of the meditative practice of contemplating feeling tones see Anālayo 2021c.

249 MN 44 at MN I 304,16.

250 See above note 224.

251 MN 44 at MN I 304,33.

252 Mahāsi 1981/2006, 98 comments that "it is hard to answer that question unless one is well-versed in the knowledge of *Ariya-magga*," that is, the attainment of the supramundane path, yet she "easily tackled the question." Regarding her exposition of the three formations, Mahāsi 1981/2006, 118 points out that her "ability to clarify those three kinds of *saṅkhāra*s, which are highly profound and philosophical, is immensely praiseworthy. Even nowadays, there will be only a few among intellectual persons well-versed in Piṭaka Buddhist scriptures, who may be able to tackle these difficult questions" on their own.

253 For a survey of such references see Anālayo 2011a, 22n56. In contrast to this assessment, Collett 2021, 100 sees a negative evaluation manifesting in Pāli commentaries, as according to her judgement the account of what preceded the discussion between Dhammadinnā and Visākha reflects "a thoroughgoing reversal of the original canonical discourse" in that Visākha "is the one with knowledge and understanding while Dhammadinnā is ignorant." Yet, this is only natural since at that point in the narrative Visākha has already become a nonreturner whereas Dhammadinnā is still a worldling and apparently hears for the first time about the Buddha's teachings. Thus, for him to have more knowledge and understanding at this point in the narrative is in keeping with the basic principle of according preeminence to spiritual realization that also underpins their discussion in the discourse, by the time of which she has surpassed him in matters of knowledge and understanding through becoming an arahant.

Another supposed problem is that, after Dhammadinnā has expressed her wish to go forth, "Visākha *took her* to the nuns" (100), a depiction seemingly depriving her of agency. For Dhammadinnā to be granted the going forth, the nuns need to ascertain that she has her husband's permission, this being one of the potential stumbling blocks to becoming a nun (for the text and a translation of the corresponding inquiry see Anālayo 2018a, 154–56). Hence, the way Ps II 357,28 depicts Visākha taking action need not be considered problematic. This and other details in the whole description appear to be simply meant to express, in line with the expectations and requirements of the ancient setting, that Visākha did his very best to facilitate her going forth. In other words, any lack of agency is probably better attributed to the actual limitations of being a married woman in the ancient setting rather than to a negative attitude by the commentarial narrators.

Yet another problem identified by Collett 2021, 100 is that "in one commentary it is the Buddha's omniscience, rather than her own individual intellect, that produces her insightful answers to Visākha's questions." Commenting on the same issue, Collett 2021, 99 notes that "[a]ccording to this commentary, the Buddha had used his omniscience to enable her to know the answers to the questions." This thereby "puts in a caveat that destabilizes this exposition of Dhammadinna as [a] wise teacher." Closer inspection shows that the reference in Thī-a 18,30 to the Buddha's omniscience does not concern an influence exerted on Dhammadinnā's actual exposition but much rather explains what stands in the background of the Buddha's placing her foremost among nuns in being a speaker of the Dharma, a position she gained herself precisely through her own powerful exposition. In fact, since omniscience is not a readily transferrable quality, it could not inform the teachings given by someone else (such as Dhammadinnā in the present case) but only those given by the one who is omniscient (that is, by the Buddha himself).

The above is certainly not meant to deny that at times pronouncedly negative attitudes toward women can manifest in the Pāli commentarial tradition (see, e.g., Anālayo 2014c). The point is only that, as far as I am able to see, Dhammadinnā's powerful exposition and profound wisdom have been adequately recognized in later tradition.

254 Thī-a 55,25. Krey 2010, 20n12 notes that Dhammadinnā's role as a teacher of other nuns is also documented in the Mahāsāṅghika *Vinaya*; see Roth 1970, 52,10.

255 Thī-a 74,27.

256 Thī 12; with counterparts in Dhp 218 and Uv 2.9, Bernhard 1965, 114.

257 Thī-a 19,1.

258 AN 10.28 at AN V 54,26; on Kajaṅgalā see also Durt 2005.

259 My rendering follows the reasoning presented by Bodhi 2012, 1838n2003.

260 On this pattern in abbreviation see Anālayo 2020e, 2021a, and 2022a.

261 AN 10.27 at AN V 50,22, EĀ 46.8 at T 2.125.778c11, and Jantrasrisalai, Lenz, Qian, and Salomon 2016, 43.

262 Pj I 75,25, commenting on Khp 2,11.

263 SN 41.8 at SN IV 299,27, with a parallel in SĀ 574 at T 2.99.152c26.

264 EĀ 46.8 at T 2.125.778c19.

265 The Chinese character used here, 念, often renders "mindfulness" or "thought," although in the present context it appears to serve rather as a translation of *saṃkalpa*; see Anālayo 2020a, 1132.

266 EĀ 46.8 at T 2.125.778c24.

267 See also Anālayo 2020c.

268 On the construction of experience in early Buddhist thought see Anālayo 2019c and 2023.

269 EĀ 46.8 at T 2.125.779a1.

270 Anālayo 2013c, 8–12 and 2022c, 199–206.

271 EĀ 46.8 at T 2.125.779a12.

272 Khp 2,14, which continues with the five aggregates of clinging, the six internal sense-spheres, the seven awakening factors, the noble eight-fold path, the nine abodes of sentient beings, and the ten factors of an arahant.

273 AN 10.27 at AN V 52,5.
274 See in more detail Nyanaponika 1981.
275 EĀ 46.8 at T 2.125.779a24.
276 AN 10.27 at AN V 52,18.
277 The Pāli editions tend to abbreviate the exposition for the sixes to eights. For ease of reading, I expand the relevant parts, in line with the text provided for the fours and fives.
278 See Anālayo 2015a, 45–46.
279 See Anālayo 2017c, 184–92.
280 EĀ 46.8 at T 2.125.779b11.
281 AN 10.27 at AN V 52,31.
282 EĀ 46.8 at T 2.125.779b26 and AN 10.27 at AN V 53,9.
283 The Pāli editions differ on whether to precede the reference to the "noble eightfold path" with an additional reference to "eight." The context makes this in my view the preferable reading, as a query about eight items requires a reply that indeed lists eight. This is the case for the eight members of the path, whereas the eightfold path as such would, strictly speaking, amount to just a single item.
284 EĀ 46.8 at T 2.125.779c9 and AN 10.27 at AN V 53,22.
285 AN 10.27 at AN V 54,13.
286 See, e.g., Anālayo 2006b.
287 EĀ 46.8 at T 2.125.779c26.
288 This has already been noted by Legittimo 2012, 368 n151, who comments that "the explanations given by the nun bear a similar meaning as the 'base text' but they are given 'in positive form,' i.e., from the perspective of what one should engage in and not from the perspective of what one should avoid."
289 This holds in particular from a comparative perspective, which shows that the faculty of mindfulness is predominantly concerned with the four establishments, the topic of memory being of only secondary relevance; see Anālayo 2020d, 28–33.
290 See in more detail Anālayo 2019b.
291 EĀ 5.2 at T 2.125.559a12.
292 AN 1.14.5 at AN I 25,24.
293 The translated portion begins in EĀ 38.11 at T 2.125.727c5; already translated in Anālayo 2015d.
294 On the Monkey Pond see Anālayo 2011b, 223n95.
295 The translation is based on adopting a variant reading.
296 DN 2 at DN I 52,21, DĀ 27 at T 1.1.108a27, T 1.22.271b25, EĀ 43.7 at T 2.125.763b4, and a discourse quotation in the *Saṅghabhedavastu*, Gnoli 1978, 220,22; see also above p. 76.
297 DN 24 at DN III 12,18 and its parallels DĀ 15 at T 1.1.67c11 and SHT IV 32.7 R, Sander and Waldschmidt 1980, 113; see also Anālayo 2015c.
298 My rendering of the nun's name as Soṇā is based on an emendation, in line with the rendering found in EĀ 5.2. Since both discourses occur in the same collection and equally consider her foremost among nuns for the same quality, I take it that they must be intending the same person.
299 An instance found apart from the early discourses would be T 4.202.420b9, which reports how Śāriputra defeated the six teachers. On the textual history of T 202 see Mair

1993 and 1993/1999. According to the *Divyāvadāna*, Cowell and Neil 1886, 160,13, Mahāmaudgalyāyana would also have been able to defeat the six teachers.

300 Thī 102 to Thī 106.

301 The translation of this line follows the Asian editions; the PTS edition differs rather substantially here.

302 EĀ 5.1 at T 2.125.559a5.

303 AN 1.14.5 at AN I 25,29; see also the accomplishments of Yasodharā in Ap 28.22–23 at Ap 586,5.

304 AN 1.14.5 at AN I 25,31 and AN 1.14.7 at AN I 26,24 reckon the nun Sigālamātā as foremost in being liberated by confidence and the female lay disciple Kātiyānī as foremost in experiential confidence (*aveccapasāda*).

305 Mp I 377,1.

306 Garling 2016, 7 reasons that "in some Pāli literature, Rahulamata ('Mother of Rahula') often appears instead [of Yasodharā]. This moniker serves to marginalize her important role in the Buddha's biography."

307 The translated portion begins in EĀ 23.1 at T 2.125.611a25; already translated in Anālayo 2014c.

308 The rendering of the name is based on adopting a variant reading.

309 Here and elsewhere, my reconstruction of Indic names is only tentative.

310 The translation "food" is based on an emendation.

311 SN 12.5 at SN II 9,15 and its parallel SĀ 366 at T 2.99.101b5 describe his insight into dependent arising. A detailed coverage of various aspects of his life can be found in DN 14 at DN II 2,16, and its main parallels Waldschmidt 1956, 69, DĀ 1 at T 1.1.1c21, T 1.2.150a19, T 1.4.159b13, and EĀ 48.4 at T 2.125.790a29.

312 The combining of a meritorious deed with an aspiration is a recurrent pattern in *apadāna*/*avadāna* literature in general; see Clark 2011, 31–32.

313 See in more detail Anālayo 2010a and 2017b.

314 The reference to the "Blessed One" is based on adopting a variant.

315 SN 15.5 at SN II 181,24 and its parallels SĀ 949 at T 2.99.242c7, SĀ² 342 at T 2.100.487c26, and EĀ 52.4 at T 2.125.825c12.

316 The rendering "if" is based on an emendation that has been suggested in the CBETA edition.

317 This occurs eleven times, beginning in Ap 28.65 at Ap 589,15 (notably the Burmese edition has "King of Dharma" instead of "Great King").

318 Walters 2014, 187 in fact wonders if the reference is "to the Buddha? the Buddha's father? someone in the text's audience?" The Sinhala tradition apparently regarded such references to intend King Suddhodana; see Obeyesekere 2009, 62 and 75 for the reasoning and for an example.

319 EĀ 5.2 at T 2.125.559a10.

320 AN 1.14.5 at AN I 25,27.

321 The assumption by Garling 2021, 199 that all arahants and bodhisattvas have perfect recall of their past lives is not correct.

322 The translated portion begins in EĀ 52.2 at T 2.125.823b19; already translated in Anālayo 2014c.

323 MN 83 at MN II 74,15; for a survey of this episode in the parallels see Anālayo 2011b, 468 and on further developments of the same motif Anālayo 2012c, 230–32.

324 The translation "parasol" is here based on an emendation, in line with the term used earlier.
325 See MĀ 32 at T 1.26.470a2, which mentions these two in a list of three such divine qualities. Although the possession of such qualities is not reported explicitly in the parallel MN 123, a comparable presentation can be found in DN 30 at DN III 146,4 as part of a list of ten such divine qualities.
326 The translation "husband and wife" is based on adopting a variant reading.
327 The translation "poem" is based on adopting a variant reading.
328 The translation "sisters" is based on adopting a variant reading.
329 The translation "also" is based on adopting a variant reading.
330 The translation "appeared" is based on adopting a variant reading.
331 The translation "Paccekabuddha" is based on adopting a variant reading.
332 Literally translated the stipulation is that his appearance "will enter my mind."
333 The translation "measure" is based on adopting a variant reading.
334 The translation "who" is based on adopting a variant reading.
335 The translation "I wish" is based on adopting a variant reading.
336 The translation "I" is based on adopting a variant reading. On the idea of transferring merit see also Anālayo 2010b.
337 The translation "either" is based on adopting a variant reading.
338 The translation "her" is based on adopting a variant reading.
339 The translation "become" is based on adopting a variant reading.
340 The eighteen transformations are a series of supernormal performances; see T 30.1579.491c6 or T 46.1912.442a29.
341 Ap 27.37 at Ap 581,13, Thi-a 66,11, and Mp I 375,22.
342 Even King Brahmadattā occurs among her tales of former lives; see Ap 27.53 at Ap 583,1.
343 According to Thī-a 66,20, Bhaddā had been reborn at the time of the Buddha Kassapa as the daughter of a very wealthy merchant in Vārāṇasī.
344 The translation "Buddha" is based on adopting a variant reading.
345 In Ap 27.57 at Ap 583,10 Kapila is instead the name of Bhaddā Kāpilānī's father.
346 The translation "resembled" and the second reference to Kapila are based on adopting variant readings.
347 Commenting on variations in spelling of the Pāli name, Malalasekera 1938/1998, 204 concludes: "The correct form is probably Pippali-māṇava."
348 According to Th-a III 132,33, they went forth at the same time, cutting off each other's hair. Having gone forth, they then separated in order to avoid that others, on seeing them still together, might form a wrong impression of their motivation. Since Mahākassapa was the first of the two to join the Buddhist monastic order, perhaps the reference in EĀ 52.2 intends more specifically the going forth in the Buddhist order.
349 Ap 27.58 at Ap 583,11 reports that an actual image had been made of gold that resembled her. According to Th-a III 130,13, the making of this golden image was due to a stratagem devised by Kassapa to avoid having to marry, as he would only marry a woman that was equal in beauty to the image. The woman who turned out to fulfill this condition was Bhaddā; for a Mūlasarvāstivāda *Vinaya* parallel to this tale see Clarke 2014, 110–11.
350 Thī-a 66,7.

351 The translation is based on adopting a variant reading without a reference to "time."
352 Thī 63 to Thī 66.
353 EĀ 7.2 at T 2.125.560b11.
354 For a comparative study that covers relevant texts in addition to the discourse parallels see Anālayo 2011b, 502–5.
355 T 4.212.650a7.
356 The translated portion begins in MĀ 216 at T 1.26.801c10, with discourse parallels in MN 87 at MN II 110,8, T 1.91.915c17, and EĀ 13.3 at T 2.125.572b21.
357 AN 1.14.7 at AN I 26,18.
358 Ud 8.8 at Ud 91,22.
359 Mp I 417,7.
360 SN 3.8 at SN I 75,3 and Ud 5.1 at Ud 47,3.
361 Spk I 140,8.
362 A somewhat different perspective on the present episode emerges when Bodhi 2000, 401n212 comments, after summarizing the commentarial explanation of what stands in the background to the king's query and presumably as a way of presenting an alternative perspective, that the present exchange "is strikingly reminiscent of the discussion between the sage Yājñavalkya and his wife Maitreyī recorded at Bṛhadāraṇyaka Upaniṣad II.4.5. (also at IV.5.6) ... It is conceivable that the Buddhist conversation is modelled after the Upaniṣad but with a different message" given by the Buddha when commenting on Pasenadi's report of exchange he had had with Mallikā.

When evaluating this interesting suggestion, it could be noted that Pasenadi and Mallikā employ the term "self" just as a reflexive pronoun. In contrast, as pointed out by Bodhi 2000, 402n212, "Yājñavalkya affirms a transcendental Self." The main point of Yājñavalkya's argument is that anyone/anything is dear due to love of the Self (= soul). In the part that precedes the first of the two occurrences of the relevant passage, Yājñavalkya informs Maitreyī of his wish to go forth (II.4.1). Maitreyī responds by declaring her lack of interest in inheriting wealth from him as she rather wants to know from him how to gain immortality (II.4.2–3). Yājñavalkya responds by saying that she is dear to him and speaks what is dear (II.4.4). The stage set by such dearness, due to the similarity between her spiritual yearnings and his own interests (evident in his wish to go forth), then leads on to the passage under discussion. In this passage, Yājñavalkya explains that a husband is not dear for his own sake, but rather *ātmanas tu kāmāya patiḥ priyo bhavati*, "a husband is dear due to love of the Self," followed by applying the same treatment to the wife, sons, wealth, brahminhood, warriorhood, the worlds, gods, sentient beings, and "all." Each of these becomes dear due to love of the permanent Self or soul. That is, Yājñavalkya employs the topic of dearness broached just before to point to the immortal Self, concluding that this Self should be realized (II.4.5).

In SN 3.8 (or Ud 5.1), however, Pasenadi is not intending to go forth and Mallikā is not in quest of immortality. Pasenadi simply asks Mallikā if she loves anyone more than she loves herself and the rest of the conversation is about such self-love, not about sons, wealth, etc. Note also that here Mallikā is the one who gives the actual teaching with her unexpected but honest reply, whereas her counterpart Maitreyī only has the role of asking for a teaching. The Buddha then takes up Mallikā's clarification in his comment, affirming the priority of self-love but endowing it with an altruistic dimension. In this way, it is not only the final message that differs (immortality or altruism). The starting point is also different, as the respective protagonists have quite different concerns and assume different roles. The main point of convergence is a teaching on what is dear that employs the term "self," but then this term carries substantially different connotations in each case. Paraphrasing without using the term self/Self to bring out the difference in the two teachings, Mallikā says: "I love Mallikā more than anyone else," whereas Yājñavalkya says: "the eternal soul is the source of all love, be it for humans, celestials, material possessions, social identities, etc." Thus, in spite of some similarities, the starting point, the actual teaching, and the final message differ substantially. In view of this, it does not seem necessary to bring in Yājñavalkya to make sense of the exchange between Pasenadi and Mallikā, as it appears quite adequate to do so in the light of the commentarial explanation, which does better justice to Mallikā's wisdom.

363 AN 1.14.7 at AN I 26,25.

364 Jantrasrisalai, Lenz, Qian, and Salomon 2016, 87.

365 The translated portion begins in AN 6.16 at AN III 295,17.

366 Mp I 400,17.

367 AN 4.55 at AN II 61,23.

368 The Pāli editions differ here; see Bodhi 2012, 1752n1277. The commentary, Mp III 349,15, supports the meaning of taking another "husband."

369 The elided part has a reference to "after my demise," which appears to be an accidental copying from the previous passage; see the discussion in Bodhi 2012, 1752n1279.

370 Bodhi 2012, 1752n1280 comments on this reference: "It is interesting that she claims to have obtained a foothold in the *dhammavinaya*, which suggests that in certain contexts *vinaya* bears a wider meaning than the code of monastic regulations."

371 Mp III 350,6.

372 See, for example, Burlingame 1917, Brown 1940, Venkatasubbiah 1940, Coomaraswamy 1944, Brown 1968, Wayman 1968, Brown 1972a and 1972b. Thompson 1998, Hara 2009, and Kong 2012.

373 More advice from the early discourses for facing such a situation can be found in Anālayo 2016d.

374 EĀ 7.2 at T 2.125.560b17.

375 AN 1.14.7 at AN I 26,21.

376 Rhys Davids 1913, 41n1, Hare 1955, 35n2, and Bodhi 2012, 1611n143 and 1779n1520 consider these two to be probably the same, whereas Malalasekera 1937/1995, 362 and 1938/1998, 935n9 considers them to be distinct persons.

377 The translated portion begins in AN 7.50 at AN IV 64,25.

378 The Pāli editions agree on mentioning "merit" but vary in regard to the additional reference to an "abundance of merit."

379 Mp IV 36,12.

380 His eminent role can be seen in Sn 557 and Ud 2.8 at Ud 17,29: see also Th 1083 and the *Divyāvadāna*, Cowell and Neil 1886: 394,22.

381 The original has the two related terms in each of these three pairs in the opposite sequence. Besides, the Pāli editions vary on the actual terms used, where my translation choice is indebted to the discussion in Bodhi 2012, 1780n1524.

382 See SN 41.1 at SN IV 282,28 and its parallel SĀ 572 at T 2.99.152a12, SN 41.5 at SN IV 292,1 and its parallel SĀ 566 at T 2.99.149b14, and SN 41.7 at SN IV 296,9 and its parallel SĀ 567 at T 2.99.149c18.

383 EĀ 7.1 at T 2.125.560b1.

384 AN 1.14.7 at AN I 26,19.

385 I am not aware of any indication regarding the two lay role models having complementary skin colors, comparable to the case of Khemā and Uppalavaṇṇā, discussed above p. 36. Perhaps a need to balance lighter and darker skin was considered mainly relevant for the case of chief monastic disciples, who naturally play a more prominent public role.

386 EĀ 9.2 at T II 562b16, with parallels in SN 17.24 at SN II 236,3, AN 2.12.2 at AN I 88,27, and AN 4.176 at AN II 164,17.

387 See above note 78.

388 The preferability of a monastic lifestyle for one wholeheartedly dedicated to progress to awakening finds expression in Sn 221 by comparing the lay life to a peacock, whereas the path of a monastic compares to a goose, whose speed of flight the peacock can never match. Note that this applies to a sagely monastic who dwells meditating in forest seclusion. In other words, if one adopts the monastic lifestyle wisely, as a container for intensive meditation, a higher speed of progress can be expected compared to remaining in the lay life.

389 Mp I 439,1.

390 See Anālayo 2022d, 55–56.

391 Mil 78,23 and T 32.1670B.716c24.

392 See in more detail Anālayo 2021e.

393 DN 33 at DN III 219,9 and its parallels in Sanskrit fragments, Stache-Rosen 1968, 85, DĀ 9 at T 1.1.50b13, and T 1.12.228a22; SN 48.23 at SN V 204,18 and its parallel SĀ 642 at T 2.99.182a15.

394 T 17.765.695c1, parallel to It 62 at It 53,2.

395 The abbreviations are my own; the Chinese original gives the full text for each of the four truths.

396 See above note 131.

397 It 62 at It 53,8: *khayasmiṃ paṭhamaṃ ñāṇaṃ, tato aññā anantarā*. The line recurs in It 102 at It 104,9 and AN 3.84 at AN I 231,15, in which case a related but differently worded counterpart can be found in SĀ 824 at T 2.99.211c7.

398 It 44 at It 38,5 and T 17.765.677a29 together with material supplemented from T 17.765.678a16.

399 It 44 at It 38,19: *tassa idh' eva ... sabbavedayitāni anabhinanditāni sītibhavissanti.*

400 The specification of being a daughter of the Buddha occurs in Thī 46, used by the nun Uttamā in reference to herself; see also Thī 336 for a similar usage by the nun Sundarī.

401 For a translation of the *Ekottarikāgama* list of eminent nuns that supplies most of the names see Anālayo 2014e.

402 EĀ 7.1 to 7.3 at T 2.125.560a29.

403 The corresponding listing of outstanding male lay disciples also mentions several kings and princes; see EĀ 6.3 at T 2.125.560a5.

References

Abeynayake, Oliver. 2003. "Reappraisal of the Position of Women in Buddhism." *Journal of the Centre for Buddhist Studies, Sri Lanka*, 1: 1–16.

Adhya, Sarmishtha. 2006. *Incense on Holy Altar: A Study of Widowhood in Ancient India*. Kolkata: Progressive Publishers.

Altekar, A. S. 1956. *The Position of Women in Hindu Civilization: From Prehistoric Times to the Present Day*. Banaras: Motilal Banarsidass.

Anālayo, Bhikkhu. 2006a. "The Buddha and Omniscience." *Indian International Journal of Buddhist Studies*, 7: 1–20.

———. 2006b. "The Saṃyukta-āgama Parallel to the Sāleyyaka-sutta." *Journal of Buddhist Ethics*, 13: 1–22.

———. 2006c. "Saṅkhārā." In *Encyclopaedia of Buddhism, Volume 7*, edited by W. G. Weeraratne, 732–37. Sri Lanka: Department of Buddhist Affairs.

———. 2007a. "Comparative Notes on the Madhyama-āgama." *Fuyan Buddhist Studies*, 2: 33–56.

———. 2007b. "Who Said It? Authorship Disagreements between Pāli and Chinese Discourses." In *Indica et Tibetica 65: Festschrift für Michael Hahn zum 65. Geburtstag von Freunden und Schülern überreicht*, edited by Konrad Klaus and Jens-Uwe Hartmann, 25–38. Wien: Arbeitskreis für tibetische und buddhistische Studien, Universität Wien.

———. 2008a. "Theories on the Foundation of the Nuns' Order: A Critical Evaluation." *Journal of the Centre for Buddhist Studies*, 6: 105–42.

———. 2008b. "Upādāna." In *Encyclopaedia of Buddhism, Volume 8*, edited by W. G. Weeraratne, 402–8. Sri Lanka: Department of Buddhist Affairs.

———. 2009a. "The Bahudhātuka-sutta and Its Parallels on Women's Inabilities." *Journal of Buddhist Ethics*, 16: 137–90.

———. 2009b. "Views and the Tathāgata: A Comparative Study and Translation of the Brahmajāla in the Chinese Dīrgha-āgama." In *Buddhist and Pali Studies in Honour of the Venerable Professor Kakkapalliye Anuruddha*, edited by K. L. Dhammajoti and Y. Karunadasa, 183–234. Hong Kong: Centre of Buddhist Studies, University of Hong Kong.

———. 2010a. *The Genesis of the Bodhisattva Ideal*. Hamburg: Hamburg University Press.

———. 2010b. "Saccaka's Challenge: A Study of the Saṃyukta-āgama Parallel to the Cūḷasaccaka-sutta in Relation to the Notion of Merit Transfer." *Chung-Hwa Buddhist Journal*, 23: 39–70.

———. 2010c. "Teachings to Lay Disciples: The Saṃyukta-āgama Parallel to the Anāthapiṇḍikovāda-sutta." *Buddhist Studies Review*, 27.1: 3–14.

———. 2010d. "Women's Renunciation in Early Buddhism:The Four Assemblies and the Foundation of the Order of Nuns." In *Dignity and Discipline: The Evolving Role of Women in Buddhism*, edited by Thea Mohr and Jampa Tsedroen, 65–97. Somerville, MA: Wisdom Publications.

———. 2011a. "Chos Sbyin Gyi Mdo: Bhikṣuṇī Dharmadinnā Proves Her Wisdom." *Chung-Hwa Buddhist Journal*, 24: 3–33.

———. 2011b. *A Comparative Study of the Majjhima-nikāya*. Taipei: Dharma Drum Publishing Corporation.

———. 2011c. "Right View and the Scheme of the Four Truths in Early Buddhism: The Saṃyukta-āgama Parallel to the Sammādiṭṭhi-sutta and the Simile of the Four Skills of a Physician." *Canadian Journal of Buddhist Studies*, 7: 11–44.

———. 2011d. "The Tale of King Ma(k)hādeva in the Ekottarika-āgama and the Cakravartin Motif." *Journal of the Centre for Buddhist Studies*, 9: 43–77.

———. 2011e. "Vakkali's Suicide in the Chinese Āgamas." *Buddhist Studies Review*, 28.2: 155–70.
———. 2012a. "The Chinese Parallels to the Dhammacakkappavattana-sutta (1)." *Journal of the Oxford Centre for Buddhist Studies*, 3: 12–46.
———. 2012b. "Dabba's Self-cremation in the Saṃyukta-āgama." *Buddhist Studies Review*, 29.2: 153–74.
———. 2012c. "The Historical Value of the Pāli Discourses." *Indo-Iranian Journal*, 55: 223–53.
———. 2013a. "The Chinese Parallels to the Dhammacakkappavattana-sutta (2)." *Journal of the Oxford Centre for Buddhist Studies*, 5: 9–41.
———. 2013b. "Debate with a Sceptic: The Dīrgha-āgama Parallel to the Pāyāsi-sutta (2)." *Indian International Journal of Buddhist Studies*, 14: 1–27.
———. 2013c. *Perspectives on Satipaṭṭhāna*. Cambridge: Windhorse Publications.
———. 2014a. "The Buddha's Last Meditation in the Dīrgha-āgama." *Indian International Journal of Buddhist Studies*, 15: 1–43.
———. 2014b. "Defying Māra: Bhikkhunīs in the Saṃyukta-āgama." In *Women in Early Indian Buddhism: Comparative Textual Studies*, edited by Alice Collett, 116–39. New York: Oxford University Press.
———. 2014c. "Karma and Female Birth." *Journal of Buddhist Ethics*, 21: 109–53.
———. 2014d. "Maitreya and the Wheel-Turning King." *Asian Literature and Translation: A Journal of Religion and Culture*, 2.7: 1–29.
———. 2014e. "Outstanding Bhikkhunīs in the Ekottarika-āgama." In *Women in Early Indian Buddhism: Comparative Textual Studies*, edited by Alice Collett, 97–115. New York: Oxford University Press.
———. 2015a. *Compassion and Emptiness in Early Buddhist Meditation*. Cambridge: Windhorse Publications.
———. 2015b. "Discourse Merger in the Ekottarika-āgama (1): The Parallel to the Bhaddāli-sutta and the Latukikopama-sutta, Together with Notes on the Chinese Translation of the Collection." *Singaporean Journal of Buddhist Studies*, 2: 5–35.

———. 2015c. "The Buddha's Fire Miracles." *Journal of the Oxford Centre for Buddhist Studies*, 10: 9–42.

———. 2015d: "Miracle-Working Nuns in the Ekottarika-āgama." *Indian International Journal of Buddhist Studies*, 16: 1–27.

———. 2016a. *The Foundation History of the Nuns' Order*. Bochum: Projektverlag.

———. 2016b. "The Gradual Path of Training in the Dīrgha-āgama: From Sense-Restraint to Imperturbability." *Indian International Journal of Buddhist Studies*, 17: 1–24.

———. 2016c. "Levitation in Early Buddhist Discourse." *Journal of the Oxford Centre for Buddhist Studies*, 10: 11–26.

———. 2016d. *Mindfully Facing Disease and Death: Compassionate Advice from Early Buddhist Texts*. Cambridge: Windhorse Publications.

———. 2017a. "Anāgāmin." In *Encyclopedia of Indian Religions: Buddhism and Jainism*, edited by K. T. S Sarao and Jeffery D. Long, 99–101. Dordrecht: Springer.

———. 2017b. *Buddhapada and the Bodhisattva Path*. Bochum: Projektverlag.

———. 2017c. *Early Buddhist Meditation Studies*. Barre: Barre Center for Buddhist Studies.

———. 2017d. *A Meditator's Life of the Buddha: Based on the Early Discourses*. Cambridge: Windhorse Publications.

———. 2017e. "What About Neutral Feelings?" *Insight Journal*, 43: 1–10.

———. 2018a. *Bhikkhunī Ordination from Ancient India to Contemporary Sri Lanka*. New Taipei City: Āgama Research Group.

———. 2018b. *Rebirth in Early Buddhism and Current Research*. Somerville, MA: Wisdom Publications.

———. 2019a. "Comparing the Tibetan and Chinese Parallels to the Cūḷavedalla-sutta." In *Investigating Principles: International Aspects of Buddhist Culture, Essays in Honour of Professor Charles Willemen*, edited by Lalji Shravak and Supriya Rai, 1–36. Hong Kong: The Buddha-Dharma Centre of Hong Kong.

———. 2019b. "Immeasurable Meditations and Mindfulness." *Mindfulness*, 10.12: 2620–28.

———. 2019c. "In the Seen Just the Seen: Mindfulness and the Construction of Experience." *Mindfulness*, 10.1: 179–84.
———. 2019d. "Rebirth and the West." *Insight Journal*, 45: 55–64.
———. 2019e. "The Role of Mindfulness in the Cultivation of Absorption." *Mindfulness*, 10.11: 2341–51.
———. 2019f. "Women in Early Buddhism." *Journal of Buddhist Studies*, 16: 33–76.
———. 2020a. "Attention and Mindfulness." *Mindfulness*, 11.5: 1131–38.
———. 2020b. "A Brief History of Buddhist Absorption." *Mindfulness*, 11.3: 571–86.
———. 2020c. "The Five 'Fingers' of Name." *Insight Journal*, 46: 27–36.
———. 2020d. *Mindfulness in Early Buddhism: Characteristics and Functions*. Cambridge: Windhorse Publications.
———. 2020e. "Peyāla in the Skandha-saṃyukta, Contraction and Expansion in Textual Transmission." In *Research on the Saṃyukta-āgama*, edited by Bhikkhunī Dhammadinnā, 53–108. Taipei: Dharma Drum Corporation.
———. 2020f. "The Tevijjavacchagotta-sutta and the Anupada-sutta in Relation to the Emergence of Abhidharma Thought." *Journal of the Centre for Buddhist Studies*, 17: 21–33.
———. 2020/2022. "The Qualities Pertinent to Awakening: Bringing Mindfulness Home." *Mindfulness*, 13, (forthcoming).
———. 2021a. "Abbreviation in the Madhyama-āgama." *Annual Report of the International Research Institute for Advanced Buddhology at Soka University*, 24: 23–38.
———. 2021b. "Dependent Arising and Interdependence." *Mindfulness*, 12.5: 1094–102.
———. 2021c. *Deepening Insight: Teachings on Vedanā in the Early Buddhist Discourses*. Washington: Pariyatti.
———. 2021d. "The Four Levels of Awakening." *Mindfulness*, 12.4: 831–40.
———. 2021e. "Hearing, Reflection, and Cultivation: Relating the Three Types of Wisdom to Mindfulness." *Religions*, 21.441: 1–12.

———. 2021f. "The Opening Debate in the Milindapañha." *Sri Lanka International Journal of Buddhist Studies*, 2021, 7.2: 15–27.

———. 2021g. *Superiority Conceit in Buddhist Traditions: A Historical Perspective.* Somerville, MA: Wisdom.

———. 2022a. "Abbreviation in the Ekottarika-āgama." *Annual Report of the International Research Institute for Advanced Buddhology at Soka University*, 25: 61–71.

———. 2022b. "Beyond the Limitations of Binary Thinking: Mindfulness and the Tetralemma." *Mindfulness*, 13 (forthcoming).

———. 2022c. *Developments in Buddhist Meditation Traditions: The Interplay between Theory and Practice.* Barre: Barre Center for Buddhist Studies.

———. 2022d. *Early Buddhist Oral Tradition: Textual Formation and Transmission*. Somerville, MA: Wisdom Publications.

———. 2022e. "Situating Mindfulness, Part 2: Early Buddhist Soteriology." *Mindfulness*, 13.4: 855–62.

———. 2023. *The Signless and the Deathless: On the Realization of Nirvana*. Somerville, MA: Wisdom Publications (forthcoming).

Bailey, H. W. 1958. "Arya." *Bulletin of the School of Oriental and African Studies*, 21.1/3: 522–45.

Bancroft, Anne. 1987. "Women in Buddhism." In *Women in the World's Religions: Past and Present*, edited by Ursula King, 81–104. New York: Paragon House.

Banerjee, Anukul Chandra. 1977. *Two Buddhist Vinaya Texts in Sanskrit: Prātimokṣa Sūtra and Bhikṣukarmavākya*. Calcutta: World Press.

Bapat, P. V. 1937. "Dhutaṅgas." *Indian Historical Quarterly*, 13: 44–51.

———. 1948. "The Śrāmaṇyaphala-Sūtra and its Different Versions in Buddhist Literature." *Indian Culture*, 15: 107–14.

Bareau, André. 1979. "La composition et les étapes de la formation progressive du Mahāparinirvāṇasūtra ancient." *Bulletin de l'École Française d'Extrême-Orient*, 66: 45–103.

Basham, A. L. 1951. *History and Doctrine of the Ājīvikas: A Vanished Indian Religion*. London: Luzac.

Bechert, Heinz. 1958. "Über das Apadānabuch. "*Wiener Zeitschrift für die Kunde Süd- und Ostasiens*, 1: 1–21.

Bechert, Heinz and Klaus Wille. 1989. *Sanskrithandschriften aus den Turfanfunden, Teil 6*. Stuttgart: Franz Steiner.

Bentor, Yael. 2008. "Can Women Attain Enlightenment through Vajrayāna Practices?" In *Karmic Passages: Israeli Scholarship on India*, edited by David Shulman and Shalva Weil, 125–40. Delhi: Oxford University Press.

Bernhard, Franz. 1965. *Udānavarga, Band 1*. Göttingen: Vandenhoeck & Ruprecht.

Bingenheimer, Marcus. 2011. *Studies in Āgama Literature: With Special Reference to the Shorter Chinese Saṃyuktāgama*. Taiwan: Shin Weng Feng Print Co.

———. 2020. "A Study and Translation of the Yakṣa-saṃukta in the Shorter Chinese Saṃyukta-āgama." In *Research on the Saṃyukta-āgama*, edited by Bhikkhunī Dhammadinnā, 763–841. Taipei: Dharma Drum Corporation.

Bluck, Robert. 2002. "The Path of the Householder: Buddhist Lay Disciples in the Pāli Canon." *Buddhist Studies Review*, 19.1: 1–18.

Bodhi, Bhikkhu. 1998. "A Critical Examination of Ñāṇavīra Thera's 'A Note on Paṭiccasamuppāda.'" *Buddhist Studies Review*, 15: 43–64 and 157–81.

———. 2000. *The Connected Discourses of the Buddha: A New Translation of the Saṃyutta Nikāya*. Somerville, MA: Wisdom Publications.

———. 2012. *The Numerical Discourses of the Buddha: A Translation of the Aṅguttara Nikāya*. Somerville, MA: Wisdom Publications.

Brick, David. 2010. "The Dharmaśāstric Debate on Widow-Burning." *Journal of the American Oriental Society*, 130.2: 203–23.

Brown, Norman W. 1940. "The Basis for the Hindu Act of Truth." *Review of Religion*, 5: 36–45.

———. 1968. "The Metaphysics of the Truth Act (*Satyakriyā)." In *Mélanges d'Indianisme à la mémoire de Louis Renou*, edited by Louis Renou, 171–77. Paris. Éditions de Boccard.

———. 1972a. "Duty as Truth in Ancient India." *Proceedings of the American Philosophical Society*, 116.3: 252–68.

———. 1972b. "Duty as Truth in the Rig Veda." In *India Major: Congratulatory Volume Presented to J. Gonda*, edited by J. Ensink and P. Gaefkke, 57–67. Leiden: Brill.

Burlingame, Eugene Watson. 1917. "The Act of Truth (Saccakiriya). A Hindu Spell and its Employment as a Psychic Motif in Hindu Fiction." *Journal of the Royal Asiatic Society*, 429–67.

Choong Mun-keat. 1999. *The Notion of Emptiness in Early Buddhism*. Delhi: Motilal Banarsidass.

Choubey, Asha. 2009. "Voices from the Yore: Therigatha Writings of the Bhikkhunis." *The Indian Review of World Literature in English*, 5.2: 1–9.

Chung Jin-il. 2008. *A Survey of the Sanskrit Fragments Corresponding to the Chinese Saṃyuktāgama*. Tokyo: Sankibo.

Church, Cornelia Dimmitt. 1975. "Temptress, Housewife, Nun: Women's Role in Early Buddhism." *Anima*, 2: 53–58.

Ciurtin, Eugen. 2009. "The Buddha's Earthquakes [I]. On Water: Earthquakes and Seaquakes in Buddhist Cosmology and Meditation, With an Appendix on Buddhist Art." *Stvdia Asiatica*, 10.1/2: 59–123.

———. 2012. "'Thus Have I Quaked': The Tempo of the Buddha's Vita and the Earliest Buddhist Fabric of Timelessness [The Buddha's Earthquakes II]." In *Figurations of Time in Asia*, edited by Dietrich Boschung and Corinna Wessels-Mevissen, 21–54. München: Wilhelm Fink Verlag.

Clark, Chris. 2011. "Karma and Karmavipāka in Early Buddhist Avadāna Literature." *Journal of the Oriental Society of Australia*, 43: 23–34.

Clarke, Shayne. 2014. *Family Matters in Indian Buddhist Monasticism*. Honolulu: University of Hawai'i Press.

Collett, Alice. 2009a. "Historio-Critical Hermeneutics in the Study of Women in Early Indian Buddhism." *Numen*, 56: 91–117.

———. 2009b: "Somā the Learned Brahmin." *Religions of South Asia*, 3.1: 93–109.

———. 2016. *Lives of Early Buddhist Nuns: Biographies as History*. Delhi: Oxford University Press.

———. 2021. *I Hear Her Words: An Introduction to Women in Buddhism*. Cambridge: Windhorse Publications.

Cone, Margaret. 2001. *A Dictionary of Pāli, Part I, a-kh*. Oxford: Pali Text Society.

Coomaraswamy, Ananda K. 1944. "Headless Magicians; And an Act of Truth." *Journal of the American Oriental Society*, 64.4: 215–17.

Courtright, Paul B. 1995. "Sati, Sacrifice, and Marriage: The Modernity of Tradition." In *From the Margins of Hindu Marriage: Essays on Gender, Religion, and Culture*, edited by Lindsay Harlan and Paul B. Courtright, 184–203. New York: Oxford University Press.

Cowell, E. B. and R. A. Neil. 1886. *The Divyāvadāna: A Collection of Early Buddhist Legends, Now First Edited from the Nepalese Sanskrit Mss. in Cambridge and Paris*. Cambridge: University Press.

Crosby, Kate. 2014. *Theravada Buddhism: Continuity, Diversity, and Identity*. Chichester: Wiley.

Dantinne, Jean. 1991. *Les qualités de l'ascète (dhutaguṇa): Étude sémantique et doctrinale*. Bruxelles: Thanh-Long.

Dash, Shobha Rani. 2008. *Mahāpajāpatī: The First Bhikkhunī*. Seoul: Blue Lotus Books.

Datta, Vishwa N. 1988. *Sati: A Historical, Social and Philosophical Enquiry into the Hindu Rite of Widow Burning*. New Delhi: Manohar Publications.

Deeg, Max. 2005. *Das Gaoseng-Faxian-Zhuan als religionsgeschichtliche Quelle: Der älteste Bericht eines chinesischen buddhistischen Pilgermönchs über seine Reise nach Indien mit Übersetzung des Textes*. Wiesbaden: Otto Harrassowitz.

de La Vallée Poussin, Louis, 1913. "Documents Sanscrits de la seconde collection M. A. Stein." *Journal of the Royal Asiatic Society*, 569–80.

Demiéville, Paul. 1924. "Les versions chinoises du Milindapañha." *Bulletin de l'École Française d'Extrême Orient*, 24: 1–258.

de Silva, Lily. 1984. "Self-identification and Associated Problems." In *Buddhist Studies in Honor of Hammalava Saddhatissa*, edited by Gatare Dhammapāla, Richard Gombrich, and K. R. Norman, 69–76. Sri Lanka: University of Jayewardenepura.

Dewaraja, Lorna. 1999. "Buddhist Women in India and Precolonial Sri Lanka." In *Buddhist Women Across Cultures: Realizations*, edited by

Karma Lekshe Tsomo, 67–77. Albany: State University of New York Press.

Dhammadinnā, Bhikkhunī. 2015. "The Parinirvāṇa of Mahāprajāpatī Gautamī and Her Followers in the Mūlasarvāstivāda Vinaya." *Indian International Journal of Buddhist Studies*, 16: 29–61.

———. 2016. "The Upasampadā of Mahāprajāpatī Gautamī in the Mūlasarvāstivāda Vinaya and a Sūtra Quotation in Śamathadeva's Abhidharmakośopāyikā-ṭīkā." *Journal of the Centre for Buddhist Studies*, 13: 91–121.

———. 2018. "When Womanhood Matters: Sex Essentialization and Pedagogical Dissonance in Buddhist Discourse." *Religions of South Asia*, 12.3: 274–313.

———. 2019. "Soreyya/ā's Double Sex Change: On Gender Relevance and Buddhist Values." *Annual Report of the International Research Institute for Advanced Buddhology at Soka University*, 22: 9–33.

———. 2020. "Bhikṣuṇī Śailā's Rebuttal of Māra's Substantialist View: The Chariot Simile in a Sūtra Quotation in the Abhidharmakośopāyika-ṭīkā." *Indian International Journal of Buddhist Studies*, 21: 1–33.

———. 2021. "The Ordination of Bhaddā Kuṇḍalakesā and the Ehibhikkhunī in the Theravāda Textual Tradition." In *Illuminating the Dharma: Buddhist Studies in Honour of Venerable Professor K. L. Dhammajoti*, edited by Tochiichi Endo, 51–98. Hong Kong: Centre of Buddhist Studies, University of Hong Kong.

Dhammanandā, Bhikkhunī. 2010. "A Need to Take a Fresh Look at Popular Interpretations of the Tripiṭaka: Theravāda Context in Thailand." In *Dignity and Discipline: The Evolving Role of Women in Buddhism*, edited by Thea Mohr and Jampa Tsedroen, 149–60. Somerville, MA: Wisdom Publications.

Dhammavihari Thera. 2002/2011. *Women in Buddhism: Studies on Her Position and Role*. Kandy: Buddhist Publication Society (online version of Wheel publication 453/454).

Dhammika, S. 2015/2018. *Nature and the Environment in Early Buddhism*. Kandy: Buddhist Publication Society.

Dhirasekara, Jotiya. 1967. "Women and the Religious Order of the Buddha." *The Maha Bodhi*, 75.5/6: 154–61.

Durt, Hubert. 2005. "Kajaṅgalā, Who Could Have Been the Last Mother of the Buddha." *Journal of the International College for Advanced Buddhist Studies*, 9: 65–90.

Dutt, Sukumar. 1957. *The Buddha and Five After-Centuries*. London: Luzac.

Engelmajer, Pascale F. 2020. "'Like a Mother Her Only Child': Mothering in the Pāli Canon." *Open Theology*, 6: 88–103.

Enomoto Fumio. 1994. *A Comprehensive Study of the Chinese Saṃyuktāgama; Part 1: Saṃgītinipāta*. Kyoto: Kacho Junior College.

Falk, Nancy Auer. 1989. "The Case of the Vanishing Nuns: The Fruits of Ambivalence in Ancient Indian Buddhism." In *Unspoken Words: Women and Religious Lives*, edited by Nancy Auer Falk and Rita Gross, 155–65. Belmont: Wadsworth.

Faure, Bernard. 2003: *The Power of Denial: Buddhism, Purity and Gender*. Princeton: Princeton University Press.

Finnegan, Damchö Diana. 2009. *'For the Sake of Women too': Ethics and Gender in the Narratives of the Mūlasarvāstivāda Vinaya*. PhD, University of Wisconsin–Madison.

Foley, Caroline A. 1894. "The Vedalla Sutta, As Illustrating the Psychological Basis of Buddhist Ethics." *Journal of the Royal Asiatic Society*, 321–33.

Frauwallner, Erich. 1956. *The Earliest Vinaya and the Beginnings of Buddhist Literature*. Rome: Istituto Italiano per il Medio ed Estremo Oriente.

Ganguly, Jayeeta. 1989. "Nisraya and Dhutanga in Buddhist Tradition." *Bulletin of Tibetology, New Series*, 2: 17–29.

Garling, Wendy. 2016. *Stars at Dawn: Forgotten Stories of Women in the Buddha's Life*. Boulder: Shambhala Publications.

———. 2021. *The Woman Who Raised the Buddha: The Extraordinary Life of Mahaprajapati*. Boulder: Shambhala Publications.

Garzilli, Enrica. 1997. "First Greek and Latin Documents on Sahagamana and Some Connected Problems." *Indo-Iranian Journal*, 40.3: 205–43 and 40.4: 339–65.

Geiger, Magdalene and Wilhelm Geiger. 1920. *Pāli Dhamma, vornehmlich in der kanonischen Literatur*. München: Bayerische Akademie der Wissenschaften.

Gethin, Rupert. 1997. "Cosmology and Meditation: From the Aggañña-Sutta to the Mahāyāna." *History of Religions*, 36: 183–217.

Gnoli, Raniero. 1978. *The Gilgit Manuscript of the Saṅghabhedavastu, Being the 17th and Last Section of the Vinaya of the Mūlasarvāstivādin, Part II.* Rome: Istituto Italiano per il Medio ed Estremo Oriente.

Gokhale, Balkrishna Govind. 1976. "The Image-world of the Thera-Therī-Gathās." In *Malalasekera Commemoration Volume*, edited by O. H. de Wijesekera, 96–110. Colombo: The Malalasekera Commemoration Volume Editorial Committee.

Griffiths, Paul J. 1986/1991. *On Being Mindless: Buddhist Meditation and the Mind-Body Problem.* Illinois, La Salle: Open Court.

Guang Xing. 2009. "The Different Chinese Versions of the Nāgasena Bhikṣu Sūtra." *Journal of the Centre for Buddhist Studies*, 7: 226–45.

Hara Minoru. 2009. "Divine Witness." *Journal of Indian Philosophy*, 37.3: 253–72.

Hare, E. M. 1955. *The Book of the Gradual Sayings: Aṅguttara Nikāya, The Book of the Sevens, Eights, and Nines, Part IV.* London: Pali Text Society.

Harris, Elizabeth J. 1999. "The Female in Buddhism." In *Buddhist Women Across Cultures: Realizations*, edited by Karma Lekshe Tsomo, 49–65. New York: State University of New York Press.

Harvey, Peter. 1983. "The Nature of the Tathāgata." In *Buddhist Studies: Ancient and Modern*, edited by Philip Denwood and Alexander Piatigorsky, 35–52. London: Curzon.

———. 1990. *An Introduction to Buddhism: Teachings, History and Practices.* Delhi: Munshiram Manoharlal.

———. 2000/2005. *An Introduction to Buddhist Ethics, Foundations, Values and Issues.* Cambridge: Cambridge University Press.

Hawley, John Stratton. 1994. *Sati, The Blessing and the Curse: The Burning of Wives in India.* New York: Oxford University Press.

Hirakawa Akira. 1997. *Buddhist Chinese-Sanskrit Dictionary.* Tokyo: Reiyukai.

Horner, I. B. 1930/1990. *Women under Primitive Buddhism: Laywomen and Almswomen.* Delhi: Motilal Banarsidass.

Jamison, Stephanie. 2006. "Women 'Between the Empires' and 'Between the Lines.'" In *Between the Empires: Society in India 300 BCE to 400 CE*, edited by Patrick Olivelle, 191–214. New York: Oxford University Press.

Jantrasrisalai, Chanida, Timothy Lenz, Lin Qian, and Richard Salomon. 2016. "Fragments of an Ekottarikāgama Manuscript in Gāndhārī." In *Manuscripts in the Schøyen Collection: Buddhist Manuscripts, Volume IV*, edited by Jens Braarvig, 1–122, Oslo: Hermes Publishing.

Jootla, Susan Elbaum. 1988. *Inspiration from Enlightened Nuns*. Kandy: Buddhist Publication Society.

Karunadasa, Y. 1994. "Nibbanic Experience: A Non-Transcendental Interpretation." *Sri Lanka Journal of Buddhist Studies*, 4: 1–13.

Kloppenborg, Ria. 1995. "Female Stereotypes in Early Buddhism: The Women of the Therīgāthā." In *Female Stereotypes in Religious Traditions*, edited by Ria Kloppenborg and Wouter J. Hanegraaff, 151–69. Leiden: Brill.

Kong Choy Fah. 2012. *Saccakiriyā: The Belief in the Power of True Speech in Theravāda Buddhist Tradition*. Singapore (self-published).

Krey, Gisela. 2010. "On Women as Teachers in Early Buddhism: Dhammadinnā and Khemā." *Buddhist Studies Review*, 27.1: 17–40.

Kusumā, Bhikkhunī. 1987/2010. *The Dasasil Nun: A Study of Women's Buddhist Religious Movement in Sri Lanka, with an Outline of Its Historical Antecedents*. Nedimala, Dehiwala: Buddhist Cultural Centre.

Lamotte, Étienne. 1949/1981. *Le Traité de la Grande Vertu de Sagesse de Nāgārjuna (Mahāprajñāpāramitāśāstra), Tome II*. Louvain-la-Neuve: Institut Orientaliste.

Lang, Karen Christina. 1986. "Lord Death's Snare: Gender-related Imagery in the Theragāthā and the Therīgāthā." *Journal of Feminist Studies in Religion*, 2.2: 63–79.

———. 2019. "Reimagining Buddhist Women in India." In *Buddhist Feminisms and Femininities*, edited by Karma Lekshe Tsomo, 27–65. Albany: Sunny Press.

Lefmann, S. 1902. *Lalita Vistara: Leben und Lehre des Çâkya-Buddha, Textausgabe mit Varianten-, Metren- und Wörterverzeichnis*. Halle: Verlag der Buchhandlung des Waisenhauses.

Legittimo, Elsa. 2012. "Buddhānusmṛti Between Worship and Meditation: Early Currents of the Chinese Ekottarika-āgama." *Asiatische Studien*, 66.2: 337–402.

Leslie, Julia. 1991. "Suttee or Satī: Victim or Victor?" In *Roles and Rituals for Hindu Women*, edited by Julia Leslie, 175–90. Rutherford: Fairleigh Dickinson University Press.

Lévi, Sylvain. 1908. "Açvaghoṣa: le Sûtrâlaṃkâra et ses sources." *Journal Asiatique*, 10.12: 57–184.

MacQueen, Graeme. 1988. *A Study of the Śrāmaṇyaphala-Sūtra*. Wiesbaden: Otto Harrassowitz.

Mahāsi Sayādaw. 1981/2006. *Cūḷavedalla Sutta: Discourse on Various Aspects of Buddha's Dhamma*. Translated by U Min Swe. Malaysia: Selangor Buddhist Vipassanā Meditation Society.

Mair, Victor H. 1993. "The Linguistic and Textual Antecedents of the Sūtra on the Wise and the Foolish." *Sino-Platonic Papers*, 38: 1–95.

———. 1993/1999. "The Khotanese Antecedents of the Sūtra of the Wise and the Foolish (Xianyu jing)." *In Buddhism across Boundaries: Chinese Buddhism and the Western Regions*, edited by John R. McRae and Jan Nattier, 361–420. Taipei: Fo Guang Shan.

Malalasekera, G. P. 1937/1995. *Dictionary of Pāli Proper Names, Vol. I.* Delhi: Munshiram Manoharlal.

———. 1938/1998. *Dictionary of Pāli Proper Names, Vol. II.* Delhi: Munshiram Manoharlal.

Mani, Lata. 1998. *Contentious Traditions: The Debate on Sati in Colonial India*. Berkeley: University of California Press.

Marciniak, Katarzyna. 2019. *The Mahāvastu: A New Edition, Vol. III.* Tokyo: International Research Institute for Advanced Buddhology at Soka University.

Meisig, Konrad. 1987. *Das Śrāmaṇyaphala-Sūtra: Synoptische Übersetzung und Glossar der chinesischen Fassungen verglichen mit dem Sanskrit und Pāli*. Wiesbaden: Otto Harrassowitz.

Minh Chau, Thich. 1964. *Milindapañha and Nāgasenabhikshusūtra: A Comparative Study Through Pāli and Chinese Sources*. Calcutta: K. L. Mukhopadyay.

Monier-Williams, M. 1899/1999. *A Sanskrit-English Dictionary, Etymologically and Philologically Arranged, with Special Reference to Cognate Indo-European Languages*. Delhi: Motilal Banarsidass.

Murcott, Susan. 1991. *The First Buddhist Women: Translations and Commentaries on the Therigatha*. Berkeley: Parallax Press.

Ñāṇananda, Bhikkhu. 2003. *Nibbāna: The Mind Stilled, Volume I*. Sri Lanka: Dharma Grantha Mudrana Bhāraya.

Nanayakkara, S. K. 1989. "Dhutaṅga." In *Encyclopaedia of Buddhism*, edited by W. G. Weeraratne, 4.4: 580–85. Sri Lanka: Department of Buddhist Affairs.

Nandy, Ashis. 1980. "Sati: A Nineteenth-Century Tale of Women, Violence and Protest." In *At the Edge of Psychology: Essays in Politics and Culture*, edited by Ashis Nandy, 1–31. Delhi: Oxford University Press.

Nyanaponika Thera. 1981. *The Four Nutriments of Life*. Kandy: Buddhist Publication Society.

Obeyesekere, Ranjini. 2001. *Portraits of Buddhist Women: Stories from the Saddharmaratnāvaliya*. Albany: State University of New York Press.

———. 2009. *Yasodharā, The Wife of the Bōdhisattva*. Albany: State University of New York Press.

Ohnuma Reiko. 2017. *Unfortunate Destiny: Animals in the Indian Buddhist Imagination*. New York: Oxford University Press.

Oldenberg, Hermann. 1912. "Studien zur Geschichte des buddhistischen Kanon." *Nachrichten von der königlichen Gesellschaft der Wissenschaften zu Göttingen, philologisch-historische Klasse aus dem Jahre 1912*, 155–217.

Pieris, Aloysius. 2003. "What Happens to Viññāṇa in the Cessation Attainment? An Exegesis of M.I. 295–296." *Bukkyō Kenkyū*, 31: 43–68.

Pradhan, P. 1967. *Abhidharmakośabhāṣya of Vasubandhu*. Patna: Kashi Prasad Jayaswal Research Institute.

Pruitt, William. 1998/1999. *The Commentary on the Verses of the Therīs (Therīgāthā-aṭṭhakathā, Paramatthadīpanī VI) by Ācariya Dhammapāla*. Oxford: Pali Text Society.

Pruitt, William and K. R. Norman. 2001. *The Pātimokkha*. Oxford: Pali Text Society.

Przyluski, Jean. 1918. "Le parinirvāṇa et le funérailles du Buddha, II: Le dernier voyage du Buddha." *Journal Asiatique*, 11.12: 401–56.

Rajapakse, Vijitha. 1995: "Therīgāthā: On Feminism, Aestheticism and Religiosity in an Early Buddhist Verse Anthology." *Buddhist Studies Review*, 12.1: 7–26 and 12.2: 135–55.

Ray, Reginald A. 1994. *Buddhist Saints in India: A Study in Buddhist Values and Orientations*. New York: Oxford University Press.

Rhys Davids, C. A. F. 1913. *Psalms of the Early Buddhists, II: Psalms of the Brethren*. London: Pali Text Society.

———. 1917/1979. *The Book of the Kindred Sayings (Saṃyutta-Nikāya) or Grouped Suttas, Part I*. London: Pali Text Society.

Roth, Gustav. 1970. *Bhikṣuṇī-Vinaya, Including Bhikṣuṇī-Prakīrṇaka and a Summary of the Bhikṣu-Prakīrṇaka of the Ārya-Mahāsāṃghika-Lokottaravādin: Edited and Annotated for the First Time, with Introduction and Two Indexes*. Patna: K. P. Jayaswal Research Institute.

Rotman, Andy. 2009. *Thus Have I Seen: Visualizing Faith in Early Indian Buddhism*. New York: Oxford University Press.

Samuels, Jeffrey. 1999. "Views of Householders and Lay Disciples in the Sutta Piṭaka: A Reconsideration of the Lay/Monastic Opposition." *Religion*, 29: 231–41.

Sander, Lore and Ernst Waldschmidt. 1980. *Sanskrithandschriften aus den Turfanfunden, Teil IV*. Wiesbaden: Franz Steiner.

———. 1985. *Sanskrithandschriften aus den Turfanfunden, Teil 5*. Wiesbaden: Franz Steiner.

Schmithausen, Lambert. 1987/2007. *Ālayavijñana: On the Origin and the Early Development of a Central Concept of Yogācāra Philosophy*. Tokyo: The International Institute for Buddhist Studies.

Schumann, Hans Wolfgang. 1982/1999. *Der historische Budddha: Leben und Lehre des Gotama*. München: Diederichs.

Senart, Émile. 1882. *Le Mahāvastu: Texte sanscrit publié pour la première fois et accompagné d'introductions et d'un commentaire, Tome premier*. Paris: Imprimerie Nationale.

———. 1897. *Le Mahāvastu: Texte sanscrit publié pour la première fois et accompagné d'introductions et d'un commentaire, Tome troisième.* Paris: Imprimerie Nationale.

Sharma, Arvind, Ajit Ray, Alaka Hejib, and Katherine K. Young. 1988/2001. *Sati: Historical and Phenomenological Essays.* Delhi: Motilal Banarsidass.

Shaw, Miranda. 2006/2007. *Buddhist Goddesses of India.* Delhi: Munshiram Manoharlal.

Silk, Jonathan A. 2008/2009. *Riven by Lust: Incest and Schism in Indian Buddhist Legend and Hagiography.* Delhi: Munshiram Manoharlal.

Skilling, Peter. 1994. *Mahāsūtras: Great Discourses of the Buddha, Volume I.* Oxford: Pali Text Society.

———. 1997. *Mahāsūtras: Great Discourses of the Buddha, Volume II.* Oxford: Pali Text Society.

———. 2001. "Eṣā Agrā: Images of Nuns in (Mūla-)Sarvāstivādin Literature." *Journal of the International Association of Buddhist Studies,* 24.2: 135–56.

Somaratne, G. A. 2009. "White-Clothed Celibate Arahants in Early Buddhism." In *Buddhist and Pali Studies in Honour of the Venerable Professor Kakkapalliye Anuruddha,* edited by K. L. Dhammajoti and Y. Karunadasa, 151–67. Hong Kong: Centre of Buddhist Studies, University of Hong Kong.

Speyer, J. S. 1909/1970. *Avadānaçataka: A Century of Edifying Tales Belonging to the Hīnayāna, Volume II.* Osnabrück: Biblio Verlag.

Sponberg, Alan. 1992. "Attitudes toward Women and the Feminine in Early Buddhism." In *Buddhism, Sexuality, and Gender,* edited by José I. Cabezón, 3–36, Delhi: Sri Satguru.

Stache-Rosen, Valentina. 1968. *Dogmatische Begriffsreihen im älteren Buddhismus II: Das Saṅgītisūtra und sein Kommentar Saṅgītiparyāya.* Berlin: Akademie Verlag.

Strong, John S. 2010. "The Triple Ladder at Saṃkāśya, Traditions about the Buddha's Descent from the Trāyastriṃśa Heaven." In *From Turfan to Ajanta: Festschrift for Dieter Schlingloff on the Occasion of His Eightieth Birthday,* edited by Eli Franco and Monika Zin, 967–78. Lumbini: Lumbini International Research Institute.

Takakusu J. 1896. "Chinese Translations of Milinda Pañho." *Journal of the Royal Asiatic Society*, 1–21.

Tatia, Nathmal. 1975. *Prātimokṣasūtram of the Lokottaravādamahāsāṅghika School*. Patna: Kashi Prasad Jayaswal Research Institute.

Thomas, Edward J. 1933/2004. *The History of Buddhist Thought*. Delhi: Munshiram Manoharlal.

Thompson, Evan. 2020. *Why I Am Not a Buddhist*. New Haven: Yale University Press.

Thompson, George. 1998. "On Truth-Acts in Vedic." *Indo-Iranian Journal*, 41.2: 125–53.

van den Bosch, Lourens P. 1995. "The Ultimate Journey: Satī and Widowhood in India." In *Between Poverty and the Pyre: Moments in the History of Widowhood*, edited by Jan Bremmer and Lourens van den Bosch, 171–203, London: Routledge.

Venkatasubbiah, A. 1940. "The Act of Truth in the Ṛgveda." *The Journal of Oriental Research*, 14: 133–65.

Vetter, Tilmann. 2000. *The 'Khandha Passages' in the Vinayapiṭaka and the Four Main Nikāyas*. Wien: Österreichische Akademie der Wissenschaften.

Vidyabhusana, Satis Chandra. 1915. *So-sor-thar-pa (khrims): Vol. V of the Dulwa Portion of the Kangyur (Leaves 1–29 and Top Line of Leaf 30), Edited and Translated*. Calcutta: Asiatic Society.

Vogel, Claus. 1970. *The Teachings of the Six Heretics, According to the Pravrajyāvastu of the Tibetan Mūlasarvāstivāda Vinaya: Edited and Rendered into English, With an Appendix Containing an English Translation of the Pertinent Sections in the Chinese Mūlasarvāstivāda Vinaya*. Wiesbaden: Franz Steiner.

von Hinüber, Oskar. 1996/1997. *A Handbook of Pāli Literature*. Delhi: Munshiram Manoharlal.

———. 2019. [Review of Anālayo 2016a]. *Indo-Iranian Journal* 62: 89–99.

von Simson, Georg. 2000. *Prātimokṣasūtra der Sarvāstivādins Teil II: Kritische Textausgabe, Übersetzung, Wortindex sowie Nachträge zu Teil I*. Göttingen: Vandenhoeck & Ruprecht.

Waldschmidt, Ernst. 1944. *Die Überlieferung vom Lebensende des Bud-*

dha: Eine vergleichende Analyse des Mahāparinirvāṇasūtra und seiner Textentsprechungen, erster Teil, Vorgangsgruppe I–IV. Göttingen: Vandenhoeck & Ruprecht.

———. 1951. *Das Mahāparinirvāṇasūtra: Text in Sanskrit und Tibetisch, verglichen mit dem Pāli nebst einer Analyse der in chinesischer Übersetzung überlieferten Parallelversion, auf Grund von Turfan-Handschriften herausgegeben, Teil II.* Berlin: Akademie Verlag.

———. 1956. *Das Mahāvadānasūtra: Ein kanonischer Text über die sieben letzten Buddhas, Sanskrit, verglichen mit dem Pāli nebst einer Analyse der in chinesischer Übersetzung überlieferten Parallelversion, auf Grund von Turfan-Handschriften herausgegeben. Teil II.* Berlin: Akademie Verlag.

———. 1968. "Ein Beitrag zur Überlieferung vom Sthavira Śroṇa Koṭiviṃśa." In *Mélanges d'Indianisme à la Mémoire de Louis Renou*, edited by Louis Renou, 773–87. Paris: Éditions de Boccard.

Walters, Jonathan S. 1994. "A Voice from the Silence: the Buddha's Mother's Story." *History of Religions*, 33: 358–79.

———. 1995. "Gotamī's Story." In *Buddhism in Practice*, edited by Donald S. Lopez, 113–38. Princeton: Princeton University Press.

———. 2014. "Apadāna: Therī-apadāna: Wives of the Saints: Marriage and Kamma in the Path to Arahantship." In *Women in Early Indian Buddhism: Comparative Textual Studies*, edited by Alice Collett, 160–91. Oxford: Oxford University Press.

Wayman, Alex. 1968. "The Hindu–Buddhist Rite of Truth: An Interpretation." In *Studies in Indian Linguistics: Professor M. B. Emenau Ṣaṣṭipūrti Volume*, edited by Bhadriraju Krishnamurti and Murray B. Emeneau, 365–69. Centres of Advanced Study in Linguistics, Deccan College, and Annamalai University in Studies in Indian Linguistics.

———. 1979. "The Twenty Reifying Views (sakkāyadiṭṭhi)." In *Studies in Pali and Buddhism: A Memorial Volume in Honor of Bhikkhu Jagdish Kashyap*, edited by A. K. Narain and L. Zwilling, 375–80. Delhi: B. R. Publishing Corporation.

Weinberger-Thomas, Catherine. 1996. *Cendres d'immortalité: la crémation des veuves en Inde.* Paris: Éditions du Seuil.

Wille, Klaus. 2008. *Sanskrithandschriften aus den Turfanfunden, Teil 10*. Stuttgart: Franz Steiner.

Wilson, Liz. 2004. "Ascetic Practices." In *Encyclopedia of Buddhism, Volume One*, edited by Robert E. Buswell, 32–34. New York: Macmillan.

———. 2011. "Sati or Female Supremacy? Feminist Appropriations of Gotami's Parinirvana." In *Engaging South Asian Religions: Boundaries, Appropriations, and Resistances*, edited by Mathew N. Schmalz and Peter Gottschalk, 133–50. Albany: State University of New York Press.

Winternitz, Moriz. 1920/1968. *Geschichte der indischen Literatur, Band 2: Die buddhistische Literatur und die heiligen Texte der Jainas*. Stuttgart: K. F. Koehler.

Wogihara Unrai. 1932. *Sphuṭārthā Abhidharmakośavyākhyā by Yaśomitra, Part I*. Tokyo: The Publishing Association of Abhidharmakośavyākhyā.

Yao Fumi. 2015. "The Story of Dharmadinnā: Ordination by Messenger in the Mūlasarvāstivāda Vinaya." *Indo-Iranian Journal*, 58: 216–53.

Young, Serinity. 2004. *Courtesans and Tantric Consorts: Sexualities in Buddhist Narrative, Iconography, and Ritual*. New York: Routledge.

Index

About the Author

BHIKKHU ANĀLAYO is a scholar of early Buddhism and a meditation teacher. He completed his PhD research on the *Satipaṭṭhānasutta* at the University of Peradeniya, Sri Lanka, in 2000, and a habilitation research with a comparative study of the *Majjhimanikāya* in the light of its Chinese, Sanskrit, and Tibetan parallels at the University of Marburg, Germany, in 2007. His over four hundred publications are for the most part based on comparative studies, with a special interest in topics related to meditation and the role of women in Buddhism.

What to Read Next from Wisdom Publications

Early Buddhist Oral Tradition
Textual Formation and Transmission
Bhikkhu Anālayo

Acclaimed scholar-monk Bhikkhu Analayo examines the impact of such oral transmission on early Buddhist texts, be these monastic rules, verses, or prose portions of the early discourses.

Superiority Conceit in Buddhist Traditions
A Historical Perspective
Bhikkhu Anālayo

"This book is a courageous call for integrity and self-reflection. Bhikkhu Anālayo argues that if Buddhism is to engage the modern world with any enduring success, it must abandon its own conceit and reckon with its internal prejudices. This book is a much-needed contribution that will help reshape the direction of the field."—Vanessa Sasson, professor, Marianopolis College

The Hidden Lamp
Stories from Twenty-Five Centuries of Awakened Women
Zenshin Florence Caplow and Reigetsu Susan Moon

"An amazing collection. This book gives the wonderful feel of the sincerity, the great range, and the nobility of the spiritual work that women are doing and have been doing, unacknowledged, for a very long time. An essential and delightful book."—John Tarrant, author of *The Light Inside the Dark: Zen, Soul, and the Spiritual Life*

Rebirth in Early Buddhism and Current Research
Bhikkhu Anālayo

"Bhikkhu Anālayo offers a detailed study of the much-debated Buddhist doctrine of rebirth and a survey of relevant evidence. He also investigates the Pāli chantings of Dhammaruwan, who at a very young age would spontaneously chant ancient and complex Buddhist suttas. I first met Dhammaruwan when he was seven years old, when my teacher, Anagarika Munindraji, and I visited him and his family in Sri Lanka. *Rebirth in Early Buddhism and Current Research* illuminates a complex topic with great clarity and understanding."—Joseph Goldstein, author of *Mindfulness: A Practical Guide to Awakening*

Dignity and Discipline
Reviving Full Ordination for Buddhist Nuns
Edited by Thea Mohr and Ven. Jampa Tsedroen

"It is essential reading for those who want to understand how Buddhists are thinking through the question of bhikkhuni ordination. I recommend this volume with warm enthusiasm."—*Journal of the American Academy of Religion*

Dharma Matters
Women, Race, and Tantra
Jan Willis

"This collection of essays by Jan Willis, penned over thirty years of study, teaching, and practice, is destined to become an authoritative resource in Buddhist scholarship and thought. Willis challenges many of our preconceptions, but asks no more and no less than what the Buddha asked: come, see, and experience for yourselves."—Sharon Salzberg, author of *Lovingkindness* and *Real Happiness*

Zen Women

Beyond Tea Ladies, Iron Maidens, and Macho Masters

Grace Schireson

"An exceptional and powerful classic with great depth, humor, and clarity."—Joan Halifax, abbess of Upaya Zen Center

About Wisdom Publications

Wisdom Publications is the leading publisher of classic and contemporary Buddhist books and practical works on mindfulness. To learn more about us or to explore our other books, please visit our website at wisdomexperience.org or contact us at the address below.

Wisdom Publications
199 Elm Street
Somerville, MA 02144 USA

We are a 501(c)(3) organization, and donations in support of our mission are tax deductible.

Wisdom Publications is affiliated with the Foundation for the Preservation of the Mahayana Tradition (FPMT).